The '8...

The '80s Resurrected

Essays on the Decade in Popular Culture Then and Now

Edited by RANDY LAIST

McFarland & Company, Inc., Publishers

Jefferson, North Carolina

This book has undergone peer review.

LIBRARY OF CONGRESS CATALOGUING-IN-PUBLICATION DATA

Names: Laist, Randy, 1974– editor.
Title: The '80s resurrected : essays on the decade in popular culture then and now / edited by Randy Laist.
Other titles: 1980s resurrected, essays on the decade in popular culture then and now
Description: Jefferson, North Carolina : McFarland & Company, Inc., Publishers, 2023. | Includes bibliographical references and index.
Identifiers: LCCN 2023002395 | ISBN 9781476686516 (paperback : acid free paper) ∞
ISBN 9781476648552 (ebook)
Subjects: LCSH: United States—Civilization—1970- | Popular culture—United States—History—20th century. | Mass media—United States—History—20th century. | Nostalgia—United States. | Nineteen eighties.
Classification: LCC E169.12 .A1885 2023 | DDC 973.927—dc23/eng/20230208
LC record available at https://lccn.loc.gov/2023002395

BRITISH LIBRARY CATALOGUING DATA ARE AVAILABLE

ISBN (print) 978-1-4766-8651-6
ISBN (ebook) 978-1-4766-4855-2

Cover images © 2023 Shutterstock

Printed in the United States of America

*McFarland & Company, Inc., Publishers
Box 611, Jefferson, North Carolina 28640
www.mcfarlandpub.com*

Table of Contents

Fight the Power: Social Justice

Introduction

RANDY LAIST

Marty McFly has his confused face on. Still reeling from his travels backward in time from 1985 to 1955 in the first *Back to the Future* movie (1985), Marty has now shot forward in time to 2015 in the giddy opening moments of *Back to the Future Part 2* (1989). Just as he's becoming acclimatized to the new styles and technologies of the 20-teens, however, he stumbles into another kind of time-portal when he wanders into The Café 80s. Marty's confusion is understandable. The '50s diner from the first movie has been redecorated with a jumble of '80s shwag: neon colors, arcade games, electric guitars, a wall of television screens playing montages of '80s footage, and Max-Headroom-style video screens of Michael Jackson, Ronald Reagan, and the Ayatollah Khomeini serving as waiters, all awash in the sounds of Michael Jackson's "Beat It." Along with Marty, we are also overwhelmed, not only by the barrage of stimuli, but also by the semantic implications of the spectacle. As a denizen of 1985, Marty himself is faced with the prospect of seeing his own self and time vanish into history and become "periodized." For contemporary audiences watching *Back to the Future 2* in November of 1989, the scene suggests that the '80s have gone from being a living moment to a historical curiosity. *Back to the Future 2* was released less than two weeks after the Berlin Wall came down, an event that marks an unofficial end to the '80s, and, because Marty is still existentially in 1985, the 1989 audience sees Marty, who, in the first movie, had represented the pinnacle of cultural evolution, absorbed into The Café 80s as a living artifact of a vanished time. Simultaneously, the scene also suggests the efforts of the filmmakers working at the end of the 1980s to predict how the 1980s would be remembered 25 years into the future. The fact that the scene is set in the '50s nostalgia-diner suggests that the '50s nostalgia that prevailed in the '80s has shifted naturally into the 20-teens' nostalgia for the 1980s, while the discrepant collage of random pop-cultural signifiers that crowd the walls of The Café 80s constitutes a mildly satirical but mostly celebratory vision of the 1980s as an effervescent swirl of consumerist fads. For a modern audience in 2021, meanwhile, all of these perspectives are folded into the question of how this prediction of 1980s nostalgia matches up with the way that the 1980s has actually come to be remembered and represented in the popular imagination of the early 21st century. The Café 80s presents a funhouse mirror of our own ongoing preoccupation with Marty McFly's home-decade.

While the prescience of *Back to the Future 2*'s representation of 2015 has been debated, the film's representation of a future market niche for '80s nostalgia is certainly one of its more accurate predictions. While '80s-themed restaurants might not be extremely common (although they do exist), popular culture retains a capacious shopping-mall-sized space in its collective imagination devoted to revisiting, relitigating, and reimagining the decade associated with the presidency of Ronald Reagan. Adam Gopnik has described a 40-year pattern of nostalgia fueled by middle-aged writers' and audiences' predilection for representations of their own childhoods, while other observers have described a 30-year "nostalgia cycle" (Van Hoof), a "20-year cycle of resuscitation" (Wilson), or a 15-year "nostalgia life cycle" (Staskiewicz). From the record of popular entertainment, the '80s seems to obey all of these patterns. Clusters of 80s–related films and television series can be observed around ten years after the '80s ended (*The Wedding Singer* [1998], *Freaks and Geeks* [1999–2000], *American Psycho* [2000], *Donnie Darko* [2001], and *Rock Star* [2001]), and again about ten years later (*Adventureland* [2009], *Hot Tub Time Machine* [2010], *Super 8* [2011], *Rock of Ages* [2012]). It also seems to be the case that the rolling boil of '80s-awareness that had been stoked by series like *The Goldbergs* (2013–present) and *The Americans* (2013–2018) and by reboots of '80s film franchises such as the three *Star Wars* sequels (2015, 2017, and 2019), the *Rocky* movies about Apollo Creed's son (2015 and 2018), and *Ghostbusters* (2016) has attained its apogee with the popularity of '80s-based titles like *Stranger Things* (2016–present), *Cobra Kai* (2018–present), *The Mandalorian* (2019–present), *Wonder Woman 1984* (2020), and *Ghostbusters: Afterlife* (2021).

The recent currency of the 1980s in popular culture has taken place against a political backdrop in which Donald Trump's presidency suggested echoes of Ronald Reagan's, most conspicuously in Trump's appropriation of Reagan's 1980 campaign slogan, "Let's make America Great Again." In the same way that Reagan's identity as an old-timey film actor evinced to 1980s voters memories of a sanitized version of a prosperous 1950s, so Trump's status as a figure associated with the affluent 1980s suggested that his presidency would signify a return to the supply-side, saber-rattling conservatism of the Reagan era. Toward the end of Trump's presidency, the image of "Ronbo" a cartoon of Ronald Reagan's face on Sylvester Stallone's body, popularized in the mid–80s as a satirical commentary of Reagan's foreign policy, became reinvented as "Trumpbo," one of the most prominent icons of the Trump 2020 movement. Trump's presidency itself might be remembered as the ultimate experiment in rebooting an '80s franchise. The fluid relationship between pop-cultural and political variations of '80s nostalgia demonstrates the extent to which these two realms interpenetrate one another in the life of mass-media society. Writing in 2011, David Sirota warned about what he saw as "the 80s fixation in our current culture" (xx), cautioning us to examine not only "why a twenty-first-century nation is still a 1980s society, but how that anachronistic reality is affecting us right now" (xxi). His thesis that the narcissism, celebrity-worship, and white privilege that characterized the '80s continue to shape our personal attitudes and political behaviors seems, in retrospect, even more relevant today than it was in 2011.

On the most obvious, rational level, a decade is a meaningless unit of historical time. It is self-evident that dividing the recent past into ten-year units is a parlor game that has little, if any, relationship to the real forces of historical phenomena. Indeed, a decade-based historiography likely does more to distort and misrepresent history than it does to illuminate it. As Jason Scott Smith explains, "the concept of the decade represents thinking about time in a punctuated, discontinuous manner. Discontinuous time encourages viewing history not as a seamless web of events, but as discrete, temporally fragmented snapshots" (263). Thinking about "the '80s," for example, as a distinct historical period occludes the sense in which the events of that decade influence and are influenced by events in the previous and subsequent decades while also overstating the degree of continuity between the early years of the decade and the later years. To think of the twentieth century as a series of discrete ten-year "chapters" prioritizes trends in fashion and popular culture while disregarding more significant macro-trends in areas of social justice, environmental history, women's rights, and geopolitical organization. It also, correspondingly, privileges the lifestyles of affluent white consumers rather than representing the perspectives of minority populations and subcultures. Despite these distortional effects of thinking about history through the lens of decades, a decade-based historiography of twentieth-century American history is ubiquitous in popular culture. Smith traces popular fascination with the decade back to the abrupt split that the Great Depression occasioned between the world before 1929 and the world after. The bafflement of Americans living under the duress of the Great Depression spurred a market for nostalgia for the 1920s, which became "the first decade"—the archetypal ten-year span characterized by a particular "style" and drenched in nostalgia for a vanished past. The election of John F. Kennedy in 1960 represented a similar cultural turning-point, drawing attention to the contrast between "the '50s" and "the '60s," and by the end of the 1960s, a popular self-consciousness regarding decade-based chronology served to provide both a shorthand for discussing the recent past as well as a frame of reference within which to understand the present moment. Popular journalism obliged by compiling retrospective articles in any year ending in a 9 that summarized "the decade in review," and, by the mid–1990s, an entire market niche had evolved around celebrating the music, fashion, and ephemera of "the '50s," "the '60s," "the '70s," and, of course, "the '80s." As each decade elapsed, the "idea" of the decade seemed to become more ingrained in the actual culture of the decade, and by 1980, when the sea-change of the transition from the Carter to the Reagan administration seemed to echo the 1960 transition from Eisenhower to Kennedy, American mass-audiences were ready to embrace their status as inhabitants of a new historical period. There is an element of self-conscious performance in "the '80s," therefore, that remains one of the signature elements of the decade, and one that, in some ways, seems to legitimize its uniqueness as a period in history. The '80s might be thought of as the implosive moment when the idea of "the decade" made the transition from being a disingenuous and meaningless historical unit to becoming a self-fulfilling prophecy and therefore a "real" force in history.

Homer Simpson articulates this hyperreal aspect of the 1980s as a unit of time in the *Simpsons* episode "I Married Marge," which, released in 1991, presents one of the first post–80s representations of the 1980s. Introducing his anecdote about meeting his wife in the 1980s, Homer reflects, "It all happened at the beginning of that turbulent decade known as the '80s. Those were idealistic days. The candidacy of John Anderson, the rise of Supertramp. It was an exciting time to be young." Homer carelessly conflates memories of his own past with clichés borrowed from Baby Boomers' nostalgic memoirs about growing up in the 1960s. Homer's use of the words "turbulent" and "idealistic" do not refer to the socio-political realities of 1980; instead, they merely ape the stereotyped language that a decade-based historiography invites, while ephemeral cultural artifacts such as the Anderson campaign and Supertramp take on a heightened significance just because they happen to have existed in a year that ends with a zero. Indeed, it is not rare to hear characters in 1980s media referring to the fact that they live in "the '80s," and trying to use that frame of reference to understand the world they inhabit. In *Xanadu*, released in 1980, Sonny champions his vision for the titular nightclub by pointing out to Gene Kelly that "This is the '80s!" and in *Can't Stop the Music*, released the same year, Samantha shares her conviction that "The '80s are going to be something wonderfully new and different, and so am I!" On the night before election day in 1980, Reagan gave an address to the nation which began with the warning that the coming decade "promises to be the most perilous decade in human history," while a few weeks later, in the final interview he gave before he was shot, John Lennon stated simply, "Let's try to make the '80s good" (Sholin and Kaye). In their own ways, fictional characters, conservative heroes, and rock legends were constructing cultural expectations for the future based on the historiographic model of the decade, making something out of nothing, and presaging a decade where television and movie characters, and maybe even real people, were prone to justifying or explaining just about anything by saying, "It's the '80s." In this strange kind of temporality, mores and social trends mingle together with pop culture references and hairstyles in a transvalued "wax museum" atmosphere that lends them the ontological status of historical artifacts even as they are still happening. The superficiality of referring to the decade as a unit of historical time lends itself to a superficial understanding of history itself, and this principle is exemplified by the "Café 80s" approach to representing the 1980s as a video collage of Rubik's Cubes, Michael Jackson gloves, and Pac-Men (or, as Al Bundy put it in a 1994 episode of *Married ... with Children* [1987–1997], "*Miami Vice*, the DeLorean, and 'Ebony and Ivory,'" or, in the words of the opening voice-over in the first episode of *The Goldbergs*, "E.T., Mr. T, and MTV").

In his landmark 1981 publication *Simulacra and Simulation*, Jean Baudrillard described the fourth order of simulation, in which the simulacrum bears no reference to any signified. The decontextualized icons in The Café 80s exemplify the Baudrillardian semantics of implosion, a condition in which '80s signifiers have no referentiality to any history outside of the "pop history" of their tautological status as '80s signifiers. The Café 80s can be read as a cartoonish critique of any decade-based approach to history—which will always necessarily be equally self-enclosed and ahistorical—but it also serves particularly effectively as a critique of the '80s themselves as a decade that is itself a hyperreal construct—a historical period held together by nothing more than its own performance of itself. In the absence of the geopolitical and domestic strife that had informed the consciousness of the '60s and '70s, the '80s are remembered as a relatively placid time, a time when fashion and fads replaced history as the most conspicuous frame of reference. The baroque hairstyles, loud clothes, and synthesizer-heavy music associated with the 1980s seem to have become popular simply because they signified "the new." If '60s and '70s hair was a political statement, the hairstyles worn by The Thompson Twins and Flock of Seagulls are apolitical statements, hairstyles that escape the gravity of time and history to float into a synthetic dimension of pure being. Big hair, spandex clothing, microwave cookery, and synthesizer music are all "'80s" phenomena that bespeak a cultural consensus that if something becomes technologically possible, it is worth doing. The '80s may turn out to be the high-water mark of popular techno-utopianism, the last decade before the earth's emerging environmental crisis became common knowledge, and it also therefore stands as the decade of "peak America," the decade when the idea of America as the techno-utopia of the future made its final stand. Representations of the 1980s such as those in *It: Chapter One* (2017), *Stranger Things* (2016–present), and *Summer of '84* (2018) that center around pre-adolescent protagonists suggest this connotation that the 1980s itself is America's last pre-oedipal stage, and that the end of the 1980s, as Don Henley plaintively crooned in a song released in 1989, represented the definitive "end of the innocence."

The first section of this book is dedicated to examining the psychological and political function of '80s nostalgia as it has been expressed across a range of media. The first four essays examine the various ways that twenty-first-century representations of the 1980s superimpose the nostalgic timeframe of the 1980s onto the lifeworld of contemporary audiences. In "'There's nothing for you back there': Reflective Nostalgia in *Stranger Things*," Valerie Surrett describes how *Stranger Things'* Upside Down operates as a kind of dark mirror that upends the series' nostalgic representation of '80s childhood, and in "*The Breakfast Club, A Nightmare on Elm Street*, and *Riverdale*'s '80s Palimpsest," Stephen Hock describes a witty instance of how classic '80s films become rewritten as ironic commentaries on the corrosive impact of nostalgia itself. In a similar vein, Lilly J. Goren's essay "*The Americans* and How We Think About the Reagan '80s" describes the sense of double-vision that pervades the show's representation of both the nostalgic and anti-nostalgic aspects of the 1980s, while Jack Anderson's contribution, "'It's just one of them things innit, there's nothing you can do about it': The Specter of Thatcherism in *This Is England '86–'90*" reflects on the "haunting" after-effects that the policies of Ronald Reagan's cross–Atlantic doppelganger, Margaret Thatcher, have inflicted on both the fictional characters in the stories and contemporary audiences. This essay then opens out to consider how the meaning of '80s nostalgia is articulated in other media. In "Remembering to Forget: 1980s Retro Gaming and the Aesthetics of Escape," John Misak explores the motives behind gamers' perennial fascination with the video game aesthetics of the 1980s, and Carrie Clanton concludes this section with "The Pop Music Montage: Nostalgia as a Function of 1980s Film Soundtracks," which considers how the pop music montage, that quintessential '80s trope, has continued to live on as an elemental strategy for configuring time and space.

The next series of essays examines the question of how the phenomenon of '80s nostalgia acts as a lens for thinking about constructions of gender, both then and now. Kristen Galvin's essay "'Cobra Kai Never Dies': Reframing Masculinities in *The Karate Kid*'s Nostalgic Transgenerational Reboot," describes how the popular series *Cobra Kai* actively critiques the style of masculinity celebrated in *The Karate Kid* films from the 1980s, while John Quinn's contribution, "Tragic Masculinities and Craig Mazin's *Chernobyl*," presents a similar argument regarding the stark contrast between the modes of male heroism on display in 1980s popular culture and the failure of "hard body" action heroism to save the day in Mazin's dramatization of a real '80s tragedy. The next pair of essays turn to the construction and representation of '80s girlhood. In "Safety, Stoneybrook, and the Sitters," Morgan E. Foster explains how the *Baby-Sitters Club* books provided an empowering model of female independence for young readers in the 1980s and considers how that spirit has been rekindled in the recent Netflix adaptation of the franchise. In "The Cutest Doll at the Arcade: Technology and (American) Girl Power," Myrna Moretti evaluates the American Girl doll, Courtney, and her accompanying narrative as a window into both the true history and the reconstructed history of how young women have been invited into and sometimes excluded from the culture of technology over the last 40 years. Ann M. Ciasullo's essay "Back to the (Gendered) Future: Feminist Nostalgia in Netflix's *Stranger Things* and *GLOW*," considers the sense in which the reconstructed representations of '80s womanhood in these two series can foster insight into how attitudes about women's roles have evolved and failed to evolve between then and now. Helena I. Gurfinkel concludes this section with her essay "A Very '80s Love Affair: Joanna Hogg's Formalist Feminism in *The Souvenir I*," which interprets Hogg's elusive 2019 film as a vindication of the protagonist's ability to assert her own identity and against a social climate that is eager to absorb and efface female agency.

The final series of essays in this collection considers how media representations of the 1980s intersect with ongoing cultural discourses about social justice, particularly with regard to racism, homophobia, and ableism. The first two essays provide a compelling contrast. In "*Jem*, *She-Ra*, and *My Little Pony*: Combating Misogyny, Homophobia, and Racism in Girl-Centered Reboots," Melanie Hurley argues that the progressive values expressed in certain cartoon franchises marketed toward young girls in the 1980s have been picked up again and reinforced in recent reboots of these franchises. Conversely, in "Nostalgia for What Always Was: Race and American Superheroes in Television and Film," Patrick L. Hamilton and Allan W. Austin argue that the superficial "multiculturalism" prevalent in 1980s superhero cartoons (marketed primarily to young boys) continues to haunt modern iterations of superhero stories, limiting their ability to deal meaningfully with racial inclusivity. Erika Tiburcio Moreno, meanwhile, inspects the racist atmosphere of white privilege, xenophobia, and lethal policing that connect the Reagan era to our own in her essay "'Dad, every serial killer is somebody's neighbor!' The Problem of White Supremacy in *Summer of '84*." The second half of this section turns to texts that represent the HIV/AIDS crisis in the 1980s. Craig Clark's essay "*Dallas Buyers Club*: Libertarian American Dreams in the Neoliberal 1980s," focuses on how Ron Woodroof's free-market approach to his medical treatment reveals the anti-individualist hypocrisy of the neoliberal worldview upheld by the Reagan Administration. The final two essays, Ilaria Biano's "Ryan Murphy's '80s and the Past as Political Postmodern Battleground" and Kylo-Patrick R. Hart's "Cinematically Satirizing AIDS Realities of the Reagan Decade in *Chocolate Babies*," examine media texts that celebrate the empowerment, activism, and diversity of the '80s-era LGBTQ+ community.

Indeed, the closer we look at the 1980s, as both a historical period and as a subject of representation, the more diversity and complexity we see. For this reason, the examination of what the 1980s "means" lends itself to the collaborative approach exemplified in this book. The international team of critics, historians, and scholars represented here provides a wealth of perspectives and insights that challenge us to look closer at a decade whose meaning seems to be continually evolving as it has been re-presented and reimagined by successive waves of artists and storytellers.

Works Cited

Gopnik, Adam. "The Forty-Year Itch." *The New Yorker*. 16 April 2012.

Kushner, Tony. *Angels in America*. New York: Theatre Communications Group, 2013.

Sholin, Dave, and Laurie Kaye. "John Lennon's Last Interview, December 8, 1980."

Sirota, David. *Back to Our Future*. Ballantine, 2011.

Smith, Jason Scott. "The Strange History of the Decade: Modernity, Nostalgia, and the Perils of Periodization." *Journal of Social History* 32(2), 1998. 263–285.

Staskiewicz, Keith. "'American Reunion': Have We Entered the Era of Late-'90s Nostalgia?" EW.com, 7 April 2012.

Van Hoof, Carolien. "Cycles of Nostalgia: A Return of the 80s." *The Sundial Press*, 25 March 2019.

Wilson, Carl. "My So-Called Adulthood." *The New York Times Magazine*, 4 August 2011.

Time After Time
The Meaning of '80s Nostalgia

"There's nothing for you back there"

Reflective Nostalgia in Stranger Things

VALERIE SURRETT

"A cinematic image of nostalgia is a double exposure, or a superimposition of two images—of home and abroad, of past and present, of dream and everyday life. The moment we try to force it into a single image, it breaks the frame or burns the surface."—Svetlana Boym[1]

Nostalgia might be the number one word associated with the Duffer Brothers' hit Netflix series, *Stranger Things*. Set in the fictional town of Hawkins, Indiana, in the mid–1980s, the show deluges viewers with the decade's aesthetics, saturating each chapter with '80s pop culture iconography, homages to classic '80s cinema, synth soundscapes, shopping malls, and analog tech.[2] If examined solely from a nostalgic standpoint, the show might discourage critical thought about the '80s (and, by extension, the 2010s) by presenting a faux version of the decade stripped of the real-life fears and injustices that plagued it. After all, nostalgia for a simpler time demands this type of erasure. But the show is equal parts nostalgia and horror, a genre that employs monstrous metaphors ("analogies!") that invite critical engagement with the existential dooms of the here and now.[3]

Season 1 begins with the opening of a gate between planes. Eleven (El), a telepathic and telekinetic child whose powers are the result of her mother's participation in MK-Ultra experiments while pregnant, unintentionally rips the fabric separating Hawkins from the Upside Down with a powerful psionic scream. Eleven was stolen from her mother at birth and raised by Dr. Brenner, aka "Papa," in Hawkins Lab, a cover for a clandestine government operation that includes wielding psionic children as Cold War weapons. The opened gate reveals the Upside Down and allows one of

11

its monsters, the Demogorgon, to traverse between planes. The Demogorgon captures a boy named Will and takes him to the Upside Down. Will's nerdy, D&D loving friends, Dustin, Lucas, and Mike—aka "the Party"—join up with the newly-escaped El on a quest to find and rescue Will. Seasons 2 and 3 follow the Party's continued efforts to hold the Upside Down's ever-more-terrifying monsters at bay and to close the gate.

The show is one of many 2010s pop culture texts to capitalize on contemporary nostalgia for the '80s; however, the show's '80s aesthetics only tell half the story of why the show resonated with 2010s American audiences the way that it did. The elements of horror explain the rest. Just as the Party's late-night bicycle rides through cul-de-sac streets tickled the zeitgeist in its portrayal of a simpler, analog childhood, the uncanny, horror-filled Upside Down and its rapacious denizens of doom also hit at exactly the right time as America's real-life political landscape was also ringing with an echo from the 1980s—"Make America Great Again." For many, this echo was less nostalgic than horror-filled.

Despite its nostalgic veneer, the series ultimately assumes an anti-nostalgic stance in its visual linking of Hawkins with the parallel dimension, the Upside Down. The Upside Down is often visually represented as an underground world, hidden just below the Earth's surface, while the dimension's flora is depicted as a massive, ever-expanding root system. The Upside Down thus symbolically functions as the foundation of the fictional town and the roots of the community. The Upside Down also mirrors Hawkins in landscape and architecture, only the buildings are dilapidated and the spore-filled atmosphere is dark, cold, and toxic. This visual layering and doubling positions Hawkins as a palimpsest constructed to obscure the older, deeper, horror-filled reality of the Upside Down. The Upside Down thus represents horrors of the past lying in wait for an opportunity to rupture nostalgic renderings of a decade marked by exploding national debt, the AIDS epidemic, the racist War on Drugs, Cold War fears, and conservative backlashes to social justice advancements of the '60s and '70s.

The visual imagery of the Upside Down connects real-world Reagan-era nostalgia for the 1950s to Trump-era nostalgia for the Reaganite '80s, a call to return to "Again" that viewers were living through as they binged seasons 1, 2, and 3. Season 2 opens in October of 1984 in the final weeks of Reagan's reelection campaign. The series explicitly and repeatedly references this context via "Reagan-Bush '84" campaign placards peppering suburban yards and "Vote Here" signs affixed to library façades.[4] In a series set in the past and saturated with iconic '80s nostalgia, such overt references to an administration that successfully promoted 1950s nostalgia as a political strategy become metacommentary on nostalgia itself. From this view, the Upside Down functions as the festering underbelly of Reaganite "Let's Make America Great Again" politics that placed hope for a brighter future in a return to an imagined, idyllic past, a palimpsest 1950s based largely on cinematic iconography. Through the Upside Down and its monsters, the series, thus far, exposes the biopolitical functions of collective nostalgia and, through the posthuman, cyborg child Eleven, argues for the political necessity of placing hope for the future *in the future*.

The Never-Place: or, Nostalgia All the Way Down

The term nostalgia is a portmanteau of the Greek *nóstos*, meaning homecoming, and *álgos*, or pain. Most contemporary scholarship aligns nostalgia with Svetlana Boym's definition: "a longing for a home that no longer exists or has never existed," (7) a sentiment captured by Gertrude Stein's observation upon returning to her childhood home that "there is no there there."[5] Nostalgia, in this sense, refers to a painful yearning to return to a romanticized, misremembered past, a never-place. Collective nostalgic longings tend to align with a phenomenon that Boym refers to as "restorative nostalgia," a reactionary discontentment that locates the solutions to today's problems in a return to an idealized past (13–15). Restorative nostalgia resists critical evaluation of the past by advocating for *nostos*. However, Boym also complicates the functions of nostalgia by creating a space for understanding nostalgia as a productive tool for self-reflection. "Reflective nostalgia," a nostalgia that "thrives on *algia*," or longing for what is lost, acknowledges imperfections and gaps intrinsic to the process of remembering (13). Asserting that "nostalgia … is not always retrospective; it can be prospective as well," Boym envisions reflective nostalgia as a critical process that acknowledges that the past for which we yearn is necessarily part fantasy; yet, through this acknowledgment, we can turn our energies to incorporating the fantastical elements of misremembered yesterdays into prospective visions of better futures, appropriating the anti-utopian sentiments of nostalgia for utopian purposes (8).

At first glance, *Stranger Things* gestures towards restorative nostalgia, particularly in its cinematic recreation of bygone analog childhoods. The freedom of the Party to hop on their bikes in the dark and pursue danger by flashlight not only pays homage to '80s classics, like *E.T.: The Extra-Terrestrial* (1982), *The Goonies* (1985), and *Stand by Me* (1986), but also reminds viewers who grew up in the '80s, like myself, that once upon a time it was possible for us to escape the parental gaze, to momentarily be unfindable. For viewers born after the '80s, the show depicts an unimaginable, seemingly fantastical time of freedom from digital surveillance—a time when it was common for parents to have no idea where their latchkey children were *and to be ok with it*.[6]

The show's romanticizing of the Party's seemingly carefree and, well, *free* childhood, combined with its saturation of '80s pop culture references and iconography, tempts a reading of the show as firmly in the camp of restorative nostalgia. Dan Hassler-Forest, for instance, argues that the show "feeds and sustains a deeply conservative cultural, social and political sensibility, in which attractions of this earlier era are exaggerated and made more spectacular, while its problems are casually papered over" (184). While Hassler-Forest's analysis of Season 1 has merit, I find that the elements of restorative nostalgia in the series' opening chapters give way to a deeper, reflective nostalgia as the series unfolds, ultimately extending into to anti-nostalgia, or a critique of nostalgia itself in Seasons 2 and 3.

Stranger Things recreates an era that was, in itself, steeped in nostalgia for "the Fifties," what Michael D. Dwyer refers to as the pop culture construction of a simpler, purer past distinct from the literal decade. For a fifteen-year period during the '70s and '80s, Americans experienced a groundswell of '50s pop culture nostalgia, including Hollywood films, period sitcoms, increased access to 1950s films and sitcoms via cable TV, and a "Golden Oldies" music craze (Dwyer). Nostalgia for the '50s in pop culture echoed and reinforced concurrent trends in political rhetoric. The rise of the New Christian Right, fueled by Jerry Falwell's Moral Majority lobby in 1979, also placed America's future in its past by insisting that the road to social and economic stability ended in a revival of the '50s suburb and its nuclear families.

The Duffer brothers' choice to create a fictional town as the setting for *Stranger Things* heightens the show's critique of restorative nostalgia. Hawkins, very literally, has never existed off-screen. Of equal importance is the show's centering of an idyllic, rust belt suburb, a place Lacey N. Smith argues has also never existed. Applying Jean Baudrillard and Fredric Jameson's concepts of postmodern simulacrum—or replicas without originals—to portrayals of suburbia in film and television since the 1950s, Smith claims that onscreen suburbia "is always a reflection of a reflection of a reflection," a never-place imbued with ideological significance (217). The suburban simulacra, a powerful mode of anti-communist Cold War propaganda, anchors the mythos of the American Dream to suburbia, representing white, middle-class, suburban spaces as normative. The suburban simulacrum is also the site of the idyllic American family, a nuclear family led by the patriarchal father.[7]

In 1980, Ronald Reagan, the actor-turned-presidential candidate, capitalized on both political and cultural nostalgia for the '50s in his "Let's Make America Great Again" campaign that promised to return the country to "traditional American values." Cinematic iconography of the '50s suburbs and their normative nuclear families was central to Reagan's message (Dwyer).[8] For Reagan, the cinematic '50s represented the height of the U.S. as a healthy biopolitical state in which internal and external Others were thoroughly held in check. The suburban simulacrum symbolized an era of strict conformity to social norms, norms that drew stark contrasts between America as a Christian capitalist state and Russia as a secular communist state. The cinematic '50s suburb is also a white space, assured by Jim Crow laws, redlining, and restrictive covenants. Finally, Reagan's evocation of the '50s hearkened back to the post-war boom, when the U.S.'s economy felt secure and the U.S.'s role as an international superpower appeared unquestioned following the atomic bombings of Hiroshima and Nagasaki.

A Return to "Again," Again

Nearly four decades after Reagan rolled out his "Let's Make America Great Again" slogan, amid a pop-culture revival of the Reagan era in film and television, another cultural-figure-turned-presidential-hopeful, Donald Trump, rebooted Reagan's 1980 campaign slogan into the 2016 directive, "Make America Great Again." While appropriating Reagan's use of political nostalgia, Trump's populist MAGA brand presented an image of America that was stripped bare of Reagan's hopeful tones, bringing to the forefront the fearful undercurrents of Reagan's seemingly optimistic campaigns. At the heart of both campaigns was fear; the American way of life was under attack by foreign enemies at the borders and an expanding welfare state within.

During his 2020 re-election bid, Trump revived yet another icon of Reagan's rhetoric—the suburbs. Painting a picture of white suburbs under siege, threatened by low-income housing developments and encroaching minorities, Trump tweeted, "The 'suburban housewife' will be voting for me. They want safety & are thrilled that I ended the long running program where low income housing would invade their neighborhood" (@realDonaldTrump). Again, Trump strips bare Reagan's more subtle rhetoric, making clear that, for both, the suburbs represent the idyllic American space where middle-class, white nuclear families can thrive in comfortable homes, free of the violence and corruption of urban spaces. For both, the image of the suburbs they invoke is an idyllic fantasy and powerful political tool.

The Monsters Within

Reagan and Trump's "Again" campaigns shed light on the biopolitical functions of restorative nostalgia in neoconservative political rhetoric.

For both, the suburban simulacrum presents the suburbs as a place of original unity and purity, threated by encroaching outside enemies, both foreign and domestic. Michel Foucault, amid a rising tide of neoliberalism in Europe and America in the '70s and '80s, formulated his theories of biopolitics, or "the new discursive regulation of populations through surveillance and control of their health, sexuality, reproduction, and so on" (*Society* 4). Biopolitical states justify their power over "life in general" by promising to safeguard citizens' lives and the health of the body politics (*Society* 253). But there's a catch. Biopolitical states regulate the body politic based on a system of norms, normalizing the individual through discipline and the population through biopower. Though biopolitical regimes purport to promote peace, prosperity, and health, Foucault suggests that perpetual intra- and inter-state wars undergird biopolitical programs (*Society* 50–51). A backdrop of perpetual inter-state war justifies what Giorgio Agamben terms state-of-exception suspensions of individual rights while also fueling nationalistic rhetoric and demanding unquestioned loyalty to the state (Agamben; Foucault *Society* 62). Perpetual intra-state war divides the body politic into groups: disciplined subjects who adhere to norms and enemy subjects who transgress them.

In *Stranger Things,* the suburban simulacrum of Hawkins embodies neoconservative uses of nostalgic rhetoric *until* El rips the veil hiding the underground, exposing Hawkins as it really is. Hawkins was not a place of original unity and purity; the threats to Hawkins were inside all along. While the Upside Down functions as a corrective to the suburban simulacrum, exposing the suburban space as always already "infected space" (Smith 218), its monsters embody the threats biopolitical states pose to their own citizen-subjects by manufacturing internal enemies, picking off non-normative subjects at the fringes, disciplining subjects via a system of norms, and conscripting the body politic in biopolitical wars.

The Vale of Shadows

The Upside Down: the dark, oozy, toxic foundation upon which the glossy, camera-ready Hawkins rests. Film critics and scholars alike have spilled much ink trying to answer the question, *what exactly is the Upside Down?* To help them understand the bizarre space that has stolen their friend, a place that is both where they are and where they cannot be, the Party references a source they know all too well, *Dungeons & Dragons* and its legend of the Vale of Shadows. As described by Dustin, "the Vale of Shadows is a dimension that is a dark reflection or echo of our world. It's a place of decay and death, a plane out of phase, a place of monsters. It is right next to you and you don't even see it" (1:5). In Season 1, when Will is in the Upside Down, he is both "here" and "not here" at once; both in his home and dispossessed of it; both next to his mother and unable to touch her. He is in a realm of decay and death that looks like his home, "but it's so dark … and empty. And it's cold!" (1:4). Its monster, the Demogorgon, is always hungry, always hunting.[9]

Thinking of the Upside Down as a parallel universe explains some of its characteristics, but also raises new questions, such as how actions in Hawkins, such as decorating the school gym for the Snow Ball dance, affect the corresponding parts of the Upside Down (*who decorated the gym in the Upside Down?*), or how Will is able to communicate between worlds using Christmas lights, stereos, and landline phones. There are other mysteries as well. El is responsible for ripping the fabric separating the two worlds. However, the gate she opened is located in the basement of Hawkins Lab. This doesn't explain how other gates begin to open around Hawkins: in trees, floors, and Joyce Byers' living room wall. In short, the Upside Down seems to be a parallel universe and *something else*, something much more connected to life in Hawkins.

Season 2, which opens against the backdrop of Reagan's re-election campaign, solidifies the visual imagery of the Upside Down as *below* Hawkins. Back at Hawkins Lab, the gate to the Upside Down El opened in Season 1 continues to grow, despite the lab agents' best efforts to burn it shut. The Upside Down is also growing underneath Hawkins, its vine-like flora carving labyrinthine tunnel systems just beneath Hawkins' surface. The Upside Down refuses to be contained, killing crops and plant life in Hawkins as it spreads below. Theoretically, if allowed to spread at will, the Upside Down's flora would carve tunnels underneath all of Hawkins, weakening the surface. The Upside Down is also much easier to access in Season 2; the Party enters the dimension simply by digging above one of the tunnels. The narrative's positioning of Hawkins on top of the Upside Down, rendering the Upside Down accessible by a little light shoveling, suggests that the Upside Down is the foundation of Hawkins. As the borders continue to thin, the Upside Down threatens to swallow the surface.

"Something's coming…. Something thirsty for blood." —Mike

The monsters of the Upside Down similarly evolve, beginning with a lone Demogorgon in Season 1, adding the Mind Flayer and its demodog minions in Season 2, and introducing the Spider Monster in Season 3. Each figure satisfies Noël Carroll's criteria of art-horror monsters; they are threatening and impure, eliciting both fear and disgust (27–35). Season 1's Demogorgon is a humanoid predator with long arms and a tooth-filled flower face. The monster hangs out in liminal spaces, picking off victims from the fringes of society: Will, Barb, and, according to Dr. Brenner, six other people we never see (1:8). Will, vaguely coded as queer, is taken from his house, which is located on the outskirts of suburbia. Barb, the clear social outsider at Steve's house party, is taken from Steve's pool.[10] The monster is drawn by blood, drawn to people who have been hurt by/within Hawkins. Looked at through a biopolitical lens, the monster preys on the non-normative, the boundary dwellers and transgressors who threaten the health of the suburban simulacrum's body politic.[11]

Season 2 introduces us to the Mind Flayer (aka Shadow Monster), a hivemind superorganism that controls all forms of life in the Upside Down through a collective consciousness. The Mind Flayer's ostensible goal is to break into Hawkins and infect human life, bending humanity to its will. According to Dustin, it "believes it's the master race" (2:8). The Shadow Monster infects Will, slowly taking over his mind and replacing Will's own memories with "now memories," connecting Will to the Mind Flayer's thoughts (2:4). Will, as the Mind Flayer's spy, begins to do its bidding, sending several Hawkins Lab soldiers to their deaths in the Upside Down. Season 3 gives rise to a new monster, the Spider Monster. The Spider Monster evokes Hobbes' Leviathan, an image of a body politic operating as a single, spider-like body made of individual citizens, a body headed by a tyrant.

Season 3 ratchets up the disgust quotient of Carroll's art-horror formula. In the opening chapter, part of the Spider Monster escapes the Upside Down and enters Hawkins.[12] This small part, working on the Mind Flayer's behalf, begins to build a great weapon, a weapon made of the guts, bones, and teeth of all life forms it infects, beginning with rats. When the Mind Flayer's weapon initially takes over a life, the possession seems very similar to Will's possession by the Mind Flayer in Season 2. The creature's mind slowly gives way to the will of the possessor. However, after eating fertilizer and chemicals for a while, and whenever the weapon deems it necessary, the possessed creature makes its way "back" to "the source" by exploding into a pile of bio ooze—bones, hair, blood, guts—before worming its way towards the weapon (3:4). The weapon then subsumes the new victim into its ever-growing body, a body made of bodies. The Spider Monster, as the Mind Flayer's weapon, is pursuing two related goals: "to build," adding more bodies to its amalgamated body of bodies, and to infect El, adding her to its collection (3:2; 3:6). The Mind Flayer regards El as the only force that can truly stop it; as such, it is determined to eradicate her powers by drawing her into itself.

The biopolitical functions of the Mind Flayer and its minions are difficult to miss. Believing itself to be the master race, the Mind Flayer is driven to bring all life under its command, disciplining all subjects to adhere to its ideals of proper life—its norms. Unlike the threats posed by the Demogorgon or demodogs—a painful death as a terrifying monster eats you alive—the Mind Flayer threatens the residents of Hawkins in a more intimate way; it threatens to consume identity and agency, turning everyone in its grasp into mindless foot soldiers marching toward war. It seeks to create one body politic, a body that acts and moves in unity, advancing the Mind Flayer's ultimate goal of dominating all life outside its network. When combined with the overt references to Reaganite politics in Season 2, the Mind Flayer, and the Upside Down it inhabits, represent anxieties about a political agenda that seeks to enforce rigid social norms and demands unquestioned, nationalistic loyalty to the state.

"I am the monster"—El

Stranger Things provides one defense against the trappings of restorative nostalgia: El, the shadow walker. As many have noted, El is a bit of a mashup of psionic figures featured in '70s and '80s horror films—a sprinkle of *Carrie* (1976), a dash of *Poltergeist* (1982), and a heaping scoop of *Firestarter* (1984). Created as a Cold War weapon, her childhood is spent in training, learning to use her telepathic powers to locate and spy on Russian intelligence and her telekinetic and biokinetic powers to kill. Her childhood in the lab is depicted as a traumatic sequence of abuse and manipulation as "Papa" pushes El to her physical, psionic, and emotional limits. If she performs as commanded, she is rewarded with praise and mild affection; if she fails, she is punished with solitary confinement. Dr. Brenner also keeps El in a state of arrested development as part of his plan to discipline her as a biopolitical weapon, as evidenced by her monosyllabic speech and stick-figure drawings.

But El escapes.

El is a cyborg. As the product of in utero experimentation, it is not possible to isolate the parts of El that are "natural" and "unnatural," "human" and "machine." She does not have an origin story of organic unity and wholeness before undergoing cyborganization. Her before-birth hybridity transgresses her biopolitical state's norms. She is also monstrous in the Foucauldian sense, defying rules of both law and of nature, both forbidden and impossible (*Abnormal*), but she is not a monster of art-horror. We do not run away in fear and disgust. In 1985, Donna Haraway proposed an ironic liberation for cyborg life in "A Cyborg Manifesto." Despite the origins of cyborgs as the "illegitimate offspring of militarism and patriarchal capitalism, not to mention state socialism," Haraway sees a potential for the cyborg to change its apocalyptic fate as a biopolitical weapon and move towards a future finally freed from humanism's hierarchical binaries and resulting endless wars (151).

Fatherless, cyborgian, psionic, monstrous: El is the antidote to restorative nostalgic thinking. In El, Dr. Brenner has created a weapon he does not understand and cannot control. The powers Dr. Brenner disciplines El to hone and master are the very powers capable of undermining his biopolitical agenda, an agenda that depends on the maintenance of Hawkins as a suburban simulacrum. But El is a shadow walker, able to traverse liminal spaces and reveal the Upside Down that has always been there.

Stranger Things might be set in the '80s, but its use of a suburban simulacrum self-consciously gestures to the nostalgic fantasy of Hawkins' surface. Its Upside Down ruptures the image, reminding us of all the things restorative nostalgia demands that we forget. The show does not suggest that tomorrow's solutions can be found in a return to the '80s; through El, the show looks forward. El is the currently-impossible future, but the future to strive for, not because of her psionic powers, but because of her hybrid nature that denies the myth of original unity and wholeness, destabilizing dualisms upon which biopolitical agendas depend. Airing against a political narrative that insists on a return to "Again," *Stranger Things,* through El, reminds us, "there's nothing for you back there" (2:7).

"Mornings are for coffee and contemplation"
—Hopper

Writing against the backdrop of Trump's presidency and the further entrenchment of MAGA's "America First" nationalism in right-wing politics, the Duffer Brothers sharpen and clarify the series' political commentaries in each season, using the ever-evolving Upside Down to critique biopolitical ideologies that demand strict adherence to norms and view all Others as enemies to be conquered or eliminated. Though political references remain subtle in Season 1, the Duffer Brothers bring the era's politics to the forefront in Seasons 2 and 3. Likewise, what at first appears to be a supersaturation of restorative nostalgia in the series' opening chapters gives way to reflective nostalgia as the Upside Down and its monsters insist that Hawkins is always already a never-place, a palimpsest creation of restorative nostalgia. In short, the show simultaneously encourages nostalgia while also insisting that the time and place for which we yearn is a false memory. In the faux-utopian landscape of Hawkins, the posthuman

El represents the possibility of a future we can't yet imagine, a future that has yet to be written. El thus invites us to participate in a nostalgia that is reflective rather than restorative. We can acknowledge that some aspects of bygone eras might have been better than the present, but the solution to the present cannot be a reactionary return. Rather, we must tear the veil of restorative nostalgia and face the horrors of the past. Only then can we incorporate what was good about yesterday into visions of wholly new futures.

Notes

1. Boym, Svetlana, "Nostalgia and Its Discontents."
2. For an exhaustive list of '80s references and allusions in *Stranger Things*, see Joseph Vogel's *Stranger Things and the '80s: The Complete Retro Guide*. Cardinal Books, 2018.
3. For an extended analysis of horror in *Stranger Things*, see Franklin S. Allaire and Krista S. Gehring's "Horror Appeals to Our Dual Nature," Adrea Zanin's "Not from Around Here," and William C. Pamerleau's "The Unique Horror of the Upside Down" in *Stranger Things and Philosophy*.
4. The series also frequently references Reagan via television and radio. For example, in Season 1, Chapter 3, El flips on Mike's TV to Reagan giving a speech following the 1983 bombing in Beirut, Lebanon that killed 241 U.S. citizens and soldiers. Similarly, when El flips through radio stations searching for white noise, she frequently passes stations relaying Reagan's voice or Cold War news.
5. Gertrude Stein. *Everybody's Autobiography*. Vintage Books, 1937.
6. For an extended analysis of nostalgia as simulacra in *Stranger Things*, see Cherise Huntingford's "To Err is Human, to Forget…Sublime" in *ST. Stranger Things and Philosophy*.
7. For a show set in an '80s suburb, effectual father figures are strikingly absent in *Stranger Things*. The show does center one stereotypical suburban nuclear family, the Wheelers; however, the family's seemingly idyllic façade quickly gives way to a thinly-veiled critique of neoconservative insistence that the nuclear family is the best safeguard against the evils that threaten American life.
8. See Lauren Berlant's discussion of how Reagan's political campaigns brought the nuclear family to the political forefront by convincing "a citizenry that the core context of politics should be the sphere of private life." *The Queen of America Goes to Washington City: Essays on Sex and Citizenship*. Duke University Press, 1997.
9. Like most features and creatures of the Upside Down, the Demogorgon gets its name from *Dungeons & Dragons*; however, it is one of the show's anachronisms. The Demogorgon was introduced in 1976, three years after the setting of Season 1.
10. For a fascinating discussion of Barb and the #JusticeForBarb social media campaign demanding the show address her death, see Eric Holmes and Jeremy Christensen's "Barb Dead, People Mad" in *Stranger Things and Philosophy*.
11. For discussions of ways the show centers outsiders, misfits, and liminal characters, see Christine Muller's "Should I Stay or Should I Go," in *Uncovering Stranger Things* and Fernando Gabriel Pagnoni Berns, Diego Foronda, and Mariana Zárate's essay, "Abnormal is the New Normal" in *Stranger Things and Philosophy*.
12. Whereas Season 1 and Season 2 place blame for the opened gate on Hawkins Lab, aka the Department of Energy, Russian operatives re-open the gate in Season 3. In addition to taking critical aim at late-stage American capitalism by setting the season's final showdown inside a brand-new shopping mall, a la the 1978 zombie classic, *Dawn of the Dead*, Season 3 also collapses differences between the U.S. government and Russia by mirroring their efforts to harness the Upside Down as a biopolitical weapon.

Works Cited

Agamben, Giorgio. *State of Exception.* Translated by Kevin Attell. University of Chicago Press, 2005.

Boym, Svetlana, "Nostalgia and Its Discontents." *The Hedgehog Review* vol. 9 no. 2, Summer 2007. pp. 7–18. *Gale Academic OneFile.* GALEIA168775861.

Carroll, Noël. *The Philosophy of Horror: or, Paradoxes of the Heart.* Routledge, 1990.

Duffer, Matt, and Ross Duffer, creators. *Stranger Things.* 21 Laps Entertainment and Netflix, 2016.

Dwyer, Michael D. *Back to the Fifties.* Oxford University Press, 2015.

Foucault, Michel. *Abnormal: Lectures at the College De France 1974–1975.* Translated by Graham Burchell. Picard, 2003.

_____. *Discipline and Punish.* Translated by Alan Sheridan. Random House, 1995.

_____. *Society Must Be Defended.* Translated by David Macey. Ed. Arnold I. Davidson. Picador, 2003.

Haraway, Donna. "A Cyborg Manifesto." *Simians, Cyborgs, and Women.* Routledge, 1991. 149–182.

Hassler-Forest, Dan. "'When you get there, you will already be there': *Stranger Things, Twin Peaks* and the Nostalgia Industry." *Science Fiction Film and Television* vol.13, no. 2, July 2020, pp. 175–195. *Project MUSE* muse.jhu.edu/article/760791.

@realDonaldTrump. "The 'suburban housewife' will be voting for me. They want safety & are thrilled that I ended the long running program where low income housing would invade their neighborhood. Biden would reinstall it, in a bigger form, with Corey Booker in charge! @foxandfriends @MariaBartiromo." *Twitter,* 12 Aug. 2020, 7:59 a.m.

Smith, Lacey N. "A nice home at the end of the cul-de-sac." *Uncovering* Stranger Things: *Essays on Eighties Nostalgia, Cynicism, and Innocence in the Series.* Ed. Kevin J. Wetmore, Jr. McFarland, 2018.

The Breakfast Club, A Nightmare on Elm Street, and Riverdale's '80s Palimpsest

STEPHEN HOCK

Since its premiere on January 26, 2017, the CW television series *Riverdale* has presented an updated treatment of classic Archie Comics characters. Beyond its adaptation of elements from its sources in Archie Comics, *Riverdale* has consistently fashioned itself as a text that draws on any number of predecessor texts, for instance, in the fact that the titles of many of its episodes allude to earlier film, television, and theater productions. This essay focuses on one such episode, "Chapter Thirty-Nine: The Midnight Club," the fourth episode of *Riverdale*'s third season. First broadcast on November 7, 2018, both the title and premise of "The Midnight Club" frame the episode as a rewriting of John Hughes' quintessential '80s teen movie *The Breakfast Club* (1985).

Like *The Breakfast Club*, "The Midnight Club" presents the story of a group of high school students bonding while spending time together in Saturday detention. Relatively quickly, however, the episode swerves into seemingly much different territory, becoming a horror story that culminates in murder. In this swerve, "The Midnight Club" jumps from teen drama to teen horror. More specifically, it brings the John Hughes teen films exemplified by *The Breakfast Club* into dialogue with another well-known set of films from the '80s, namely, the *Nightmare on Elm Street* films, through an allusion to that series' third installment, *A Nightmare on Elm Street 3: Dream Warriors* (1987). In doing so, "The Midnight Club" highlights affinities between these two intertexts in terms of their treatment of relationships between teenagers and their parents.

"The Midnight Club" further puts its textual present in dialogue with the textual past signified by *The Breakfast Club* and the *Nightmare on Elm*

Street films by framing itself as a flashback set in the '80s. In that '80s setting, the present visually rewrites itself over the past by virtue of the fact that, in this flashback, the young actors who play *Riverdale*'s teen characters portray their characters' parents as teens. As such, "The Midnight Club" functions as a palimpsest, in which the present inscribes itself on top of the semi-effaced traces of past texts, including *The Breakfast Club*, the *Nightmare on Elm Street* films, and the '80s that those films metonymically stand for. Ultimately, *Riverdale*'s '80s palimpsest suggests a cycle of generational continuity in which teens unavoidably become their parents. This dynamic of generational continuity, in turn, reflects the contemporary sense of the generational return of the '80s, the era of Reagan, in the Trump era in which *Riverdale* was made.

"Are we gonna be like our parents?"

"The Midnight Club" never precisely states that the flashback that makes up the bulk of the episode takes place in the '80s. In fact, the *Spoilertv.com* page for the episode quotes a press release, which it attributes to the CW, that describes the flashback as being set "in the early 90's" (qtd. in Benjamin). Likewise, the voiceover narration that accompanies the flashback, provided by Mädchen Amick in her role as Betty's mother, Alice Cooper, sets the stage for the flashback by noting that "everything smelled like teen spirit," which would seem to point to a setting no earlier than the 1991 release date of Nirvana's "Smells Like Teen Spirit." However, the fact that Archie's father, Fred Andrews, appears in the flashback as a high school student, combined with the fact that the series establishes elsewhere that Fred was born in 1970 (for instance, in the memorial plaque at the Fred Andrews Community Center seen in "Chapter Sixty-Four: The Ice Storm," the seventh episode of *Riverdale*'s fourth season, first broadcast on November 20, 2019), indicates an '80s setting. Regardless of the intricacies of maintaining continuity in episodic television, the cultural milieu of "The Midnight Club" is unmistakably the '80s. The episode's soundtrack, for instance, consists entirely of songs from the '80s, ranging from A-ha's "Take On Me" to Spandau Ballet's "True," without a hint of nineties grunge, Alice's voiceover notwithstanding.

Beyond those musical cues, "The Midnight Club" most obviously engages with the '80s by virtue of the fact that it takes its premise of students from different high school cliques bonding while in Saturday detention from *The Breakfast Club*, the quintessential teen film by the filmmaker who defined the '80s teen film as a genre, John Hughes. As Elissa H. Nelson observes, "Films featuring teen characters in primary roles have been a mainstay in Hollywood for decades. However, it was in the 1980s that these films started to form a more unified genre, that the semantic and syntactic rules became more fully codified, and that the structural elements became more discernable" (52). Hughes has been widely recognized as the master of this genre. As Susannah Gora puts it, "Starting in 1984 with *Sixteen Candles*, and ending in 1987 with *Some Kind of Wonderful*, John Hughes remade American teenhood in his own image" (4). Apropos of "The Midnight Club," *The Breakfast Club* has been singled out among Hughes' teen films as a particularly exemplary model of a film that takes issues facing '80s teens seriously. Gora argues:

> Because Hughes had his finger on the pulse of young America, it's only fitting that the cross-section of personalities inhabiting the library in *The Breakfast Club* represented what was happening in the lives of many real-life teenagers across the country in the 1980s. Claire was a child of impending divorce; 1980s teens' parents were getting divorced at an unprecedented rate. Allison was a lonely youth ignored by her parents; this was the era of latchkey kids, adolescents who came home to an empty house and often were their own primary caregivers. Brian was a teen considering suicide; 1980s teens killed themselves at a rate triple that of their 1950s counterparts [65].

In both the popular and critical imagination, *The Breakfast Club* stands as a period signifier of '80s teen films, making it a particularly apt vehicle for *Riverdale*'s flashback to the high school years of the parents of its teen characters.

Fraught relationships between teens and their parents lie at the heart of *The Breakfast Club*. Even though the parents appear only at the very beginning of the film, to drop their children off at Saturday detention, and then at the very end, to pick them up again, the teens' relationships with their parents come up repeatedly. Claire, the "princess" played by Molly Ringwald, expresses her frustration with her parents by telling Bender, the "criminal" played by Judd Nelson, "I mean, I don't think either one of them gives a shit about me. It's like they use me just to get back at each other." A moment later, Bender follows up by asking Andy, the "athlete" of the group, played by Emilio Estevez, "You get along with your parents?" to which Andy responds, "Well, if I say yes, I'm an idiot, right?" "You're an idiot anyway," Bender replies, "but if you say you get along with your parents, well, you're a liar, too." As Bender and Andy face off, Brian, the "brain" played by Anthony Michael Hall, tries to create a connection by sharing, "I don't like my parents, either." In a later scene, the remaining member of the Breakfast Club, Allison, the "basket case" played by Ally Sheedy, offers that she might have to run away because, as she puts it, "My home life is unsatisfying," after which Andy observes, "Well, everyone's home life is unsatisfying. If it wasn't, people would live with their parents forever." Over the course of the film, across the barriers of social class and high school clique that separate the members of the Breakfast Club, fractured relationships with parents stand as the strongest of the shared experiences that unite them.

That shared experience later motivates Andy to pose the starkest question the members of the Breakfast Club face during their day in detention: "Are we gonna be like our parents?" Claire defiantly replies, "Not me. Ever," in response to which Bender nods in affirmation. Claire's determination is almost immediately undercut, however, by the follow-up comment made by Allison, "It's unavoidable. Just happens." Notably, less than a minute later, Brian asks, "What is gonna happen to us on Monday?" In other words, will the members of the Breakfast Club still be friends after they are no longer forced to be together in detention? The juxtaposition of Andy's and Brian's questions reveals them to be two versions of the same question: will these teens be able to break out of the identities imposed on them by their parents and their existing groups of friends, to forge more authentic connections across lines of social class and high school clique, based on the insights that they now have into each other's genuine selves? This is the key question *The Breakfast Club* poses.

Nelson argues that the fact that *The Breakfast Club* does not answer this question is one of the sources of its enduring power. Reading Hughes' films as "coming-of-age myths" (98), Nelson contends:

> Interestingly, while *The Breakfast Club* functions as myth, what it does specifically that keeps it alive is leave off the explicit happy ending. Audiences do not know what will happen when school starts again. All the eternal conflicts the film addresses about how teens brave the coming-of-age process and all the questions about how they will mature into adults are left hanging [99].

Of course, the ambiguity of the ending has not stopped fans of *The Breakfast Club* from reading it in more uplifting terms. As Jennifer Hays notes, "The preferred (dominant) reading of this text is that despite major differences in interests and values and lifestyles, people can suddenly stop disagreeing and instantly bond as friends, and even lovers, if they will just be open and honest," even though such a reading overlooks just how "very unrealistic" it is (234). Writing in terms echoing the enthusiasm for the film felt by the many members of Generation X who have identified with the members of the Breakfast Club since the film first came out, Gora reads the iconic closing shot of the film, in which Bender raises his fist triumphantly, as follows:

> Long after that last image of Judd Nelson flickered on the screen, the meaning of it stayed with us. Nelson's exuberantly raised fist, we thought, meant this: The world may label us: "jock" or "brain" as teenagers, and different but

equally limiting labels over the course of our adult lives. But if we are bold enough, we can break through. We can see one another, and ourselves, however we like [7].

Gora's description of the final shot of *The Breakfast Club* certainly fits the way that many of the film's fans have read that final shot, taking its hope for the future at face value, the well-known cynicism of Generation X notwithstanding.[1]

Still, keeping in mind Robin Wood's cautionary note that "affirmation in the 80s is never free of cynicism" (340), we might wonder, just how hopeful is that ending of *The Breakfast Club*? Bender's triumphant pose follows the kiss he shares with Claire as the two part at the end of the day, a kiss that is accompanied by her giving him one of her diamond earrings, all while Simple Minds' "Don't You (Forget about Me)" plays. All the elements of the film at this moment seem to suggest the hopeful reading that Gora outlines. Watching the film from a vantage point removed from the gender politics of the '80s, however, it becomes harder to overlook the fact that Bender and Claire's romantic coupling comes after he sexually harasses her throughout the day, as well as the infamous scene in which he takes advantage of hiding under the desk at which Claire is sitting to look up her skirt and sexually assault her. As Nelson notes, "The message is that his abusive behavior is not only tolerated, it is romanticized" (60).[2] Beyond that troubling element of the film, it is also worth remembering something Bender says shortly before the ending of the film, when Claire kisses him in the closet he's been confined to: "You know how you said before, how your parents use you to get back at each other? Wouldn't I be *outstanding* in that capacity?" While the film does not pursue the implications of that line—namely, that Claire might be using Bender to get back at her parents, regardless of whatever attraction she may feel to him—it does at least allow for the possibility that her later public kissing of him and giving him her diamond earring might, to some degree, constitute a cynical performance on her part, suggesting that she's learned all too well her parents' lessons on how to press the emotional buttons of family members. In other words, the ending of *The Breakfast Club* just might be showing that Claire is well on her way to being like her parents, after all.[3]

"Remember when this was our lives?"

The reading of *The Breakfast Club* in which its members do, in fact, go on to be like their parents is one that "The Midnight Club" endorses in a number of ways. The first has to do with the casting of the episode. As noted earlier, the bulk of "The Midnight Club" takes the form of a flashback to the '80s, specifically, a time when the parents of *Riverdale*'s teen characters are themselves high school students who bond over the experience of Saturday detention. The conceit of the casting for the episode is that those parents' younger selves are played by the actors who ordinarily play their children. For instance, K.J. Apa, who plays Archie, plays the teen version of his father, Fred Andrews (portrayed as an adult by Luke Perry), while Camila Mendes, who plays Veronica, plays the younger version of her mother, Hermione Lodge (portrayed as an adult by Marisol Nichols). This palimpsestic casting has the ironic effect of affirming through its visual logic that these teens—both the '80s teens portrayed in the flashback as well as the contemporary teens portrayed in *Riverdale*'s main storyline—will, indeed, become their parents. The teen versions of *Riverdale*'s parents seen in "The Midnight Club" further this sense in their dialogue, much of which ironically foreshadows what the audience already knows to be their fates. For example, when young Penelope Blossom, portrayed in the flashback by Madelaine Petsch (who ordinarily plays Penelope's daughter, Cheryl) explains to the other teens that the Blossoms are "terrible people," viewers know that Penelope will herself become a terrible parent in turn, repeating the cycle of oppressive parenting that plagues so many of *Riverdale*'s characters. Further emphasizing the effect of this palimpsestic casting, Principal Featherhead, who presides over detention in "The Midnight Club," is played by Anthony Michael Hall, the same actor who played Brian over thirty years earlier in *The Breakfast Club*. Moreover, much of Principal Featherhead's dialogue in "The Midnight Club" echoes dialogue spoken in *The Breakfast Club* by Vice Principal Vernon (played by Paul Gleason), giving us the uncanny experience of seeing one of the members of the Breakfast Club apparently having grown up into precisely the sort of uncaring authority figure he rebelled against as a teen.

The casting of Anthony Michael Hall as Principal Featherhead echoes another bit of casting that likewise reinforces the sense *Riverdale* gives that '80s teens will indeed grow up to be like their parents, namely, the fact that Archie's mother, Mary Andrews, is played by none other than Molly Ringwald.[4] While Ringwald's Mary Andrews is a much more sympathetic character than Claire's parents in *The Breakfast Club*—in fact, she is presented as one of the few genuinely good parents to the contemporary generation of *Riverdale* teens—the failure of Mary's marriage to Archie's father, Fred, leads Archie to act out in various ways over the course of *Riverdale*, a dynamic that ironically echoes Claire's anxieties about her parents in *The Breakfast Club* and thereby puts Ringwald in the position of being a member of the Breakfast Club who has seemingly grown up to be like her parents. Consider the first episode in which Mary appears (albeit only in the episode's final scene), "Chapter Ten: The Lost Weekend" (the tenth episode of *Riverdale's* first season, first broadcast on April 13, 2017). In this episode, Fred has gone out of town to finalize his divorce from Mary.[5] At one point, Fred calls Archie and explains that he has not seen Mary yet, as they have decided not to meet without their lawyers, to which Archie responds, "'Cause things are so bad you can't talk without a mediator." Archie goes on to get drunk while throwing a party that, predictably, gets out of control and ends in violence.

Fig. 1. In *The Breakfast Club* (Universal Pictures, 1985), Molly Ringwald's (left) Claire and Ally Sheedy's Allison, along with the other members of the Breakfast Club, dance to Karla DeVito's "We Are Not Alone" to signify their attempt to liberate themselves from the confining identities forced on them by parents and high school cliques, in an affirmation of the hope that they can avoid being like their parents.

Mary and Fred go on to develop a more amicable relationship over the remainder of the episodes of *Riverdale* that were produced before the untimely death of Luke Perry led the series to kill off Fred, but there

Fig. 2. In *Riverdale's* "Chapter Eleven: To Riverdale and Back Again" (Warner Bros. Television/CBS Studios, 2017), when Molly Ringwald's Mary dances with Luke Perry's Fred to Imperial Mammoth's cover of Wang Chung's already-nostalgic '80s hit "Dance Hall Days," it signifies their regret that their youthful hopes for the future did not pan out.

remains a cloud of wistful regret over their separation. In Mary's first full episode, "Chapter Eleven: To Riverdale and Back Again" (the eleventh episode of *Riverdale*'s first season, first broadcast on April 27, 2017), that wistful nostalgia is filtered through signifiers that evoke Ringwald's status as an '80s teen idol. Mary and Fred decide to attend the aptly named Blast from the Past homecoming dance—attending the dance, awkwardly enough, with Veronica's mother Hermione, with whom Fred has just broken off an affair. Mary, Fred, and Hermione arrive at the dance while Rogue Wave's cover of "Bette Davis Eyes," a song popularized by Kim Carnes in 1981, is playing, and later scenes at the dance are set to other '80s songs, including New Order's "Blue Monday" and a performance of Kim Wilde's "Kids in America" by Archie and Veronica. Just after arriving, Mary exclaims to Fred and Hermione, "Remember when this was our *lives*?" and Fred replies, "The best of times." Given the fact that the actors playing Mary and Fred, Molly Ringwald and Luke Perry, were both teen idols, it is all too tempting to read that line not simply as referring to the characters' shared history at Riverdale High but also as offering metacommentary on the actors' professional history in teen dramas and the trajectory of their *Riverdale* characters' lives in comparison to the hopes of the teen characters they once played.[6] In *The Breakfast Club*, Ringwald's Claire and the other members of the Breakfast Club dance to Karla DeVito's "We Are Not Alone" to signify their attempt to liberate themselves from the confining identities forced on them by parents and high school cliques in an affirmation of the hope that they can avoid being like their parents (see fig. 1). By contrast, when Ringwald's Mary dances with Fred to Imperial Mammoth's cover of Wang Chung's already-nostalgic '80s hit "Dance Hall Days," it signifies their regret that their youthful hopes for the future did not pan out (see fig. 2).

"And now we're paying for their sins"

The reliance on '80s musical cues to set up the nostalgic feeling surrounding Ringwald's introduction as Archie's mother, as well as the similar function of '80s songs to establish the timeframe of the flashback in "The Midnight Club," fits with the second way, beyond the episode's casting decisions, that "The Midnight Club" endorses a pessimistic reading of *The Breakfast Club* and its characters' likelihood of growing up to be like their parents: the fact that, relatively early, the episode swerves from modeling itself on a John Hughes teen drama to modeling itself on a different subgenre of '80s teen movie, namely, teen horror. This swerve happens when the *Riverdale* '80s teens discover a copy of the fantasy game

Gryphons and Gargoyles while in detention. At this point in the main storyline of *Riverdale*, this game is ensnaring the contemporary teens in its grip, in a clear reference to '80s-era paranoia about teens playing Dungeons & Dragons. The game likewise comes to exert a captivating influence over the '80s *Riverdale* teens, who soon take to breaking into the school at night to play the game, hence calling themselves the Midnight Club. In this way, "The Midnight Club" presents a reversal of *The Breakfast Club*'s scenario of being forced to stay in school, while also moving away from *The Breakfast Club*'s ideal of self-revelation in favor of a plot in which the characters lose themselves in the fantasy of the game. The ultimate instance in which the members of the Midnight Club lose themselves in fantasy comes on the so-called Ascension Night, when all of them but Alice get high, and the mood drifts toward horror. This drift toward horror is itself marked by a musical cue that points to a specific '80s film, namely, the performance by the teen version of Fred and his band the Fred Heads[7] of Dokken's "Dream Warriors," the theme song to *A Nightmare on Elm Street 3: Dream Warriors* (1987).[8]

On the face of it, this appears to be an abrupt shift in genre: John Hughes films like *The Breakfast Club* and the slasher horror of the *Nightmare on Elm Street* series seem, at first glance, to be at opposite ends of the spectrum of teen films produced in the '80s.[9] By juxtaposing *The Breakfast Club* with *Dream Warriors*, however, "The Midnight Club" reminds us that these two genres have more in common than audiences might initially remember, specifically, when it comes to relationships between teens and their parents. In both sets of films, the parents are ineffectual at best, actively threatening at worst. As William Paul writes of the original *A Nightmare on Elm Street* (1984), which establishes the series' pattern of presenting parents who deny their children's warnings about the dangers lurking in their dreams, "So, what's wrong with the parents in this film? They are mostly absent, as in earlier films, but here they are specifically tagged as being emotionally absent. As the children are the only ones who seem to know what is going on, the film works a kind of inversion on parents and children" (404). The same line of analysis could, of course, apply to *The Breakfast Club*. Indeed, Kyle Christensen explicitly frames the concerns of slasher films like *A Nightmare on Elm Street* in the terms offered by *The Breakfast Club*: "Popular films of the 1980s (slasher films, teen comedies, coming-of-age chronicles, and so forth) tended to feature teenage characters who express resentment toward adults and dread becoming exactly like their parents" (37).

Just as *Riverdale*'s treatment of *The Breakfast Club* affirms the inevitability of becoming one's parents, however, so, too, do the films of the *Nightmare on Elm Street* series demonstrate that same sense of generational continuity. Indeed, the basic premise of the *Nightmare on Elm Street* films has to do with the crimes of one generation being revisited upon the next. The specific installment in the series that "The Midnight Club" alludes to, *A Nightmare on Elm Street 3: Dream Warriors*, lays it out as clearly as any of the films in the series when Nancy Thompson (played by Heather Langenkamp), the only teen to survive the first film in the series, returns as an adult trying to help an institutionalized group of teens being menaced by Freddy Krueger (played by Robert Englund), the deceased child murderer who seeks out his victims in their dreams. When the teens ask why Freddy is after them, Nancy explains, "It's not you. Your parents, my parents, they burned him alive. And now we're paying for their sins. You are the last of the Elm Street children." By this point, Nancy has already begun her own path of becoming like her parents, insofar as the climax of the first film in the series sees Nancy pull Freddy out of the dream and into reality, where she sets him on fire, just as her parents' generation is said to have done. Similarly, just as Nancy's parents' generation thought they had protected their children from Freddy by killing him, so, too, does Nancy at the end of *Dream Warriors* seemingly help to vanquish Freddy and save the remaining teens, only for Freddy to return and kill all of the surviving teens from *Dream Warriors* in the next film in the series, *A Nightmare on Elm Street 4: The Dream Master* (1988). Just as Nancy's parents' generation ultimately fails to protect Nancy and her friends from Freddy, so, too, does Nancy ultimately fail to save "the last of the Elm Street children" from being killed in their dreams.[10]

Fittingly enough, Nancy's death at the end of *Dream Warriors* comes when Freddy appears to her disguised as her own father.[11] Telling her he's "crossed over," he explains, "I couldn't go without telling you how sorry I am for all the things I've done. I love you so much. I'll always love you," prompting Nancy to embrace him, whereupon he reveals himself as Freddy and kills her. As Tony Williams observes in his discussion of this scene, "The films all make clear that submission to any form of family authority results in death" (176). This theme is only heightened in the later films of the series, which, as Ian Conrich notes (129), increasingly frame Freddy as a father figure. Whether abandoned to Freddy by their parents' failures or threatened by Freddy in his own role a parental figure, the teens of the *Nightmare on Elm Street* films share with the teens of *The Breakfast Club* the sense that, ultimately, the real threat lies in one's parents and the possibility of becoming just like them.

In the end, the swerve to '80s teen horror in "The Midnight Club" picks up on the cycle of failure repeated from one generation to the next in the *Nightmare on Elm Street* series, as the chaos of Ascension Night culminates in the death of Principal Featherhead, apparently at the hands of the demonic Gargoyle King, a character from the Gryphons and Gargoyles game seemingly come to life, who, like Freddy, later returns not just to threaten the lives of the contemporary *Riverdale* teens, but, indeed, to kill a number of them.

"Everybody Wants to Rule the World"

The '80s flashback in "The Midnight Club" ends, inevitably, with the teen members of the Midnight Club poised to become the parents we know them as from the main *Riverdale* storyline. Instead of the promise implicit in the title of the song that plays over the final moments of *The Breakfast Club*, Simple Minds' "Don't You (Forget About Me)," the story of the Midnight Club wraps up to the tune of a rather different '80s song, Tears for Fears' "Everybody Wants to Rule the World," an apt commentary on the desire for money, power, and control that drives most of the members of the Midnight Club into what Alice's voiceover describes, with respect to Hermione, as "a lifetime of compromises."[12] Archie's father, Fred, avoids the dark fate of his fellow members of the Midnight Club insofar as *Riverdale* presents him, like Mary, as one of the few genuinely good parents to the contemporary generation of teens.[13] As noted above, however, Fred's good intentions cannot keep the effects of his separation from Mary from adversely affecting Archie, and the ending of "The Midnight Club" shows that even Fred winds up becoming a version of his father, as he abandons his dreams of a life making music and instead takes over his family's business following his father's death. On a broader level, Alice's voiceover wraps up the flashback with the blunt declaration, "And when the Midnight Club passed each other in the halls, we didn't so much as smile. We'd become strangers again." "The Midnight Club" thereby offers a palimpsestic rewriting of the ending of *The Breakfast Club* in decidedly cynical terms, effacing the ambiguous but hopeful ending of that '80s John Hughes film, via a detour through '80s horror, in favor of a despair at the impossibility of breaking free from generational patterns of behavior that all too often lead to abuse and terror.[14]

Riverdale's '80s palimpsest offers an apt document of its historical moment, when an icon of the '80s, Donald Trump, reemerged from that decade of Ronald Reagan, John Hughes, and Freddy Krueger to dominate the cultural and political landscape as he assumed the office of the President of the United States. Of course, Trump himself is a John Hughes character, of a sort, by virtue of his cameo appearance in the Hughes-written *Home Alone 2: Lost in New York* (1992).[15] Though Trump's presence in Hughes' body of work stems from the period of Hughes' post–80s turn away from teen films, the President Trump who performed indifference and idolized a particular version of masculine strength as hundreds of thousands of Americans died of a pandemic fits well with the mode of parenting presented to us by *The Breakfast Club* and the *Nightmare on Elm Street* films, assuming the role of the ultimate threatening parent whose patterns of behavior we as a nation need to grow out of, but whose mistakes we may well be doomed to repeat.[16] "Everybody Wants to Rule the World," indeed.

NOTES

1. As Nelson writes in her discussion of generational conflict in *The Breakfast Club*, "while the boomers are associated with idealism in youth, Generation X is associated with cynicism" (64).

2. For further discussion of the gender politics of Hughes' films in the context of the '80s, see Ann De Vaney's "Pretty in Pink? John Hughes Reinscribes Daddy's Girl in Homes and Schools." For a more personal response to the experience of re-watching *The Breakfast Club* and other John Hughes movies in light of contemporary gender politics, see Molly Ringwald's "What about 'The Breakfast Club'? Revisiting the Movies of My Youth in the Age of #MeToo."

3. Hughes offers his own revisionary take on Claire's gift of her earring to Bender in *Some Kind of Wonderful* (1987), a film he wrote but which was directed by Howard Deutch. The final scene of that movie, like the final scene of *The Breakfast Club*, features an unattainable "princess" character, Amanda Jones (played by Lea Thompson), handing a pair of diamond earrings to a working-class outcast, Keith Nelson (played by Eric Stoltz). In this case, the earrings are originally a gift from Keith to Amanda, who he has pursued romantically throughout the film. In returning the earrings to Keith, Amanda allows for the film's happy ending, which sees Keith realize his romantic love for his fellow outcast Watts (played by Mary Stuart Masterson). As it happens, *Some Kind of Wonderful* has often been read as—and manifestly is—a gender-flipped reworking of *Pretty in Pink* (1986), another film written by Hughes and directed by Deutch. In the standard reading, *Some Kind of Wonderful*'s revision of *Pretty in Pink* allows its protagonist to make the correct—and, indeed, corrected—choice of romantic partner in the end; see, for instance, Gora's discussion of the two films in *You Couldn't Ignore Me If You Tried* (129–55, 203–29). Reading the return of the earrings in *Some Kind of Wonderful* not in terms of a revision of *Pretty in Pink* but rather as a revision of *The Breakfast Club*, however, fits a more cynical reading of the ending of *The Breakfast Club*: insofar as the act of Amanda's giving the earrings back to Keith signifies the end of their relationship, it also reminds viewers of the possibility that Claire's gift of her earring to Bender might well be the final act in their relationship, too, in the event that the "relationship" does not outlive the Saturday they spend together in detention.

4. It is worth noting that Hall and Ringwald are the only two members of the Breakfast Club to appear in more than one John Hughes movie. Both appear in *Sixteen Candles* (1984), while Hall also appears in *Weird Science* (1985). Ringwald also appears in *Pretty in Pink* (1986), which, as noted above, was written by Hughes but directed by Howard Deutch. The fact that these are the two members of the Breakfast Club who appear in *Riverdale* thereby serves to emphasize the connection specifically to the John Hughes teen films of the '80s.

5. Apropos of the setting of Hughes' '80s teen films in the suburbs of Chicago, Mary lives in Chicago.

6. Perry's time as a teen idol, of course, came somewhat later than Ringwald's, since his role as Dylan McKay on *Beverly Hills, 90210* did not originate until 1990.

7. It is fortuitous that Fred shares his name with the monster who haunts the *Nightmare on Elm Street* films, allowing the name of his band, the Fred Heads, both to identify the band as his and also to signify his apparent status as a fan of the films.

8. In a further connection to the *Nightmare on Elm Street* films, the teen version of Penelope Blossom in "The Midnight Club" mentions at one point that Riverdale also has an Elm Street. In fact, as shown in "Chapter Eleven: To Riverdale and Back Again," Betty lives on Elm Street, which is all too appropriate, since her father, Hal Cooper, turns out to be the serial killer the Black Hood. Hal is played by Lochlyn Munro, who plays the role of Deputy Stubbs in the *Nightmare on Elm Street* crossover with the *Friday the 13th* series, *Freddy vs. Jason* (2003).

9. There is at least one onscreen connection between the *Nightmare on Elm Street* films and *The Breakfast Club*, albeit tangential: Jesse Walsh, the protagonist of *A Nightmare on Elm Street 2: Freddy's Revenge* (1985), played by Mark Patton, has a Simple Minds poster hanging above his bed that reads, in large all-capitalized letters, "Don't you forget about these," followed by images of *Sparkle in the Rain* and *New Gold Dream (81/82/83/84)*, the two Simple Minds albums that immediately preceded the band's big break with "Don't You (Forget about Me)" on *The Breakfast Club*'s soundtrack. The logic of the poster seems to be to remind record-buyers not to overlook work by Simple Minds that could be eclipsed by the success of "Don't You (Forget about Me)," similar to the logic of "The Midnight Club" that asks its audience not to overlook the affinities between *The Breakfast Club* and teen slasher films like those in the *Nightmare on Elm Street* series.

10. Later films in the *Nightmare on Elm Street* series likewise continue the theme of children becoming their parents, even as the next generation must pay for its parents' sins. In the climax of *Freddy's Dead: The Final Nightmare* (1991), Freddy's adult daughter, Maggie (played by Lisa Zane), must don his iconic glove and stab him with it, becoming a murderer like her father. Later, the metacinematic *Wes Craven's New Nightmare* (1994) sees Heather Langenkamp, playing a fictionalized version of herself, realize that her role as Nancy in the first and third *Nightmare on Elm Street* films has exposed her son, Dylan (played by Miko Hughes), to the threat posed by a new version of Freddy. She ends the threat by destroying Freddy in a fire, just as Nancy's parents' generation does in the films' backstory.

11. In keeping with my reading of the ironic effect of casting former teen stars of John Hughes movies in *Riverdale*, it is worth noting the fact that, as Timothy Shary observes (25, 59), Nancy's father in the *Nightmare on Elm Street* films is played by John Saxon, himself a former teen idol.

12. "Everybody Wants to Rule the World" serves a similar function in Zack Snyder's 2009 film adaptation of Alan Moore and Dave Gibbons' classic '80s comic book *Watchmen*. In that '80s-set film, the song appears in the form of elevator music in a scene where Adrian Veidt (played by Matthew Goode) is talking with a number of titans of industry, underscoring the desires of the scene's characters for money, power, and control.

13. Notably, Fred likewise stands out from the rest of the Midnight Club insofar as he appears to have a good relationship with his father.

14. On one level, it is profoundly unsatisfying that neither Ringwald nor a teen version of her character appears in "The Midnight Club," to bring *Riverdale*'s palimpsestic rewriting of *The Breakfast Club* full circle. Of course, it might be suspected that any Generation X members of *Riverdale*'s audience would not really be interested in seeing a contemporary young actress playing a version of Molly Ringwald's character from *The Breakfast Club*. Rather, those putative Generation X *Riverdale* fans might instead prefer to get back to that moment of their lives when it was possible to believe in the idealistic hopes of the teenager played by the actual Molly Ringwald in *The Breakfast Club*, a moment that "The Midnight Club" argues is long gone.

15. For a reading of Trump's cameo in *Home Alone 2*, see Ashleigh Hardin's "Trump Traces: Examining Donald Trump's Film and Television Cameos (1990–2004)" (131–32).

16. For a reading of Trump's appeal as a father figure in the context of another text offering a representation of the '80s, see Caitlin R. Duffy's "Trump as 'Daddy': *American Psycho* and Hero Worship in the Neoliberal Era."

Works Cited

Benjamin, Sam. "Riverdale—Episode 3.04—The Midnight Club." *Spoilertv.com*, 7 Nov. 2018.

Christensen, Kyle. "The Final Girl versus Wes Craven's *A Nightmare on Elm Street*: Proposing a Stronger Model of Feminism in Slasher Horror Cinema." *Studies in Popular Culture*, vol. 34, no. 1, 2011, pp. 23–47.

Conrich, Ian. "Seducing the Subject: Freddy Krueger, Popular Culture and the *Nightmare on Elm Street* Films." *Trash Aesthetics: Popular Culture and Its Audience*, edited by Deborah Cartmell, I.Q. Hunter, Heidi Kaye, and Imelda Whelehan. Pluto Press, 1997, pp. 118–31.

De Vaney, Ann. "Pretty in Pink? John Hughes Reinscribes Daddy's Girl in Homes and Schools." *Sugar, Spice, and Everything Nice: Cinemas of Girlhood*, edited by Frances Gateward and Murray Pomerance. Wayne State University Press, 2002, pp. 201–15.

Duffy, Caitlin R. "Trump as 'Daddy': *American Psycho* and Hero Worship in the Neoliberal Era." *Trump Fiction: Essays on Donald Trump in Literature, Film, and Television*, edited by Stephen Hock. Lexington Books, 2020, pp. 39–52.

Gora, Susannah. *You Couldn't Ignore Me If You Tried: The Brat Pack, John Hughes, and Their Impact on a Generation*. Three Rivers Press, 2010.

Hardin, Ashleigh. "Trump Traces: Examining Donald Trump's Film and Television Cameos (1990–2004)." *Trump Fiction: Essays on Donald Trump in Literature, Film, and Television*, edited by Stephen Hock. Lexington Books, 2020, pp. 127–43.

Hays, Jennifer. "'Five Total Strangers, with Nothing in Common': Using Galician's Seven-Step Dis-illusioning Directions to Think Critically about *The Breakfast Club*." *Critical Thinking about Sex, Love, and Romance in the Mass Media: Media Literacy Applications*, edited by Mary-Lou Galician and Debra L. Merskin. Routledge, 2007, pp. 229–38.

Nelson, Elissa H. *The Breakfast Club: John Hughes, Hollywood, and the Golden Age of the Teen Film*. Routledge, 2019.

Paul, William. *Laughing Screaming: Modern Hollywood Horror and Comedy*. Columbia University Press, 1994.

Ringwald, Molly. "What about 'The Breakfast Club'? Revisiting the Movies of My Youth in the Age of #MeToo." *New Yorker*, 6 April 2018.

Shary, Timothy. *Teen Movies: American Youth on Screen*. Wallflower, 2005.

Williams, Tony. "Trying to Survive on the Darker Side: 1980s Family Horror." *The Dread of Difference: Gender and the Horror Film*, edited by Barry Keith Grant. University of Texas Press, 1996, pp. 164–80.

Wood, Robin. "Images and Women." *Issues in Feminist Film Criticism*, edited by Patricia Erens. Indiana University Press, 1990, pp. 337–52.

The Americans and How We Think About the Reagan '80s

LILLY J. GOREN

FX's drama *The Americans* depicts the 1980s not only through representations of the images and ideas of that decade, but also through a kind of double vision, since the representation of Reagan's America is presented from both the American as well as from the Soviet perspective. The narrative of *The Americans* centers on the lives of two sleeper Soviet agents in the United States during the Reagan Administration, facilitating a complex and multi-dimensional exploration of many facets of the 1980s. The audience is presented with nuanced competing ideas about this period, since Philip and Elizabeth Jennings have different attachments and loyalties even as they continue to do the bidding of their Soviet spymasters. In his analysis of the role of nationalism in the television show *Mad Men* (2007–2015), Lawrence Heyman points out that "real-life events … serve two purposes: as 'mile marker' references to where we are in the era, and also as dramatic tools" (120). In *The Americans*, the writers and show runners use the historical setting in a similar fashion, but also in a strangely bifurcated way, since Philip and Elizabeth are loyal to the Soviet Union even as they develop attachments within the United States. Thus, in exploring *The Americans*, we face a complexity of considerations, from the conflicted patriotism of the main characters to the show's wider, multifaceted perspectives on the Reagan Era, encompassing politics, popular culture, music, and narratives about home, family, consumption, and friendship.

The Americans is intricately layered in its representations of the political dimensions of the Reagan '80s, involving the themes of global anti-communism and the Cold War, the popularity of American individualism and self-help culture, and the rise of the yuppy, as well as gender clashes and racism. The series is threaded with televisual and musical touchstones of the 1980s, from the newly developed video game Pong to the film *The Day After* (1983) to the synthpop music of Yaz/Yazoo, while it also portrays a stark contrast between the shoulder pads, cascading hair dos, and pleated jeans sported by those in the United States and the color-less, heartless, and depressing imagery of scenes set in the Soviet Union. The contrasts between these two societies are experienced not only by the audience watching the series through our twenty-first-century lenses, but also by the situated Soviet spies who live and raise their children in the United States.

Philip and Elizabeth Jennings were recruited and trained at a very young age by the KGB to become "sleeper agents" in the United States.[1] As Directorate S/KGB recruits, they were trained in combat, espionage, surveil-lance, seduction, and the like, and a marriage was arranged by the Director-ate for the two of them. As young newlyweds, they were sent to the United States to establish cover identities and to become "normal suburban" Amer-icans. They were instructed to have a child, Paige, and then another, Henry, and they were provided with capital to start a business, a travel agency, which gave them a cover so they could operate in the United States (and else-where). The audience meets Philip and Elizabeth when their children are on the verge of being teenagers in the early 1980s, and, while they have been married for about fifteen years and have created this life together, Philip and Elizabeth don't quite trust each other as we come upon them.

A significant source of their marital tension comes from the relation-ship that Philip and Elizabeth have, separately, with the United States and the kind of life they live in the U.S. Although he is a Soviet spy, Philip takes to the opportunities to enjoy life as a middle-class American dad. As he says in *Trust Me* (1.6), "I fit in, like I am supposed to, and yes, I like it, so what?" We also see him square dancing, going to the mall to help Paige pick out a dress for her baptism, and luxuriating in the aspects of life that he never experienced growing up in the desperate post–World War II Soviet Union.

In the second season, Philip buys a new white Camaro Z28, and Eliz-abeth is rendered speechless when he arrives at their suburban house with this clearly capitalist talisman, the new car, as the Stray Cats' *Rock This Town* plays in the background (fig. 1).

When they are by themselves, plotting their next approach to getting FBI information, Philip and Elizabeth have a fascinating dialogue that pulls the viewer into the complexity of their experiences in the U.S. and the tension they experience between their commitment to the communist ideology of the Soviet Union and the lives they lead as their cover, where they need to operate as Americans within an economic system that values these kinds of acquisitions (new cars, shoes, comfort, etc.).

Fig. 1. Philip Jennings (Matthew Rhys) arrives home with the new Camaro in "New Car," 2.8 (FX Productions, 2014).

> ELIZABETH: I want you to be happy.
> PHILIP: Don't you enjoy any of this, this house, your clothes, all those beautiful shoes?? Don't you ever like it?
> ELIZABETH: That's not why I am here.
> PHILIP: Don't you ever like it?
> ELIZABETH: We have to live this way. For our job for our cover. Five miles from here there are people who are living....
> PHILIP: Do you like it?
> ELIZABETH: You know how I grew up. It is nicer here, It's easier. It's not better [2.8: *New Car*].

Their dialogue reflects the manner in which Philip is attracted to the rising consumer culture that characterized the Reagan Administration's advocacy for freer markets at the same time that the Jenningses try to manage their internal commitments to the austerity of the communist country in which they were raised and to which they have a nationalistic loyalty.

Philip's affinity for his adopted American lifestyle contrasts with Elizabeth's more unflinching commitment to the moral rectitude of Soviet communism. The audience learns quite quickly that Elizabeth is more loyal to Mother Russia, and, over the seasons, we see that she is, literally, more cut-throat. Philip is menacing in his own way, but his ideological commitment is tempered by his obvious enjoyment of his capitalist surroundings. He questions his own commitment to the lives he and Elizabeth have been living and his willingness to continue to act as a spy for the Soviet Union. The audience is pulled into the 1980s through the different ways that Philip and Elizabeth each interpret the life they see all around them.

This tension between Philip and Elizabeth echoes the geopolitical tension stoked by the Reagan Administration. In 1983, Ronald Reagan called the Soviet Union an "evil empire," painting the confrontation
between these superpowers as a binary battle between good and evil.[2] Reagan's words are integrated into the series with some frequency, and Reagan's rhetoric typically compels Elizabeth to become more committed to
her mission to destroy the country that has positioned the U.S.S.R. as a
moral and political enemy. Elizabeth maintains her unwavering commitment to the Soviet Union over the course of six seasons, until the very end
of the series, as the Soviet Union itself starts to change under Mikhail Gorbachev, and communism is pushed aside by *Glasnost* and *Perestroika*.

Season 1 includes a small narrative arc involving Secretary of Defense
Caspar Weinberger's maid Viola Johnson, whom the Jenningses threaten,
blackmailing her into putting a listening device in Weinberger's home
office (1.2: *The Clock*). They sicken Viola's son with a poison to which only
they have an antidote, and they threaten to withhold the antidote if she
does not place the listening device in Weinberger's house. This is a small
example of how Philip and Elizabeth interact with real and fictional poli-
cymakers in the Reagan Administration, figures who represent the "mile
markers" of history and policy as they are woven throughout the series. It
also provides an entry point to understanding the level of espionage that
the Jenningses are tasked with by their Soviet handlers. We see the lengths
they are willing to go to: almost killing a young man who has nothing to
do with the Administration or politics in an effort to compel his mother to
cooperate in their plan. Thus, in *The Americans*, we get a high-level view
into the workings of the Reagan Administration, as well as into the lives of
many lower-level individuals who become involved in traitorous activities
as Philip and Elizabeth manipulate them. As the series continues, Philip
and Elizabeth's unique perspective on the secret under-history of Reagan's America problematizes any nostalgic or mythologized narrative of
the Reagan era. While the affluence of their suburban lifestyle might prove
enticing to Philip, *The Americans* repeatedly reminds audiences of the sinister geopolitical policies that underwrite '80s prosperity.

The Reagan Administration's involvement in Central America provides a conspicuous example of such a policy. With the United States trying to contain or defeat communist uprisings in Nicaragua, El Salvador,
Honduras, and other Central American countries, this area of the world
became a proxy battlefield for the United States in pushing against the
U.S.S.R., especially following the American withdrawal from Vietnam and
Southeast Asia. *The Americans* integrates aspects of this hot and cold war,
especially as it was being fought by proxies for the U.S. and the U.S.S.R.,
into the Jenningses' lives and their espionage work. This is especially the

case in the first three seasons of the series, mirroring the time when the U.S. was engaged in secret warfare in these areas, training Central American anti-communist fighters in U.S. military strategies and techniques. Ultimately, some of this engagement would evolve into the Iran-Contra scandal that almost brought down the Reagan Administration.

One of the narrative arcs in the middle of the second season involves Philip gaining access to one of the military training sites in the United States that was being used to help train these fighters. The Jenningses were sent in to get images of the training sites to expose them to the world. A prevailing narrative of the Reagan Administration prioritized the moral fight against communism, including the increase in defense spending during this period and the militaristic posture towards those organizations and countries who were inclined to sympathize with communist causes in places other than the Soviet Union and the Eastern Bloc. *The Americans* brings in Reagan himself in *New Car* (2.8) to make this case for the defense build-up and for aggressive American militarism. In the midst of trying to get the means to expose the secret Contra training sites, Philip and Elizabeth also learn that their most recent job, stealing and passing along plans for submarine rotors, had been compromised; they had been duped by American intelligence with bad plans, leading to the death of all of the crew members aboard a Soviet submarine. They discuss this while Reagan is on TV, in a dinner jacket, talking about America's resurgent military prowess, noting how he promised, on the campaign trail, that if faced with "either balancing the budget or restoring our national defenses, he would respond with the answer to restore national defense." Elizabeth sits and watches Reagan's speech with an eerie stillness as she becomes more infuriated with Reagan, finally protesting in exasperation, "Kids, nuns, journalists, he doesn't care" (2.8: *New Car*). Elizabeth's comment refers to the nuns who had been killed in Central America,[3] the Soviet soldiers on the submarine, and the journalists who had been killed trying to cover the civil war in El Salvador and in other hot spots around Central America. Elizabeth criticizes Reagan not only from her Soviet perspective as a political enemy, but also through a humanitarian perspective, decrying the president's indifference to the loss of life that his policies have brought about. In this critique, Elizabeth echoes the sentiments of other contemporary critics who accused Reagan and the Reagan Administration of ignoring the deadly consequences of the Central American shadow-war, deflecting attacks while continuing to position themselves, especially in the geopolitical conflict with communism, as being right, good, moral, and virtuous.[4]

All of this is woven around a narrative about the United States' clandestine training and equipping of the Nicaraguan Contras.[5] The character

Lucia Chena, a Sandinista fighter from Nicaragua who blames covert American fighters for killing her family, is also working undercover in the United States, posing as a Costa Rican student (2.2: *Cardinal*), and she calls on Elizabeth for help and mentoring while she is in Washington, D.C. This narrative arc in Season 2 incorporates Reagan's military build-up, the covert wars that were killing communists as well as civilians in Central America, and the slaughter of Catholic nuns and various journalists who were covering some of these events. Philip manages to infiltrate the camp and take photos of the training of Contras by U.S. military personnel (2.9: *Martial Eagle*). These photos are then sent back to Moscow, where they make their way to newspapers in Central and South America, and circle back to the United States government, exposing the U.S.'s covert activities in Central America. Thus, secret American anti-communist activities in Central America become a focal point for a significant portion of the second season on *The Americans*. These duplicitous actions undermine the Reagan Administration's argument that the United States represents the moral force for good in this superpower standoff.

The Central American storyline of exposing covert warfare quickly moves to Central Asia and the U.S. effort to support, again in another form of covert warfare, the Mujahadeen, who are fighting against the Soviet invasion of Afghanistan. In one of the many storylines that wrap around this proxy war in Afghanistan, there is a long and involved arc in Season 3 where Philip, in disguise (as always!), begins a relationship with Kimmy, whose absent father is head of the CIA's Afghanistan division. This is a high priority target for the agents, as the Center in Moscow is desperate to be able to provide intelligence to the Soviet military so they can better combat the Mujahadeen in Afghanistan, as the Soviets are suffering huge casualties. Philip is to install a hidden tape recorder in Kimmy's father's briefcase, and then to change out the tapes every couple of weeks. Kimmy is about the same age as Philip's daughter Paige, and this whole affair, where Philip does everything he can to avoid actually having sex with Kimmy, is an avenue for Philip to get into Kimmy's house and gain access to the briefcase on a regular basis.

While there is a clear political reason for the U.S.S.R. to want to be able to learn what the Americans are planning in Afghanistan, as the Soviet Union has become stuck in this military quagmire, this storyline also brings up the social dynamics of the 1980s. Kimmy's homelife clearly reflects the stereotypical upper-middle-class white family of the time,[6] with a privileged daughter who behaves wildly without any concern for consequences, smoking pot, getting fake IDs, drinking, going out with her friends, and pursuing a sexual relationship with Philip, who is a much older man. Kimmy's unsupervised exploits present an ironic perspective on the supposedly conservative values of the Reagan 1980s, which touted the strength of family and religion[7] and the integration of the Christian Right/Moral Majority into the Reagan Administration (Moen), even as members of that Administration were not always abiding by the family values advertised in Republican campaign slogans.

In parallel to this storyline with Kimmy, the Jenningses are faced with their own dilemma, also within this same cultural and social construction. Paige Jennings, their high-school-age daughter, meets a teenager who brings her to church and starts to engage her in developing a relationship with Jesus and the Church. While Paige's newfound Christianity is very much part of the social and cultural messaging of the Reagan Administration, as noted, Paige's newfound Christian faith is anathema to her parents, who are, at their hearts, communists and atheists. So, Kimmy, the daughter of a member of the Executive branch, is demonstrating the vacuousness of the sloganeering of this decade, while Paige, unaware that she is the daughter of avowed Soviet atheists, is eagerly looking to become a faithful member of the Christian church. She goes so far as to ask to be baptized as her birthday present. Both young women are coming of age and trying to figure out who they are in the midst of this decade that politicized the family.

The Americans unpacks and explores the layers of the Reagan '80s through a kind of warped nostalgic lens. The perspective of the show is unique in that it takes a multidimensional look at this period of time through the double vision of Soviet spies who have been living and working in the United States for decades. Because Philip and Elizabeth are spies, so much of the political world around them is tinged with aspects of the Reagan Administration policies, both domestic and foreign. Paige nearly gets arrested when she and her church go to protest nuclear weapons. And because the Jenningses live across the street from FBI Agent Stan Beeman, we are also given the alternative perspective of those working inside U.S. counterintelligence trying to manage Soviet threats to the American homeland. *The Americans* does not nostalgize the Reagan years as uncomplicated, either from an American perspective or from a Soviet perspective, which is one of the strengths of the show, making the granular focus on politics during this time more enticing to the viewer. The show's historical and political context provides both the "mile markers" that help us to keep track of what is going on at the time, as well as the dramatic tools that shape the narrative itself, giving the Jenningses their marching orders in terms of the tasks they are given by the directorate back in Moscow. As any number of critics noted during the series' run, *The Americans* may be the only television series that invited American audiences to root for Soviet agents working to bring down America.

The Americans highlights a variety of aspects of the Reagan Era, not least the superpower struggle between the United States and the U.S.S.R.

Part of Philip's difficulty throughout the series is his attraction to the "yuppy" life that is his cover, but it is also his lived experience. He has a much more difficult time than Elizabeth in disconnecting himself from the pleasure that he finds in being a father to Paige and Henry, and in buying country music albums and nice cars. Elizabeth and Philip, later in the series, must eventually tell Paige who they really are and what they actually do as Soviet spies. Philip is frightened of crossing this bridge because he is legitimately scared that Paige will come to hate them. The episode in which Philip wrestles with this decision is one of the most stunning episodes of the series (3.10: *Stingers*), and it exposes the complexity of the life that Philip and Elizabeth have been living, while also encompassing the geopolitical stakes involved between the United States and the U.S.S.R. during the Reagan Era (fig. 2). Philip and Elizabeth Jennings and their children, Paige and Henry, are all soldiers in this Cold War that comes to an end as the series concludes, and through them, we learn to see the moral and political complexity of the Reagan Era. *The Americans* represents the 1980s from so many different perspectives as all these different characters try to make sense of the world around them through their own interpretive lenses. In the process, the show presents twenty-first-century audiences with a picture of the 1980s that encompasses the tensions and contradictions of the period.

Fig. 2. Philip (Matthew Rhyes) and Elizabeth Jennings (Keri Russell) face their daughter's questioning about their secret lives. *Stingers*, 4.10 (FX Productions, 2016).

Notes

1. This was based on a program that actually positioned Soviet "illegals" in the United States (Barry).

2. Speech by President Ronald Reagan to the National Association of Evangelicals, March 8, 1983, in Orlando Florida.

3. See, for example, Krauss. There were quite a number of incidents of this kind during the late 1970s and throughout the 1980s, in El Salvador and throughout Central America.

4. On election night in November 1980, President-elect Ronald Reagan gave his famous "city on a hill" speech, taking the term from John Winthrop, who had used it in the 1600s when the Puritans arrived in Massachusetts. In context, the United States is seen as an example, a shining city on a hill, that projects a kind of virtue and goodness that others are drawn to and want to follow.

5. See, for example, LeoGrande.

6. As portrayed in films like *Ordinary People* (1980), *Risky Business* (1983), *Ferris Bueller's Day Off* (1986), etc.

7. President Ronald Reagan Radio Address to the Nation on the American Family, December 3, 1983.

Works Cited

Baev, Pavel K. "How Afghanistan Was Broken: The Disaster of the Soviet Intervention." *International Area Studies Review* 15, no. 3 (September 2012): 249–62.

Barry, Ellen. "'Illegals' Spy Ring Famed in Lore of Russian Spying," *New York Times,* June 29, 2010.

Heyman, Lawrence. "Appearances, Social Norms, and Life in Modern America" in *Mad Men and Politics: Nostalgia and the Remaking of Modern American,* edited by Linda Beail and Lilly J. Goren. Bloomsbury Academic, 2015.

Krauss, Clifford. "How U.S. Actions Helped Hide Salvador Human Rights Abuses," *The New York Times,* March 21, 1993.

LeoGrande, William M. *Our Own Backyard: The United States in Central America, 1977–1992.* University of North Carolina Press, 2009.

Matthew C. Moen "Ronald Reagan and the Social Issues: Rhetorical Support for the Christian Right," *The Social Science Journal,* 27:2, 1990, pp. 199–207, DOI: 10.1016/0362–3319(90)90036-J.

"It's just one of them things innit, there's nothing you can do about it"

The Specter of Thatcherism in This Is England '86–'90

JACK ANDERSON

At his trial in December 2002, Paul Kelleher admitted to decapitating a 7' 2", two-and-a-half-ton marble sculpture of Margaret Thatcher, stating rather plainly: "I lopped off the head of Mrs. Thatcher and of that there is no dispute." A *pro se* defendant, Kelleher told the jury: "The prosecution will attempt to convince you that my actions amount to criminal damage, whereas my defense will center around artistic expression and my right to interact with this broken world." Four years later, another statue of Thatcher was erected in the House of Commons, and again it was attacked. This persistent iconoclastic defacement of Thatcher's image, argue Louisa Hadley and Elizabeth Ho, "presents Margaret Thatcher as a powerful personality and an equally powerful obstacle that occludes a foreclosed engagement with the political and social conditions of Thatcherism that continue to affect the present" (5).

Margaret Thatcher died of a stroke on April 8, 2013, aged 87. The singular reality of her physical passing was accompanied by a torrent of symbolic (re)deaths. Across the United Kingdom, communities spontaneously came together to celebrate the event. In the pit village of Goldsmith in South Yorkshire, a mock funeral was held in which an effigy of Thatcher was burned alongside the word "scab" spelled out in flowers. Perhaps a more notable act of iconoclasm was the irreverent repurposing of *The Wizard of Oz* (1939) song, "Ding Dong! The Witch Is Dead," which became the number two chart entry in the April 14, 2013, UK music chart.

Posthumously, Thatcher has continued to haunt popular culture and other forms of ephemera, with the "meme-ification of Thatcher's death" showing her remarkable prominence at the locus of contemporary memory (Dinning). These cycles of death elucidate the spectral, unabating nature of Thatcher and Thatcherism. That the legacy of Thatcher remains so neuralgic bespeaks "the traumatic effects that the former prime minister continues to generate on the present" (Hadley & Ho, 1).

In Cathy Caruth's definition of trauma, the traumatic episode is experienced "too soon, too unexpectedly, to be fully unknown and is therefore not available to consciousness until it imposes itself again, repeatedly, in nightmares and repetitive actions of the survivor," generating an internal wound that constitutes a "breach in the mind's experiences of time, self and the world" (4). Considered within the discourse of trauma, Thatcher and Thatcherism must be approached as an unhealing "internal wound" in the contemporary imagination. An originary trauma, Thatcher(ism), haunts the present through the persistence of the past, creating a traumatic obstacle in the future. Andreas Huyssen diagnoses Western society with a "fundamental crisis in the imagination of alternative futures," a state devoid of temporality that looks to "deny human agency and lock us into compulsive repetition" (2–6). What is at stake then, is "the need to remember and revisit the originary moment of rupture as its peculiar and persistent nature forms the basis of … an understanding of contemporary Britain as a community imagined around trauma" (Hadley and Ho 3). Doing so requires making an attempt to work through and resolve the traumatic rupture that Thatcherism was and continues to be.

This essay explores the work of contemporary British auteur Shane Meadows, examining his revisitation to the 1980s through the optic of this trauma and the legacy of Thatcherite neoliberalism. It will focus on his highly acclaimed, yet under-studied, television series *This Is England '86–'90* (2010–2015). Characterized by the persistence of the past, ghostly manifestations of the repressed, distortions of temporality, and cycles of uncanny return, the legacy of Thatcher(ism) in *This Is England '86–'90* is represented in hauntological terms as a traumatic obstacle, in which temporality, as Jacques Derrida, writes is "deeply out of joint." Meadows' engagement with (post)trauma as a haunting device adroitly navigates the poetics of returning to the Thatcherite '80s. While he delineates interminable Thatcherism as our *de facto* condition, the "Meadowsian" mode also offers a rare modulation in dealing with the wound of Thatcher and her legacy. Finding hope and redemption in the vestigial acts of daily working-class lives that negate neoliberal philosophy, Meadows outlines the potential efficacy of traumatic return through using its haunting as a potentially transformative device.

"I am Shane Meadows, Nottingham's premier director—please don't harm me"

In his own words, he is "Nottingham's premier director," and, in the words of James Leggot, he is "arguably the most influential realist British filmmaker of the era" (74). Since his first directorial feature, *Small Time* (1996), Shane Meadows has been widely extolled as one of Britain's finest contemporary auteurs, the heir apparent to the tradition of British socialist realism personified by Mike Leigh, Alan Clark, and Ken Loach—a vanguard of filmmakers who use art as a critical means of (re)conceptualizing Thatcherism. Meadows' "realist" style is an essential aspect of his films, with his work defined by that "deeply and perennially unfashionable" region of England: the Midlands. Obsessively returning to these regional "non-places," he documents the pathological melancholia of Middle England's sink estates, depicting a society "ravaged by the inexorable march of post-industrialisation" (FitzGerald 155).

Yet, alongside contemporaries such as Andrea Arnold, Paweł Pawlikowski, and Lynne Ramsay, Meadows also represents a departure "towards a more poetic form of realism that rejects didacticism and explicit explorations of social issues, in favor of a more ambiguous image-led narration" (Forrest 37). The result in Meadows' work is symbiotic; the mise-en-scène of traditional British socialist realism becomes a substratum, a familiar space made unfamiliar through his juxtaposition of the hyper-socialist realism of the working class with the supernaturality of Thatcher's ghost. Clair Schwarz employs the term "liminal realism" (Schwarz 7) to describe Meadows' approach to representing the past.

In Meadows' liminal style of realist representation, trauma is reconfigured through its narrative dissociation into metaphor: the spectral and the figure of the ghost. The hauntological transmutation of traumatic memory into the figure of the ghost offers a clear link to the past as the primary site of pain. Implicit in the spectral is the conflicting state(s) of temporality. The ghost disorientates linear time, being a figure directly out of the past in which the past is permitted to exist in the present, a symptom of repressed knowledge that simultaneously challenges the possibility of a future based on the evasion of the past. Undertaking the admittedly obfuscatory job of translating trauma to the screen, Meadows succeeds through his affinity with the subject matter. The efficacy of his articulation of the traumatic comes from a dialectic synthesis of trauma in both a theoretical and an experiential capacity, resulting in an authentic, *realistic* portrayal of (post)trauma that also mediates the complexity of its ghostly and uncanny properties.

Return, Remembrance, and Realization: "When you gonna tell her? She needs to know I'm back, love"

If to return to a place is to haunt it, the oeuvre of Shane Meadows haunts the Midlands. Julian Wolfreys argues that "to tell a story is always to invoke ghosts, to open a space through which something other returns" (3), and while Meadows' work is defined by this spatial return, it is also markedly delineated temporally by the 1980s. For Meadows' Thatcherism is *the* primary site of public and personal trauma. The unending specter of Thatcher and her legacy is an omnipresent principle in all of Meadows' work, yet it is only in the *This is England* quartet (the film and subsequent serials), that Meadows revisits this originary "rupture" with spatiotemporal authenticity. Meadows' directorial corpus is haunted by cycles of return to, and (post)traumatic memory of, the '80s and the socio-political legacy of Margaret Thatcher.

The authorial power in the naturalistic methodology of Meadowsian return comes from the filmmaker's position as a "native insider" growing up on the "social and geographical margins" during and after Thatcher (Fradley 290). Hyper-realistic—"halfway between cinema and documentary"—his work replicates his relationship with memory, using his authorial position both to represent his own experiences as well as to control "the biographies of those he knew through their representation in his films" (Schwarz 216). While the original feature film *This Is England* (2007) can be rightly interpreted as an autobiographical *Bildungsroman*, the subsequent TV series broaden the narratological framework of the poetics of return. In doing so, they become significantly more complex, developing into a humanistic, multi-faceted set of reflections on the passing of time, or rather, on the inability of time to pass. Meadows explores this stagnant temporality as a product of neoliberal interminability, but also as a psychosocial haunting device. His thematic tropes—ghostly reiterations, the persistence of the past, and the disavowing character of the future—posit the hauntological complexion of his approach. Indeed, Fradley, Godfrey, and Williams point out that, understood as "spectral traces of a recent political past.... Meadows' films are haunted both thematically and textually, displaying (post)traumatic symptoms of repetition and a therapeutic working-through of histories both personal and socio-political" (11).

A neologism first coined in his 1993 *Spectres of Marx*, hauntology was a reaction by Jacques Derrida to the triumphalism of neoliberal theorist Francis Fukuyama's declaring that the dissolution of the Soviet Union marked "the end of history." Derrida contended that unchecked capitalism was riddled with undead phantoms: "ideas thought to be buried returning, albeit in specter like traces" (Riley 18). Derridian hauntology explores a deconstructive perspective on time itself: ghosts "disturb chronology and the order of precedence it establishes … [while] haunting transforms the linear time of the calendar into a time of waiting and uncertainty, of not knowing" (Lorek-Jeziṅska and Więckowska 19). This disjointment is thus a constitutive dislocation—a fundamentally disruptive phenomenon—which proactively raises the issue of the unresolved, and the notion that the returning past is something that must be worked through. Hauntology then simultaneously offers a new way of concurrently conceptualizing our repressed past while coming to terms with our failed future. As Mark Fischer writes, "the failure of the future meant the acceptance of a situation in which culture would continue without really changing, and where politics was reduced to the administration of an already established (capitalist) system" (16).

In Meadows' portrayals of the past, disjointed "distortions of temporality" structurally and thematically organize the text through traumatic cyclicity (Forrest 39). A totalizing force, the specter of trauma persists with agitational omnipresence in a way that overwhelms normative structural time. As trauma theorist Gina Nordini argues, the psychological totality of the condition "becomes all-encompassing—absorbing experience in a way that leaves little room for existence *outside* of the trauma" (21). As depicted by Meadows, trauma is a ubiquitous condition that aggregates the larger historical enterprise of socio-economic Thatcherism with the personal annals of tragedy for its victims. The depressive urban environments and dysfunctional familial relationships interact to constitute a traumatic inheritance on both a macro and micro level from the violent impacts of an economic system that has left them behind.

Meadows' series of transmedia television narratives on Channel Four, *This Is England '86, '88,* and *'90,* act as sequels to the original *This Is England* film. The larger scope of the television medium in terms of both the physical running time and the productions' multi-year timespan allows the elaboration of a hauntological representation of the past. Rolinson and Woods point out that the primary thematic concerns of the serials include "the weight of the past as revealed in returns, hauntings and traumatic memory" (186). Throughout the series, the specter of Thatcherism challenges a pleasurable view of the past, as pop cultural nostalgia becomes "problematized by more complex and disturbing representations of the past shown in archive footage or embodied in references to challenging dramas from the period" (191). In Meadows' chronicle of Thatcherism, the unabating force of the past reiterates itself over the years as the characters are plagued by the cyclical nature of (post)traumatic return. The serials are centered around these narratological acts of return and revisitation, consequential comedowns from the violent explosion of political Thatcherism in the film. The specter of the purgatorial Combo (Stephen Graham) "destabilizes space as well as time, and encourages an existential orientation in the haunted subject" (Shaw 2). He is the harbinger of an unresolved past and a symptom of repressed knowledge. Incarcerated after his racially-motivated assault of Milky (Andrew Shim), Combo's path to redemption is coupled with the serials' tragic centralization of Lol's (Vicky McClure) nightmarish (re)encounters with her pater familias.

The unexpected return of Lol's absentee father, Mick (Johnny Harris), to the domestic fold triggers cataclysmic emotional and psychological fallout, prompting Lol's psychological fragmentation and a profound schism among her formerly close-knit group of friends (Fradley & Kingston 76). Mick is configured as an unabating specter of horror, continually returning as a semiotic reminder of the unresolved past. Initially, in '86, he is ghoulish in a metaphorical sense, reappearing from the past to dominate, destabilize, and denounce Lol's current and historical narrative. After his death, Mick returns as her literal tormenting ghost. Both in a physical and metaphysical manifestation, the enduring presence of Mick is a persistent symbol of unprocessed trauma. Meadows explores the ghostly manifestation of psychological trauma as a liminal spatiotemporal experience characterized by "the hauntings of and by characters, the traces that return and retreat" (Holdsworth 38). Lol's encysted trauma from her sexual abuse and the feelings of guilt attached to Combo's false incarceration for the murder return to haunt them as their memories are transformed into living experiences.

This experience of being haunted constitutes an encounter with something that is not known and that possibly cannot be comprehended, and whose appearance produces "a breakdown in cognitive functions" (Lorek-Jezińska & Więckowska 19). Lol's initial reaction to the arbitrary apparitions of her dead father is to deny the presence of the ghost and to try to occupy a "normal" spatiotemporal setting. During her second spectral encounter in the bathroom towards the end of the first episode of '88, Lol refuses to acknowledge the ghostly manifestation of her repressed trauma. She assures, herself, "this isn't real ... this isn't happening.... I'll be ok," as she proceeds to walk out of the room. This apparition epitomizes Clair Schwartz's observation that "the figure of the ghost becomes the participative dead subject who impinges on the living world" (215). Yet, while these ghosts may be interpreted as rational expressions of trauma, what then of the uncanny leakages away from the material that question the rationality of such an interpretation? In '88, the ghost of Mick haunts each scene, even after Lol leaves. As Schwartz put is, "If his ghost is a pure psychological manifestation of her mind, why does he linger in the bathroom, the sitting room, the church and the hospital even after the means of his manifestation has left?" (214). This uncanny apparition represents a classic instance of Meadowsian hauntology in which to view the haunting is to partake in the haunting, to be haunted both "by our own ghosts and those of others" (Lorek-Jezińska & Więckowska 19).

"Is this England?" Towards a Redemptive Hauntology of Thatcherism

In an interview in *The Guardian*, Meadows, discussing revenge as a principal thematic undercurrent in his oeuvre, pointed out that "It's not about revenge for revenge's sake ... it's about empathy for people." Indeed, in his work, revenge (and its negation) takes on a distinctly Meadowsian signature: a humanistic tapestry of causality, personal pay-offs, and redemptive ruminations. At what cost does revenge come? What forms can redemption take? Can we ever really be at peace? Such questions haunt Meadows' oeuvre, signaling the cyclical nature of life in the post-industrial mire, a condition marked by a future that has failed and a past that has persisted. This trauma stains the landscape as well as the personal histories of Combo, Lol, Woody, Kelly, and the gang. An act of revenge can suggest a certain degree of agency: a retaliation against the ghosts of the past and the evils of the present—an irrecoverable act of change, or at least a chance at mollification. "Meadows' worldview," writes Martin Fradley, "is best understood in political terms as a form of resistance to neoliberal ideology" (55). The essence of this resistance, however, is found in negation rather than in the act of revenge, in learning from our ghosts rather than repeating their mistakes, and in abandoning the violence of neoliberalism rather than participating in it (Anderson 60). While the dramatic structure of Meadows' terrain is organized around the motif of reckoning with past wrongs (much of the time through violent transgressions), it is in the poetics of psychospiritual redemption that Meadows and his characters breach the boundaries of something more meaningful. In a hauntological sense, we see how dialogue with the ghost can forcefully announce the need for a transformation; for *something to be done*. In line with the ethics of haunting as a cathartic experience, such an encounter can result not merely in "a return to the past but a reckoning with its repression in the present, a reckoning with that which we have lost but never had" (Gordon 183). In the *This Is England* serials, we see Meadows exploring the specter of repressed memory and the consequentiality of its return, oscillating between the desire for revenge and the need for redemption.

For Meadows, acts of revenge are partly explored through the ethics of virtue. No matter what the justification, retributive violence comes at a price, and Meadows focuses on the psychological fallout of revenge as a restorative device. In *This Is England '88*, we learn that, rather than extirpating the arbitrary presence of Lol's abuser, "Mick's presence is not erased with his death, as '88 manifests Lol's mental deterioration through her father's apparition, her past folding in on and stifling in her present" (Rolinson & Woods 198). In this context, Mick's murder in '86 can be read as a failed exorcism. Unable to continue in her depressive state of demonic liminality, Lol attempts to take her own life on Christmas Eve. In narratological terms, Meadows frames the violent pumping of her stomach as a cathartic purging of her pain, with the attempt to save her life coming "across as more of an exorcism than a medical procedure" (Murphy 205). The religious overtones of the montage are introduced with Evelyn's voiceover in her prayer "for a sick friend," which itself is drowned out by the nightmarish cacophony of warped sounds, a call back to the ominous glossolalia of the ghostly Mick. The stomach pumping becomes a form of return: an abstract mosaic of interspersed collective, intertextual, and personal memory, as Lol's writhing body intercuts with archival news footage of starving children, innocent scenes of the gang at the swimming pool, scattered images of Combo, Woody, and Milky, and the distressed muffled screams of her mother in the waiting room. The haunting montage is punctuated with scenes of Mick raping Trev, whispering inaudible threats, and attacking and being murdered by Lol. His evil presence is juxtaposed with flashes of Christian symbolism—the priest at the altar, the wooden crucifixes, the stained-glass window in the church—all configuring the montage as a spiritual battle for Lol's soul (fig. 2).

In the hyper-religious tonality of the montage, Lol's suffering becomes analogous with the redemptive suffering of Christ on the cross, an implication that is elucidated by the statue of the crucifixion included towards the culmination of the montage. Indeed, the inclusion of archival news footage and intertextual scenes from *This Is England '83–'88* encompasses both collective memories and shared experiences, which by extension have made Lol's haunting also *our* haunting (Anderson 63). As David Rolinson and Faye Woods astutely point out:

> During this montage, Mick says to camera (Lol), "You're the only one who knows." Given that some of the images from the film and '86 featured in the montage were not seen by Lol, the sequence can be read as a traumatic memory montage for the omniscient viewer who has experienced these events across the film and television narratives. This lends a darker [*hauntological*] meaning to Mick's comment to camera (the viewer) [200].

With the removal of Lol's tube, the frenzied montage subsides as the calm prayer returns, with Evelyn pleading: "I ask that you give mercy and grace to Lorraine. Nourish her spirit and her soul in this time of suffering and comfort her with your presence." In this numinous moment, the darkness which has haunted the story is purged for both the viewer and Lol, with further solace found in her reconciliation with Woody in the closing scene of '88.

Indeed, through poetic realism and naturalism, Meadows captures that signature of feeling, an aesthetic realization of the spirit and humor of the everyday. Woody's value-based, community-oriented sociology challenges the status of neoliberalism as a vehicle for working-class social mobility and as an authentic political force. In this sense, he is reminiscent of Martin Freeman's Timothy Canterbury from *The Office* (2001–2003), a self-deprecating, everyday "anti-hero" capable of seeing through the fraudulent camaraderie of the post-industrial workplace that seems to function as the logical extension of "the end of history." Woody, like Timothy, fulfills the role of the Jungian archetype, the trickster, functioning "as a contemporary trickster who uses strategies of liminality to negotiate the difficult intersection between the worthiness of the social realist project and the seeming vacuity of contemporary culture, all the while sustained by a homosocial environment" (Schwarz 12).

We rejoin Lol and gang again for what appears to be the final installment, *This Is England '90*, which is set against the backdrop of burgeoning rave culture and the 1990 Fifa World Cup. Released in 2015, the four-part series is both tonally and temporally aligned with the different seasons of the year. Now living together and finally married, it seems that Lol and Woody have been able to realize a trail beyond the dark recesses of the past: a road to redemption. While Lol is no longer plagued by the demonic apparitions of Mick, the specter *remains*—an (un)spoken reverberation echoing through the corridors of what was and what has yet to be. Indeed, the weight of the past continues to manifest itself, with the focus now shifting to Lol's younger sister Kelly (Chanel Cresswell) and her attempts to reconcile the revelations from '86 and '88 about her father and his murder. The legacy of the past also remains in a state of redemptive and narratological tension, with Milky forced to keep the "promises" that were made to get revenge for Combo's brutal assault in the 1983 film. These retributive actions imply the unresolved compulsion to repeat the past.

Conclusion

England has become a country obsessed with its most recent past. "Hauntology," writes Katy Shaw, "is a peculiarly English phenomenon ... [with] English culture seemingly more concerned with co-opting the past than embracing the future" (1). This spectrality has become an increasingly tangible and highly contentious battleground in recent years, symptomatic in the referendum on the European Union, the political re-centralization of Thatcherism in the Conservative Party, and, across the Atlantic, the 2016 election of Donald Trump. As this regressive (re) imagination of the past maps itself onto contemporary culture forms, it produces an ever-bleaker commercially mediated economy of nostalgia—underscored in the safe spaces of "Netflix's algorithmic reification of collective memory" (Fradley 246). *Stranger Things*, for example, reduces the fractious 1980s to a largely apolitical safety blanket, making it increasingly difficult to see what is at stake in the representation of the past.

As we slip into this cultural and political epoch of amnesia, we risk forgetting the magnitude of the break that Thatcherism was, and the profound rupture it represents. For the post–Thatcherite generation, there proves to be little urgency to understand that there was even a "break" at all, a slip that shows the efficacy of Prime Minister Thatcher. As Francis Beckett writes, "today few people under 40 remember a time when trade unions were a real force in the land; when the public sector controlled large swathes of the economy; when local councils controlled education and other local services; when benefits were considered rights of citizenship" (qtd. in "Thatcher and Attlee"). With the persistence of the Thatcherite past as our unequivocal condition, the *This Is England* television series documents a past, present, and future laden with dark Meadowsian melancholia. Meadows' dramas provide personal indictments of a violent neoliberalism and haunting reminders that, despite Fukayama's thesis, the future has never come to pass. They are much more than that, however: despite portraying a depressive topography haunted by the ceaseless cycles of the past, Meadows explores the poetics of haunting, and within the horror he finds hope, seeing in the ghosts that haunt us an ethical potential and a cathartic potency. And as the waves of creative destruction unleashed by Margaret Thatcher continue to erode the present, the politics of memory and the memory of politics become increasingly urgent.

Works Cited

Anderson, Jack. "Return, Remembrance and Redemption: Hauntology and the Topography of Trauma in This is England '88 and The Virtues," *Journal of British Cinema and Television*, 19:1, pp. 45–66.

Caruth, Cathy. Unclaimed Experience: Trauma, Narrative, and History. Johns Hopkins University Press, 1996.

Dinning, Alexandra. When Will Thatcher's Death Die? i-D, 2020, www.i-d.vice.com.

Fisher, Martin. "What Is Hauntology?," *Film Quarterly*, 66:1, 2012, pp. 16–2.

Forrest, David. "Twenty-first-Century Social Realism: Shane Meadows and New British

Realism." *Shane Meadows: Critical Essays,* edited by Martin Fradley, Sarah Godfrey and Melanie Williams. Edinburgh University Press, 2013, pp. 35–49.

Fradley, Martin. "Shane Meadows." *Fifty Contemporary Film Directors,* edited by Yvonne Tasker. Routledge, 2010, pp.280–288.

Fradley, Martin, Sarah Godfrey, and Melanie Williams. "Introduction: Shane's World." *Shane Meadows,* edited by Martin Fradley, Sarah Godfrey and Melanie Williams (eds). Edinburgh University Press, 2013, pp. 1–20.

Fradley, Martin. "Netflix Nostalgia: Screening the Past on Demand, edited by Kathryn Pallister, and The Aesthetics of Nostalgia TV: Production Design and the Boomer Era, by Alex Bevan." Book review. *Journal of Film and Screen Media,* no. 19, 2020, pp. 230–241.

Gordon, Avery. *Ghostly Matters: Haunting and the Sociological Imagination.* Minnesota University Press, 2003.

Holdsworth, Amy. "Haunting the Memory: Moments of Return in Television Drama." In *Television, Memory and Nostalgia. Palgrave Macmillan Memory Studies.* Palgrave Macmillan.

Huyssen, Andreas. *Present Pasts: Urban Palimpsests and the Politics of Memory.* Stanford University Press, 2003.

Leggott, James. *Contemporary British Cinema: From Heritage to Horror.* Wallflower, 2008.

Lincoln, Bruce, and Martha Lincoln. "Toward a Critical Hauntology: Bare Afterlife and the Ghosts of Ba Chúc," *Comparative Studies in Society and History,* 57.1, 2015, pp. 191–220.

Lorek-Jezińska, Edyta, and Katarzyna Więckowska. "Hauntology and Cognition: Questions of Knowledge, Pasts and Futures." *Theoria et Historia Scientiarum,* 14:1, 2017, pp. 7–23.

Murphy, Robert. (2013), "After Laughter Comes Tears: Passion and Redemption in *This is England '88*" in Martin Fradley, Sarah Godfrey and MelanieWilliams (eds), *Shane Meadows: Critical Essays.* Edinburgh University Press, pp. 203–9.

Nordini, Gina. *Haunted by History: Interpreting Traumatic Memory Through Ghosts in Film and Literature.* 2016. All Regis University, PhD.

Riley, John. "Hauntology, Ruins, and the Failure of the Future in Andrei Tarkovsky's *Stalker." Journal of Film and Video,* 61:1, 2017, pp. 18–26.

Rolinson, David, and Faye Woods. "Is This England '86 and '88? Memory, Haunting and Return through Television Seriality." in *Shane Meadows: Critical Essays,* edited by Martin Fradley, Sarah Godfrey and Melanie Williams. Edinburgh University Press, 2013, pp. 186–202.

Schwarz, Clair. "'An object of an indecipherable bastard—a true monster': Homosociality, Homoeroticism and Generic Hybridity in Dead Man's Shoes." *Shane Meadows: Critical Essays,* edited by Martin Fradley, Sarah Godfrey and Melanie Williams. Edinburgh University Press, 2013, pp. 95–110.

Schwarz, Clair. *Shane Meadows: Representations of Liminality, Masculinity and Class.* University of the West of England, PhD, 2013.

Shaw, Katy. *Hauntology: The Presence of the Past in Twenty-First Century Literature.* Palgrave Macmillan, 2018.

Wolfreys, Julian. *Victorian Hauntings: Spectrality, Gothic, the Uncanny and Literature.* Palgrave, 2002.

Remembering to Forget

1980s Retro Gaming and the Aesthetics of Escape

John Misak

The enduring popularity of 1980s aesthetics is vividly reflected in today's video gaming culture. Retro gamers—those who either play classic games or current recreations of past game design—overwhelmingly prefer games from the '80s. Both Generation X and their children continue to breathe life into this period's games. Nostalgia fuels some of their popularity but cannot explain why teenagers today split their time between the advanced graphics of *Fortnite* (2017) and the pixelated *Metroid* (1986) or '80s-inspired titles like *Dead Cells* (2018), or why retro game designers opt for 8-bit graphics in a time of hyper-realism. The '80s gaming aesthetic—including visuals, sounds, and gameplay elements combined—remains popular during a time of tremendous technological advancements in gaming hardware. The appeal of retro gaming may lie in the absence of complications, technologically and otherwise. These games offer players a chance to actively explore well-developed fantasy realms with simple entry points, and they provide easily accessed haptic experiences. The 1980s represents a sweet spot in terms of the mix that games from this era achieve between aesthetic simplicity and complexity.

That sweet spot rests between the Golden Era of arcades (1978–1983) and the more advanced games of the mid–1990s and beyond. For the purposes of this essay the most important aspect of the Golden Era is the Video Game Crash of 1983.[1] After the popularity of *Pac-Man, Donkey Kong,* and *Space Invaders,* manufacturers flooded the market with knock-offs and titles rushed to store shelves. As a result, the market crashed. Atari relied on its 2600 console for too long, new players like Coleco got caught in licensing quagmires, and players tired of sub-par offerings. The cornerstone moment—one that clearly illustrates the greed that drove manufacturers—was Atari's release of its *E.T.* game. The game was designed in roughly six weeks rather than the standard six months, and players rejected it, leaving Atari with millions of unwanted cartridges and stuck in a dire financial position. Aesthetically, home console games from 1977 to 1983 didn't advance much. In the arcade, *Space Invaders* (1978) looked antiquated next to *Robotron: 2084* (1982). However, their ports to home consoles looked similar due to the fact that they ran on the same hardware. Though nostalgia exists for the arcade classics and some home games from the first few years of the 1980s, the attraction cannot match that for what I will refer to as the 8-bit Era. This era enabled a synergy between arcade and home games, and it opened the door for a radical shift in how games were made, sold, and played.

Every crisis provides an opportunity. Nintendo, an arcade and handheld game manufacturer, had long wanted to enter the home console market. They originally sought out Atari, but this potential merger failed because, by 1983, Atari had already lost half a billion dollars and did not have the capital for such a partnership (Cifaldi). Nintendo decided to release their own console and needed to overcome the bad taste retailers still had from the crash. Their persistence paid off, as did their attention to software quality and fair licensing agreements. Players for the first time experienced arcade-quality graphics on their home consoles. Although the Nintendo Entertainment System (NES) used 8-bit processors like its ancestors, faster computing speed and graphics technology enabled developers to master 8-bit aesthetics. This created a moment in gaming history that serves as the original point of reference for retro gaming. For instance, *Donkey Kong*'s port to Mattel's Intellivision and Atari's 2600 was vastly different from the source material. Yet, playing the original *Mario Bros.* on the NES replicated the experience completely, creating game moments that could be remembered for a lifetime. Singlehandedly, Nintendo revitalized a stagnant video game market (Potts).

Nintendo's entry to the home market constitutes a critical development in the story of retro-gaming, as much of the 8-bit retro phenomenon refers back to the graphics created and replicated on the NES. Atari, Mattel, and Coleco all released 8-bit consoles in the late '70s and early '80s, but when one thinks about the aesthetics of the 8-bit Era,[2] images from *Kung-Fu* or *Super Mario Bros.* come to mind. Games from before the 8-bit Era lack the complexity to compel today's players and designers because of their overly-simplistic graphic design, sound, depth, and gameplay. The 8-bit Era ushered in games with stylized graphics and detailed gameplay, enabling players to experience epic moments that fuel both personal nostalgia and the collective revival these games enjoy today.

Nineteen eighty-five sits at the center point of video game culture as the time most commonly associated with '80s games and 8-bit aesthetics. Although classic games from earlier in the decade receive attention,

Asteroids' current popularity is minuscule compared to that of *Super Mario Bros.* or *Paperboy!* or *Gauntlet.* But why? Much of the explanation has to do with the evolution of 8-bit game design, along with the cultural acceptance of gaming as a hobby. Before 1985, Atari's 2600 sold over 30 million units in the Golden Era (Ciesla 162), ten times more than second-place's Mattel Intellivision. Still, the greater impact of gaming on American culture came from the arcades, which became a cornerstone of teenage social gatherings. Recapturing this experience at home remained elusive to console manufacturers, and when early classics finally saw realistic home console ports in the mid- to late '80s, the teenagers of the Golden Era had jobs, families, and seemingly little interest in nudging their children off the couch to play *Pac-Man*.[3] Their children, however, grew up on the NES and the ancillary media promoting it in the form of Saturday morning cartoons based on NES games. The NES sat attached to televisions in thirty percent of American households (Kohler). So, much like in *Back to the Future*, 1985 serves as a focal point on the timeline for retro gaming, the genesis for what is now considered 8-bit aesthetics.

The Attraction to 8-bit Era Games

One point should be made from the outset: 8-bit Era games do not outperform the games of today. Still, something about '80s games continues to capture gamers' imaginations in a way earlier and later games do not. The '80s game aesthetic involves three key areas: graphics, sound, and gameplay mechanics. The visuals are the most recognizable, but the three, both individually and as a group, explain the endurance of this era's popularity. Today's game aesthetic can trace its roots back to the aesthetic advancements of this period.

Graphics, first and foremost, make 8-bit Era games recognizable. The 8-bit Era sits between the blocky, low-res games of Atari, and the prototypical 3D games of the 1990s. Game designers found a way to refine 8-bit graphics on the NES. This allowed gameplay akin to that of the arcade without the interference of subpar graphics. When gamers in 1985 played the NES *Mario Bros.* (which came free with the system), the visuals matched the arcade version almost perfectly.[4] For the retro gamer, there's no need to play the 2600 version of *Pac-Man* or *Donkey Kong* when NES versions or emulators exist.[5] Pre-8-bit Era versions have little retro value other than for those nostalgic for them specifically. The 8-bit Era game aesthetic, which includes original NES games and near-perfect arcade ports of earlier games, attracts players from a wider range of ages.

Dubbed "pixel art," the visual aesthetic of these 8-bit games follows a pattern started in the '70s. The beauty of pixel art lies in the simplic-ity of 8-bit Era graphics that draw today's players to such titles. "Pixel art games made a comeback because … [of] the simplicity, the minimalism, the lightness of the pixels that's so alluring" (Kordic). "Simplicity" does not directly correlate to a lack of depth. The games from the 8-bit Era offer graphic fidelity from the very nature of their pixelization. For a time in game design, more pixels meant more detail. The smaller, more defined pixels of 8-bit Era games make them translatable for today's hardware and screens. They also can be used in current games without detracting from the gameplay, making the visual aesthetic of pixel art games palatable for today's players and central to the retro gaming boom.

The sound design of video games helps immerse players in the game experience. Games from the 8-bit Era have a unique sound, one that is often replicated in today's throwback games. Once again, today's retro developers do not reach back past the 8-bit era because earlier games do not provide much in the way of identifiable sound. Even games like *Donkey Kong* for the Intellivision console, which had decent sound, get over-looked because later consoles replicated the arcade version.[6] Pre-NES titles often had more noise than sound, with the rare soundtrack coming through. There just wasn't enough storage on the cartridge nor memory in the console to include compelling ambient sound or music. Although the noisy sound of these older consoles has its own aesthetic value, it does not get replicated in the same way that 8-bit Era sound does.

As game design progressed, sound became an integral part of the expe-rience, and many players refer to the ambient music of their favorite games from the 8-bit Era. With more storage, memory, and dedicated sound pro-cessors, designers could focus on making unique sounds, differentiating the 8-bit Era from the games before, which often had different variations of the same sound for games. Fans of the 8-bit Era instantly recognize the ring when collecting a coin in *Super Mario Bros.*, the triumph of a newspaper hitting a porch in *Paperboy!*, and the running music in *Kung-Fu*. Players from the era fondly remember these sounds, and many young players instantly recog-nize these classic sound effects. This advance in technology helped create the 8-bit sound aesthetic often recreated in music today. It has become a genre of music, "chip tunes," in the same way that pixel art has become a popular style in visual media. Again, the complexity within the outward simplicity of the aesthetic makes it attractive to creators and consumers of this form of media, facilitating its current popularity. A common practice today involves artists creating 8-bit versions of pop hits, meshing the past and present.

Gameplay design also made significant advancements during the 8-bit Era. More processing power enabled more realistic experiences helping game developers nearly perfect the arcade port in the 8-bit Era.

Conquering this Holy Grail of gaming inspired designers to go further. The home experience lent itself to longer play periods, and for the first time, consumers showed a preference for home games versus playing in the arcade.[7] Most arcade games were built to have short life spans at their locations and relied on gaming difficulty to require the player to keep popping in quarters. At home, with no limit on plays, this design didn't work as well. Therefore, early in the tenure of the NES, designers decided to create experiences unique to the home. The arcade release of *Gauntlet*, a four-player hack-and-slash game that represented the pinnacle of short arcade location life and quarter-popping game design, likely inspired the home game designers to include more depth. Similarly, 1983's *Dragon's Lair*, a title which received homage in the second season of *Stranger Things*, also went in and out of arcade locations because, although it told a story, the gameplay involved little more than pushing left or right or pressing a button at the right time. Players' expectations evolved, and the mid–80s saw the perfect combination of players and designers wearying of arcade ports at the same time technology became available to provide players with detailed experiences games like *Gauntlet* and *Dragon's Lair* teased. A key element of '80s games followed: intricate gameplay and stories that gave players a "reason" to play beyond simple entertainment.

Likely inspired by the success of fantasy-themed arcade games, designers like legendary *Donkey Kong* and *Super Mario Bros.* creator Shigeru Miyamoto created *The Legend of Zelda*, a game whose legacy thrives today. The *Zelda* series broke ground in several areas, most notably the telling of a complex story and the ability to save a game. It incorporated puzzles, adventure, fighting, and exploration. Such depth in a game created memorable experiences not unlike those in real life. Games had not achieved this complexity on such a scale before. Roleplaying games (RPGs) already existed, but *Zelda* paved the way for the modern console RPG, and many players see it as the true ancestor of the genre. *Zelda*'s accomplishment explains the pull games from the 8-bit Era have on today's players, both older ones seeking nostalgia and younger looking to discover gaming's past. The *Zelda* series and the games it inspired helped to create a design aesthetic based on complex yet easy-to-learn mechanics, while allowing players to unfold a detailed story they would remember. Hacking and slashing through *Gauntlet* in the arcade was mindless fun in the moment. The *Zelda* player had a clear mission with plot pieces helping them move forward with purpose.

Non-linear game design, in which certain areas can only be accessed after performing specific tasks or acquiring certain items, also debuted during the mid–1980s. Ushered in by titles like *Metroid* and *Castlevania,* this retro style of game has its own moniker, "Metroidvania." These design elements represent a key '80s game aesthetic, a unique sense of exploration infused with achievement, simplicity with underlying complexity. Current Metroidvania titles like *Dead Cells* top download charts each year, illustrating this concept's popularity. Metroidvania games illustrate the attraction to '80s game aesthetics. One of the designers of Metroid, Yoshio Sakamoto, when asked about the game's aesthetics, said, "It was dark, with a well-built player-character who hurls through enemies.[8] That was all there" (Sakamoto and Kiyotake). This design highlights the common '80s game theme of a lone, nearly supernatural hero conquering evil. The player overcomes the enemy with the help of unrelenting optimism. This visceral sense of accomplishment epitomizes the '80s gameplay aesthetic that players still seek. Retro games created today blend the original aesthetic of the 8-bit Era with the more complex game mechanics enabled by today's control methods. Add the Metroidvania gameplay dynamic, and today's indie games offer surface simplicity that belies the complex mechanics underneath. Nearly anyone can play such games on a base level; mastering the intricacies, however, requires practice and experimentation. Playing without learning advanced techniques does not diminish the gaming experience, and this accessibility attracts a wide variety of players, unlike today's games, which can be intimidatingly complex.

Recreating the Past: Why the '80s Rule Retro Gaming

The creators of *Shovel Knight*, an open homage to NES games like *Zelda*, indicated they chose to design the game with a mid–80s aesthetic to recreate the games of their youth (Turi). Matt Raithel, Studio Director of Graphite Lab, makers of *Hive Jump*, echoes this sentiment: "I grew up in that era. So, in my case, some of the appeal is probably nostalgia creeping in. Something else to consider that is more universal is the general simplicity of games back then. The hardware and tools were less robust so the experiences (though amazing for the time) were simpler in nature" (D'Aprile). The games of the 8-bit Era served as a digital playground for players in the 1980s, acting as the sites of positive memories they seek to return to as adults, both as players and as designers. Playing these games today serves as a portal into this vanished playground. The game itself creates an environment away from the current world's difficulties, and the act of replaying conjures deeper memories. The player may remember the beginnings and endings of games but likely not the events in between. Playing again allows gamers to access long-forgotten game events of their childhood. A player may forever recall starting out on the journey and ultimately defeating Ganon in *Zelda* but may not remember having received the Magical Boomerang a third of the way through.

Re-experiencing a moment like this creates a genuine nostalgic encounter—often a positive and unique one—that feeds the desire for more and undergirds the attraction of retro gaming for the older player.

Retro gaming as nostalgia involves revisiting one's past through repeated action. The experience may be different since the player has aged and since repeating never equates to perfect experiential replication. A young player in the '80s likely did not notice a game's references to the politics of the Cold War at the time. Retro-aesthetic games often whitewash the tarnish of the decade, the social inequality, wanton violence, and fear. Yet, those who played games from the 8-bit Era experience a transit back to the time period and can note the cultural and political changes that separate then from now. Playing 8-bit Era games enables players to revisit the '80s through the lens of lived experiences, resulting in a rich synthesis of past nostalgia and present understanding. "It may not be about the game per se, but instead what the game does. It serves as a reminder of consequential life experiences." (McFerren). Although often considered a mixed emotion (Wulf; Rieger and Frischlich), nostalgia has also been described as a positive resource for the self (Vess; Arndt and Routledge; Wulf, Bowman and Rieger). McFerren writes that "When people are nostalgic, they are reflecting on personally significant or momentous past experiences. Research demonstrates that engaging in nostalgic reflection increases positive mood, self-esteem, feelings of belongingness, and a sense of existential meaning." Playing the old games and experiencing a rush of memories equates to a kind of time travel, rife with many of the same paradoxes. One cannot perfectly relive the past, but one can revisit it and get the flavor of what once was through more mature taste buds. Retro gaming feels less like recapturing youth and more like reliving its experiences as an adult. The player retraces their digital steps in a way that they cannot with their physical ones. This immersive experience weaves together the past and present, allowing retro-gamers to contextualize their personal experiences within the wider frame of historical change.

Nostalgia can help to explain retro gaming's attraction for older players. But what about current teenagers? They have little connection to these classic games. Rather, the appeal of '80s-era game aesthetics for them may have to do with the style's relative simplicity. Today's teenagers have more challenges to navigate, technologically and socially, and they are likely aware of it. The complicated outside world creeps into their hobbies, as games have become a connected experience, for good and bad. Merely playing an online game can become a practice in political debate as players chat about the events of the day or stream political podcasts as they play. Teenagers from the '80s who sought solace from the politics of high school life in an arcade at least had the blaring sounds from the games to drown this chatter out. Today's teenagers have a mute button, but having to negotiate the political element of group-play can make playing games—supposedly an act of escape—more work than it should be. In addition, today's games involve more sophisticated functions than simply moving and performing actions. Many can be as complicated as real life, requiring micromanagement on a level that would make an office supervisor proud.

Games from the 8-bit Era—and those inspired by them—strip away this complexity and offer a focused mission and simple controls. Whereas conquering today's games requires diverse skills, succeeding in 8-bit Era games rarely involves more than mastering button and movement combinations. The goal remains forever in sight: a looming boss battle, the accumulation of items to open new areas, and the saving of the princess, world, or what have you. No one buzzes in the player's head about current events, there's no need to keep an eye on several different elements, and most 8-bit games are designed to be completed in a sitting or two. It takes little to get invested in the game and requires minimal skill or practice to play successfully. For today's teenagers, retro gaming is about an escape from not only the complexity of today's world, but also its games. The act of playing a current game involves constant software updates, driver downloads, configuring controller inputs, and other complexities. Playing an NES game requires a cartridge insert and power button switch. The retro gaming console only plays games. Some devices for today's games (PCs and smartphones) perform other duties for work, socialization, etc., and these can interrupt the escape games should provide. Although other reasons may exist for today's teenagers to play retro games, simplicity stands as the most salient.

From the Gen-Xer looking for nostalgia to a current teenager seeking simplicity in complicated times, games from the 1980s continue to attract players. The NES developed such a positive following that it still influences today's market, as evidenced by the popularity of the NES Mini and emulation both on current consoles, phones, and PCs. The NES' legacy reaches even further, inspiring pixel art visual media and chip tune music, along with major movie releases based on games from the time period. Though the games before and after have some popularity today, the games of the 8-bit Era enjoy perennial currency, illustrating their near-perfect execution of the initial simplicity and underlying complexity that gamers and designers still respond to today.

NOTES

1. For an in-depth look at this major event in gaming history, see (Video Game Crash of 1983) which provides a good background and several reliable sources in its references.

2. As stated, 8-bit technology drove nearly every console released before the NES. However, the 8-bit era often refers to the release of the NES up to its successor, the Super Nintendo. This period generally spans 1985–1991.

3. It's of interest to note the popularity of Microsoft's *Return of Arcade* series in the mid-'90s, which included early arcade classics like *Pac-Man, Asteroids,* and others in true arcade format. These titles clearly targeted computer users old enough to have played the originals in the arcade.

4. Although nearly three years passed between arcade and NES versions of Mario Bros. the title had impact because, relative to the time period, consumers were used to waiting for home versions of media. It often took almost two years for VHS versions of movies to come to the home screen.

5. Emulators do what it sounds like they do: they emulate hardware to run software. So, for instance, a computer user can download MAME (Multi Arcade Machine Emulator), locate the proper software (called a ROM), and have their computer recreate the experience near-perfectly. Of course, some games should not be downloaded due to copyright law, but several thousand of them are available at archive.org's site in the name of historical preservation.

6. I feel compelled to note that this is not like music, where some purists prefer vinyl records over CDs. The games from the pre–NES era are more similar to cassettes, which had bad sound quality when compared to any other medium.

7. Games for the NES ranged between $40 and $50. At 25 cents per play in the arcade, it became apparent some cartridges weren't worth 200 quarters to nearly recreate the experience.

8. Samus, the main character of Metroid, was female. Players who completed the game saw the character remove their helmet, revealing a female. So, this "well-built hero" resembling '80s action stars illustrated flipped expectations. Female characters were rare in this time, and many players consider it a most defining moment in their gaming history.

WORKS CITED

Cheng, Roger. "AT&T makes new predictions after 1993 'You Will' ads come true." 28 November 2018. *c|net.* 1 March 2021.

Ciesla, Robert. *Mostly Codeless Game Development: New School Game Engines.* Apress, 2017.

Cifaldi, Frank. "In Their Words: Remembering the Launch of the Nintendo Entertainment System." 19 October 2015. *IGN.*

D'Aprile, Jason. "Indie Games and The Loce of the Retro Aesthetic." 30 January 2019. *The Indie Game Website.*

Kohler, Chris. "Parents Didn't Just Dislike Super Nintendo 25 Years Ago—They Thought It Was a Scam." 28 August 2016. *Wired.*

Kordic, Angie. "What Exactly is Pixel Art and How Did It Come Back to Life?" 7 November 2015. *Widewalls.*

McFerren, Damien. "Crippled by Nostalgia: The Fraud of Retro Gaming." 12 September 2012. *Eurogamer.*

Potts, Mark. "Home-Video Games Have Bounced Back." *Minneapolis Star and Tribune.* 9 July 1987.

"Retro Culture." 21 February 2021. *Wikipedia.*

Sakamoto, Yoshio, and Hiroji Kiyotake. "NES Classic Edition Developer Interview: Metroid." *Akinori Sao.* n.d.

Turi, Tim. "*Shovel Knight* Devs Discuss Co-Op, Pogo Jumping, And Beyond." 29 July 2014. *Game Informer.*

Vess, Matthew et al. "Nostalgia as a Resource for the Self." Self and Identity 11.3 (2012): 273–284.

"Video Game Crash of 1983." 28 February 2021. *Wikipedia.*

Wulf, Tim, et al. "Video Games as Time Machines: Video Game Nostalgia and the Success of Retro Gaming." *Media and Communication 6.2* (2018): 60–68.

_____. "Wallowing in Media-Past: Personal and Collective Triggers of Media-Induced Nostalgia." International Communication Association 65th Annual Conference. 2015. 1–32.

The Pop Music Montage

Nostalgia as a Function of 1980s Film Soundtracks

CARRIE CLANTON

"We wear all the music we have ever heard; we are the product of all the music that we have ever listened to."—Rupert Hine

The 1980s saw soundtracks proliferate in various forms at both the public and personal level, from music videos to mix tapes. Indeed, our contemporary understanding of the concept of the soundtrack can be said to have originated during the 1980s, the era when composed film scores gave way to soundtracks compiled of popular songs that would often became stand-alone music albums in their own right.

This use of pop songs within film led to a notable montage technique of the 1980s, particularly in coming-of-age films, in which a particular song doesn't just functionally "score" a series of moments to move the film's action forward, but which may be said to exist as a cinematic moment in its own right. A number of contemporary coming-of-age films pay homage to the specific way in which 1980s pop-song film montages solidified and broadened our understanding of the concept of soundtracks, while, beyond the cinema, digital editing technologies now allow for the creation of new forms of soundtracks that play with the notions of montage and nostalgia through the remixing of images, pop songs, and soundscapes of the era.

Pop-song-scored montages in films of the 1980s therefore offer a particular insight into the relationship between the conceptualization of the soundtrack and its relation to nostalgia about the era, with implications for popular media and culture more generally in the present. Below I will trace some of the various connections between pop music and moving images as they came to be incorporated into our modern understanding of the soundtrack. I will then delve into some examples of 1980s pop music film montages and their relation to nostalgia and discuss some examples of contemporary soundtracked montages that call into question the function of media-generated nostalgia.

The Pop Music Soundtrack of the 1980s and Beyond

The use of popular songs as soundtrack material didn't originate in the 1980s. As Jeff Smith argues in his book about film music and commerce, popular songs were used more frequently within feature films beginning in the 1950s, less for aesthetic purposes than for economic ones: with film studios often having music production under the same roof, it made sense to produce and cross-promote both music and film. Likewise, the idea of the music video—a medium in which a pop song accompanies a short movie, usually produced to commercially promote the song—was not a new concept in the 1980s. Feature narrative films such as Elvis' *Jailhouse Rock* (1957) and the Beatles' *A Hard Day's Night* (1964) were vehicles for their stars and their songs, and were the precedents of 1980s films such as Prince's *Purple Rain* (1984), which would essentially cross-promote his album of the same name. However, it was during the 1980s that one-song music videos would become a commercial art form widely broadcast on MTV, which launched in 1981. Aesthetically, music videos and the pop-song montage helped legitimize the notion of the pop song as soundtrack. Their emergence and co-existence during the 1980s would redefine the parameters of what constitutes a soundtrack, which would in turn come to encompass various forms of media, and which would become a personal concept as well, with implications for the ways in which nostalgia is used as a cultural form in contemporary times.

Many music videos of the 1980s followed narrative formats, functioning as mini-movies unto themselves with the featured pop song serving as soundtrack. Michael Jackson's 1983 John Landis-directed horror-dance video for "Thriller" (known as *Michael Jackson's Thriller*), with its cinematic musical zombie story, complete with narration from Vincent Price, is one of the better-known examples of a narrative music video, but Mike + the Mechanics' 1985 sci-fi fascism-tinged fourteen-minute video for "Silent Running (On Dangerous Ground)" is also worth mentioning here for reasons to be discussed below. Meanwhile, the proliferation of music videos allowed for new forms of cross-promotional opportunities for pop music and feature film. Cyndi Lauper's video for her song "Goonies 'r' Good Enough," commissioned for the film *The Goonies* (1986), saw the pop musician, her wrestler father, and his colleagues acting in their own narrative co-starring the teen actors from the film. Other videos, such as Madonna's "Get into the Groove" from the film *Desperately Seeking Susan*

(1986) and Phil Collins' "Take a Look at Me Now (Against All Odds)" from the film *Against All Odds* (1984), consist of montages of spliced-together footage from the films.

Outside of film and beyond the 1980s, the idea of the pop-music soundtrack—now more commonly referred to as the "compilation" soundtrack—would cross over into the gaming world and to social media, as pop music began to saturate more of life's personal media experiences. From its earliest versions in 1997, the popular crime-adventure game *Grand Theft Auto* allowed players to control the soundtrack of game play through the diegetic use of pop music, with songs experienced in the background of bars or on the fictional radio stations (changeable by the player) piped into stolen cars. Many other games, particularly racing and sports games, now allow players to curate their personal playing soundtrack from a pre-selected playlist of pop songs licensed to the game. The soundtrack of *Madden NFL 20*, for example, consists of a playlist of specially commissioned hip-hop tracks that is customizable by players and "has been specifically built with *Madden NFL* and football as the foundation for the aesthetic of the sound, the tone, and the feel" ("Turn Up with the Madden 20 Soundtrack").

Social media likewise has incorporated pop music as soundtrack into its functionality. LiveJournal and Facebook of the early- to mid-2000s allowed users to flag the song and artist they were listening to (if not play or broadcast the actual track) while posting a journal entry or status update, along with some indication of mood. This personalization of the pop-music soundtrack had already started analogically during the early 1980s with the emergence of mix tapes, which in the early days were usually created by individuals using cassette recorders to capture their favorite songs as they were broadcast on commercial radio. A mix tape is of course also a soundtrack—an individually-curated album for oneself or a gift of love for others—and we continue to make them today with evolved technologies, whether passively, through auto-generated Spotify playlists, or actively, through our chosen playlists for our daily commute, parties, running, or road trips.

Technological developments, particularly digital, have massively expanded the way in which we think about, create, and consume pop soundtracks and music videos since their 1980s inception. Today, it takes nearly no time or effort to create and consume personal soundtracks and montages using digital media, such as the music-videos-in-miniature of TikTok, which gives users access to a vast catalogue of pop music paired with phone-camera footage or re-assembled commercial media. Music videos, as they have manifested variously since the 1980s, have hence determined the way in which we have come to understand the concept of the soundtrack. A popular song is rarely heard independently of some other context, and it is almost always accompanied in some way by images or activity; it is not generally a stand-alone text, but a text attached to something else, whether a playlist, a video, a blog entry, or a movie soundtrack, or even a memory.

A song becomes a soundtrack by virtue of becoming attached to something else, whether a media text or a personal recollection. When we hear certain songs and think, "I loved dancing to this song at the party," or "Here's that song from that movie," or "This song was the soundtrack to my summer," the implication is that pop songs are texts that are inherently layered with a montage of particular memories for which they serve as the soundtrack. A soundtrack is hence always linked to memory, with the concept of montage—essentially an aesthetic representation of the passing of time—serving, in its 1980s form, as a significant representational mode of that era that has resonated into the present.

The 1980s Pop Music Montage and Its Legacies

Pop music filmic montages of the 1980s constituted stand-alone music video clips embedded within larger films. Like any montage, they were used to denote the passing of time via edited footage of key events, but unlike montages of previous decades, 1980s film montages were frequently also used to evoke the emotional state of the characters as well as to evoke emotion in the viewer. Most memorable today are perhaps sports training montages (for example those in various iterations of the *Rocky* movies or in the film *Footloose*, in which the main character trains for a dance competition), and falling-in-love montages, often found in films aimed at and featuring teenage characters coming of age in some way.[1] Modern English's "I Melt with You," as used in a montage in Martha Coolidge's *Valley Girl* (1983), is an earlier example of a falling-in-love pop music montage that set the precedent for the use of similar montage sequences in subsequent teen films of the 1980s, such as the use of Howard Jones' "Like to Get to Know You Well" in 1985's *Better Off Dead*.[2]

The "I Melt with You" montage features scenes of the two main characters, Julie and Randy, as they go on various dates, fall in love, and make out among local points of interest in their respective and contrasting neighborhoods of "the Valley" and Hollywood. The montage doesn't just imply the passing of time, the strengthening of the characters' feelings for each other, and the merging of their suburban and urban backgrounds. Rather, it transforms the song "I Melt with You" into a soundtrack, the "theme" song for the film as well as for viewers for whom the song might later evoke nostalgia specifically because of its accompanying filmic montage. The song is perhaps nostalgic today for those who were teenage viewers of the film in the 1980s, and, in its coupling with the film's imagery, it already contained a built-in nostalgia in its present. As a soundtrack, its function was always to evoke nostalgia for the soon-to-be past in the present as well as in the future.

The very idea of montage—with its implication of time passing—is related to temporality more generally, and hence already associated with nostalgia. Christian Surh and Rane Willerslev write of the potentially radical disruptive possibilities of media montage that may occur when different elements are brought together, arguing that something "extra" is produced that stands as a disruption to the accepted order of things. Montage always evokes something invisible beyond its constituent sounds and images parts, raising issues related to representation and time. Film, they write, can evoke hidden dimensions of reality, with the coupling of recorded sounds and images as montage functioning as a technique to disrupt observational realism. Similarly, Bliss Cua Lim understands film as being able to depict the coexistence of other modes of being alongside and within the modern present, underscoring the variant temporalities that actually make up apparently homogenous time.

The pop song montages of 1980s teen films can be understood as a metaphor for the way in which many of us nostalgically incorporate the music of our past into our personal soundtracks as a way of making our memories into something "extra": palatable montages of a past that exists separately to our present and future, even as their function is to inform those times. A number of contemporary films and television shows have drawn upon the potency of 1980s pop music montages and the legacy of nostalgia they have fostered. Luca Guadagnino's 1980s-set *Call Me by Your Name* (2017) utilizes the Psychedelic Furs' "Love My Way" (1982) a number of times over the course of the film to soundtrack the two main characters, Ellio and Oliver, falling in love and to evoke an emotional response in its audience in the present. "Love My Way" serves as a harbinger of the inevitable nostalgia the men will feel about the song later in their lives; for the audience, for whom the song is already of a different time, the temporal effect is perhaps disorienting, evoking a new nostalgia for a temporality that exists, as Lim suggests, outside of homogenous time.

Todd Solondz's 1995 *Welcome to the Dollhouse* offers another example of drawing upon 1980s pop soundtracks to evoke nostalgia with a scene in which the film's nerdy main character, Dawn Weiner, has been coerced into meeting up with Brandon, a bully from her junior high school who keeps threatening to rape her. In the scene, Debbie Gibson's "Lost in Your Eyes" (1989) plays on in the background as the two awkwardly exchange a few words, and eventually kiss. For many viewers who were children or teens during the 1980s, early romantic fantasies may have been soundtracked by Debbie Gibson and Tiffany, but real life looked as awkward, if hopefully not as threatening, as Solondz (who is said to have been influenced by the disparity between media representations of the 1950s and his own childhood during that era) depicts it.

Other examples of the potency of 1980s film soundtracks include the 1980s-set 2001 cult film *Donnie Darko*, which, in addition to a storyline that calls existing modes of temporality into question, also features a number of 1980s song montages that seem to critically reflect upon aspects of coming-of-age during the Reagan era.[3] Contemporary filmic representations of the 1980s have not only evoked nostalgia for the era. Rather, they have literately and at times critically used nostalgia as a function of pop music soundtracks (especially as facilitated by montage), raising questions about the representational function of nostalgia more generally.

The Function of Nostalgia: Some Conclusions

Perhaps no contemporary depiction of the 1980s is as intentionally steeped in nostalgia as *Cobra Kai* (2018–2021), the action-drama television series based upon the 1980s *Karate Kid* movies, picking up the storyline of the main characters of Daniel and Johnny (teens in the original series, and now adults) in the present day. *Cobra Kai*'s adult characters constantly wax lyrical or angrily about their pasts, an obsessive focus that inevitably influences their teenager offspring and karate students in significant ways. No moment in the show is immune from 1980s nostalgia, which ranges from in-jokes about Minute Maid (an allusion to the product placement requirements of 1980s films) to sneaking into a Twisted Sister concert. Music plays an important role: Johnny has a sensual dream about his neighbor that is a re-imagined montage of the music video of Whitesnake's 1987 "Here I Go Again." Music from the band Chicago—whose "Glory of Love" was a key song on the soundtrack for *Karate Kid II*—seems to swell during Daniel's romantic moments with his wife. Daniel and Johnny both frequently find themselves overcome by musical nostalgia, for example, when turning on the car radio and catching a song from their 1980s pasts. Viewing *Cobra Kai* can give the impression that the decade of the 1980s was always already about nostalgia.

Indeed, the 1980s—the era when the pop music montage helped define the concept of the personal soundtrack and shaped how we perceive and temporally organize our pasts through music—seems to have spawned a particular aesthetic of nostalgia, one in which nostalgia for some past experience or memory is played out again and again. At the end of *Cobra Kai*'s second season, a new version of the 1984 Bananarama song that featured in the original film, "Cruel Summer," is heard, and a quick search of YouTube turns up countless music videos montages of this song coupled with various scenes from the television show. These fan-made videos are in the style of the 1980s music video film tie-ins discussed above, and many contemporary popular media texts—particularly those enjoyed by young adults—will have these peripheral fan-made music videos that seem designed to keep some essential nostalgic moment or theme of the original source's key songs and images alive via pop song montage.

The same was true following the release of *Call Me by Your Name*, with the original video for the Psychedelic Furs' "Love My Way" superseded by dozens of fan-made montages edited from footage from the film. Various 1980s songs from the 1980s-set television series *Stranger Things* have had the same treatment, including a DJ Yoda "mixtape" featuring songs from the series with sound clips of dialogue edited into the mix as a sort of audio-montage of the series. While media relating to the 1980s is certainly not the only media to receive this sort of treatment, it's notable that fan-made media nonetheless continue to follow the patterns and methods set out in the decade of the 1980s when pop music soundtracks and montages came to the fore.

More recently, following the storming of the U.S. Capitol in January 2021, Donald Trump supporters have left comments under the video of Mike + the Mechanics' song "Silent Running," mentioned above, suggesting the song as a "theme song for our times," presumably due to its lyrics about nationalism and taking up guns under a perceived threat; a link to a montage featuring the song accompanied by images of Trump and citizens rallying with weapons, including a white couple brandishing guns at a Black Lives Matter march, is more or less reminiscent of 1980s-style montages. While it functions as a type of nostalgia, its purpose is more on par with early Soviet montage, the goal being an emotional evocation through political symbolism to rally the masses. Our 1980s-dervied form of pop music montage may manifest in different ways, leaving the function of nostalgia up for debate.

Beyond the various music video montages created by political supporters or fans, other forms of engaging with nostalgia as it relates to 1980s pop music soundtracks and montage have emerged. In 2009, Oneohtrix Point Never (the electronic musician Daniel Lopatin) posted a clip to YouTube of an eerily slowed-down version of Chris de Burgh's "Lady in Red," called "Nobody Here." This was followed by a DVD-R album of similar re-imaginings of 1980s soundscapes and images, with others artists subsequently producing similar experiments using pop songs and other familiar sounds of the 1980s, re-mixed or "chopped and screwed" (heavily edited and slowed down) in order to (arguably) critique or celebrate 1980s nostalgia through re-imagined soundtracks of the era.[4] Such experiments, primarily posted as YouTube videos and sometimes accompanied by footage of empty shopping malls or other signifying 1980s imagery (known as "aesthetics"), would come to be classified as "vaporwave" and "mallsoft," and generated some debate about their function as a critique of 1980s capitalism or a celebration of it via nostalgic longing for more conservative aspects of the Reagan years.

For Robert Hewison, nostalgia shows the past to be something with which we no longer have to live, an "other" way of living for which we are not responsible and which has no bearing on the present except as a contrast. Hewison (47) writes that "through the filter of nostalgia we change the past, and through the conservative impulse we seek to change the present. The question then becomes what kind of past have we chosen to preserve and what does that say about our present?" Hewison was writing of heritage, but his sentiments could be a reflection on the way in which the nostalgia generated by 1980s media and the ongoing influence of its formats, fundamentally shaped the ways in which we come to understand soundtracks and their relation to nostalgia in our daily lives. But Hewison's comments also come to bear on the content of the representations of the 1980s that generate the nostalgia in question.[5]

Furthermore, what are the pitfalls of nostalgia as it relates to music in the present? The early 2000s saw a wave of music criticism, such as Simon Reynolds' concern with a "retromania" defined not only by vaporware and mallsoft, but also the swathes of new bands that all sounded just like Joy Division, along with the proliferation of box sets, collectors' items, and reunion tours in lieu of anything truly new. Similarly, the late Mark Fisher's frequent assertion that pop music no longer exists, and that everything is simply a remix of something else—borrowed, plundered, and never thrown away to make room for new music and experiences in the present time—raises a genuine concern about nostalgia for, and emanating from, representations relating to the 1980s from both the past and in the present.

An alternative way of thinking about the inevitability of nostalgia within media representations comes from Laura Mulvey, who has written about the ways in which new media technologies allow viewers to control both image and story, so that, for example, films meant to be seen collectively and followed in a linear fashion may be manipulated technologically, yielding unexpected and even unintended pleasures. Presumably, fan music video montages, as well as YouTube multimedia experiments, are capable of coupling nostalgia with media manipulation and potentially achieving Surh and Willerslev's previously discussed view of montage as "disruptive" in that juxtapositions of elements outside of homogenous time may stand as a form of social and cultural critique. Similarly for Giorgio Agamben, the moving images of cinema constitute modernity, but this movement has less to do with the images (or sounds) of cinema itself, and more to do with the critical act of editing: the process of juxtaposing media in ways that call into question notions of temporality and space and allow time not just to be suspended but to come into being as something altogether new that is able to stand as a critique.

Nostalgia has been crucial to our understanding of the soundtrack and the montage, media forms that came into their own in the 1980s and clearly continue to define the ways in which we interact with media representations in the present. As Frederic Jameson (82) has noted, "if nostalgia as a political motivation is most frequently associated with Fascism, there is no reason why a nostalgia conscious of itself, a lucid and remorseless dissatisfaction with the present on the grounds of some remembered plenitude, cannot furnish as adequate a revolutionary stimulus as any other." The aim of our engagements with nostalgia shouldn't be mourning some "lost future," but aiming towards a utopia in the present, or at least toward Mulvey's unintended pleasures of our media engagements. If we're going to look back, we may as well make something new and wonderful with what we dredge from the past in the process.

Notes

1. Coming-of-age pop song montages in 1980s films were not always about falling in love. In *Real Genius* (1985), The Cosmat Angels' "Falling" (1985) was used to soundtrack a montage of scenes of the main characters' experiencing the trials and wonders of college life as they try to build a laser for their professor in order to pass their class and graduate to adulthood.

2. The *Better Off Dead* soundtrack also features commissioned pop songs and an incidental score by the prolific musician and music producer Rupert Hine. Two of Hine's songs featuring him on vocals would accompany another falling-in-love sequence ("Arrested By You") and an epilogue sequence ("Starlight (With One Look)), while the film also includes a school dance scene featuring Elizabeth Daily, who had recently appeared in *Valley Girl*, performing the Hine-penned "Better Off Dead"; a ski training montage (set to Martin Ansell's Duran Duran soundalike, "Shine"), and even a Frankenstein-inspired claymation segment featuring hamburgers soundtracked by Van Halen's "Everybody Wants Some." The film is a notable example of how the lines between the compiled pop music soundtrack and the composed film score had become blurred by the1980s.

3. See for example the montage of the school's sexualized pre-teen dance club featuring Duran Duran's "Notorious," as well as the film's opening, featuring Tears for Fears' "Head Over Heels" and scenes of the local high school in all its cliquish glory.

4. See for example Hypersonic flash's "scared (Halloween vaporwave)," which includes a montage of 1980s Halloween cartoons and advertisements paired with the vaporwave artist Telan Devik's remix of Howard Jones' "Things Can Only Get Better."

5. For example, the settings and characters of the 1980s coming-of-age films on which so much of contemporary nostalgic culture in the present is based are overwhelmingly

white, and from relatively middle-class neighbourhoods. While class divides often fuelled romantic strife, there was no sense of the immense diversity of the U.S., let alone poverty. What does it mean to feel nostalgic for this era today?

Works Cited

Agamben, Giorgio. *Means without End: Notes on Politics*. University of Minnesota Press, 2000.

Fisher, Mark. *Ghosts of My Life: Writings on Depression, Hauntology, and Lost Futures*. Zero Books, 2014.

Hewison, Robert. *The Heritage Industry*. Methuen, 1987.

Jameson, Frederic. *Marxism and Form: Twentieth-century Dialectical Theories of Literature*. Princeton University Press, 1974.

Lim, Bliss Cua. *Translating Time: Cinema, the Fantastic and Cultural Critique*. Duke University Press, 2009.

Mulvey, Laura. *Death x 24x Second: Stillness and the Moving Image*. Reaktion Books, 2006.

Reynolds, Simon. *Retromania: Pop Culture's Addiction to Itself*. Faber & Faber, 2010.

Smith, Jeff. *The Sounds of Commerce: Marketing Popular Film Music*. Columbia University Press, 1998.

Surh, Christian, and Rane Willerslev. "Can Film Show the Invisible? The Work of Montage in Ethnographic Filmmaking." *Current Anthropology*, vol. 53, no. 3, June 2012, pp. 282–301.

Men Without Hats
and Material Girls

"Cobra Kai Never Dies"

Reframing Masculinities in The Karate Kid's
Nostalgic Transgenerational Reboot

Kristen Galvin

In 1984, *The Karate Kid* was Hollywood's sleeper hit of the year, cost-ing only $8 million to make and raking in $90 million at the box office. Despite its stiff summer competition from releases such as *Ghostbusters, Gremlins,* and prequels and sequels such as *Indiana Jones and the Tem-ple of Doom* and *Conan the Destroyer, The Karate Kid* went on to be the fifth highest grossing film of 1984. The film centers on the mentorship of "new kid in town" Daniel LaRusso (Ralph Macchio) by his apartment complex's maintenance man and martial arts expert, Mr. Miyagi (Nori-yuki "Pat" Morita). LaRusso learns karate to protect himself from his high school bully, Johnny Lawrence (William Zabka), ringleader of the Cobra Kai dojo, who also happens to be the ex-boyfriend of LaRusso's new love interest. At the film's climax, the two rivals square off at the All-Valley Under-18 Karate Tournament Championship. After a (questionably legal) "crane kick" to the head, the unlikely hero defeats his high school tor-mentor in a moment of pure 1980s screen magic that would, in turn, send kids from all over the United States to enroll in karate classes at their local dojos.

Yet, when considering other film trends that were emerging during the decade, *The Karate Kid*'s success story becomes much less surpris-ing. The summer of 1984 also offered John Hughes' directorial debut, *Six-teen Candles,* which launched the teen film auteur's career alongside a new genre that blended romance and comedy in its depictions of Amer-ican suburban teen life. This golden era of the teen film spawned a pub-lic fascination with the Generation X cohort of the "Hollywood Brat Pack" (e.g., Molly Ringwald, Judd Nelson), who would define "cool" in the 1980s, onscreen and off, across music, fashion, and nightlife. Sports films were also on the rise in the 1980s: it was the decade of the *Rocky* franchise, which produced four sequels between 1979 and 1990. Aside from sharing *Rocky's* status as an American classic sports film, *The Karate Kid* was also directed by John G. Avildsen, the Academy Award-winning director of *Rocky* (1976), also known as "King of the Underdogs."[1] When we do our 1980s math here, *The Karate Kid,* which generated two sequels of its own in 1986 and 1989, tapped into a 1980s zeitgeist as a quintessential film because it so skillfully synthesized and forecasted the decade's entertainment and cultural trends as a hybrid generic film.

Representative of teen films of the 1980s, *The Karate Kid* presents alternative and offbeat heroes, and moreover, onscreen masculinities that stand in stark contrast to the normative hypermasculine characters and bodies of the decade's sports, action, science fiction, and fantasy films. Hypermasculinity of the 1980s is epitomized by Sylvester Stallone in the *Rocky* and *Rambo* franchises (1979, 1982, 1985, 1988, 1990), and Arnold Schwarzenegger in the *Conan* films (1982, 1984), followed by his onslaught of action movies including *The Terminator* (1984) *Commando* (1985) and *Predator* (1987). Jumping ahead a couple of decades, this essay examines how the popular streaming television series, *Cobra Kai,* remediates the original *Karate Kid* franchise in its (re)performances of onscreen masculinities that center upon an epic pop cultural male (sports) rivalry.[2] With the 1980s film franchise serving as canon, and *Cobra Kai's* bittersweet celluloid memory bank, the digital update is a lovingly crafted and cleverly detailed nostalgic program that flashes-forward as a sequel television series and continuity reboot. The "new" action dramedy resurrects pop-cultural fossils of the 1980s—along with the decade's hypermasculine ideals—to reframe gendered tropes in the present through a radical expansion of *The Karate Kid's* story universe for transgenerational appeal.

With its very own "underdog" media success story, *Cobra Kai's* first two seasons debuted on YouTube Red beginning in 2018. Due to a change in YouTube's original programming strategy, the show was dropped only to be acquired in 2020 by Netflix. Purchasing the rights to the entire series, it swiftly rebranded *Cobra Kai* as a "Netflix Original," streaming the first two seasons and hyping the third's release on New Year's Day 2021. The power of the "Netflix Effect" skyrocketed the popularity of the show and its regular cast, with the show renewed for two more seasons (a fifth is on its way). Season four's release week in January of 2022 topped Netflix's global rankings for television, with an impressive 120 million hours viewed in just three days (Maas). Moreover, the series is a true work of fan fiction by self-proclaimed *Karate Kid* fanboys, co-creators Josh Heald, Jon Hurwitz, and Hayden Schlossberg. Together, they are collectively responsible for the oddball buddy and/or nostalgic comedy franchises of *Harold and Kumar* (2004, 2008, 2011) and *Hot Tub Time Machine*. As we move through *Cobra Kai's* four seasons, each judiciously revives "legacy" characters from the original franchise to expand its story universe. The series constantly draws upon the canonic past to develop plot twists and existing character arcs, while also adding totally new ones. Furthermore, the increased duration of screen time of a television serial allows the creators to deeply dive into the past to inventively develop the backstories of main characters across generations.

Inverting the franchise's repeated concentration on the long-shot heroics of LaRusso, the series shifts perspective to the "anti-hero" and the once-antagonistic bully, Lawrence, who is currently getting his own ass kicked by life. Lawrence, the embodiment of 1980s winning (country-club rich, white, heterosexual, athletic, classically handsome, popular, aggressive, abusive), has been on a 34-year losing streak since failing to defend his championship title against his archnemesis. In a flip of class and entitlement, Lawrence now struggles to maintain odd-jobs employment, sobriety, and any kind of relationship as a divorcee and deadbeat dad, while LaRusso is happily married with kids and owns a successful car dealership. This is plainly communicated in the first minutes of the series' pilot episode, which recuts the original film footage of Lawrence's stunning loss and inserts a new shot of him face down on the mat while the camera circles in to emphasize his "agony of defeat." After a title card indicating a time lapse and a drastic tonal shift to a somber musical soundtrack, Lawrence is found face down on his bed surrounded by chips, warm beer, and take-out sauce packets. This is the first glimpse of Lawrence in his down-and-out eternal bachelor state, which sets the tone for his future anti-hero redemption. Importantly, in the pilot episode, the viewer is introduced to LaRusso through Lawrence's eyeroll, when he sees yet another cheesy billboard for LaRusso's car dealership looming above him—with his image "kicking the competition."

While the first two *Karate Kid* films do depict a few sympathetic moments for Lawrence in relation to his domineering sensei John Kreese (Martin Kove), for the most part, his character is uncomplex with the lines between winner/loser and good/bad very clear-cut. In the series, however, Lawrence transforms into a highly sympathetic, flawed yet likeable, multi-dimensional character. The series does not merely depict a wish-fulfillment fantasy of a bully's rightful demise, but instead, enacts a Dickensian play with redemption and temporality, albeit with very different types of "hauntings." What opportunities do such role-reversals and reimaginings open in *Cobra Kai's* constant "redoings" and "undoings"? How does the text walk a fine line between revalorizing and/or criticizing dominant American white patriarchal ideologies that the original film initially challenged? This essay parses the ideological continuities and ruptures of the series, assessing the ways in which it pokes fun at, reaffirms, and challenges gender norms originating from a paradigm of 1980s Hollywood hypermasculinity.

Cobra Kai's *Deployment of Nostalgia*

Cobra Kai mobilizes various types of nostalgias to resituate onscreen masculinities of the 1980s in the present to demonstrate how media nostalgias can be nuanced and complex, and at once progressive and regressive. The series probes a collective indulgence in both the failures and guilty pleasures of 1980s pop cultural masculinities, as well as its culture of "awesome" signifiers, which are most visibly concentrated in Lawrence's personal tastes (e.g., his love of hair metal, muscle cars, karate, *Iron Eagle* [1986], beer, hot bikini babes, kicking ass). The centralization of the character of Lawrence also comes with an escalation of narrative attention to the hypermasculine antics and military backstory of his old sensei, Kreese, and his war buddy Terry Silver (Thomas Ian Griffith). Such tactics reveal the problems and pleasures of "nostalgizing" hypermasculinity in popular culture. The show astutely points to how such representations still remain pertinent and resonant in the divisive present time of culture wars in the United States, outlined by buzzwords such as toxic masculinity, popular feminism, cancel culture, and generation wars.

Cobra Kai also lies within two larger trends of the "nostalgia industry." The first is the authentic reprisal of the roles and arcs of lead and supporting characters in the continuity reboot, which must be played by the original cast members. This consistency conveys the bona fide flash-forward as a continuous sequel, while simultaneously offering a spin-off that aims for transgenerational appeal, often by introducing a younger and more diverse generation of "parallel" main characters (e.g., *Creed, Bill & Ted Face the Music* [2020], *Coming 2 America* [2021], *Saved by the Bell* [2020–present]). The second is Netflix's own success story in relation to "original" nostalgia programming, or its algorithmic reliance upon and thereby perpetuation of 1980s media nostalgias (e.g., *Stranger Things, GLOW, The Dirt* [2019], *Black Mirror: Bandersnatch* [2018]). In general, nostalgia programming also extends to the recent entry of media giants into the streaming game (e.g., *The Mandalorian, WandaVision* [2021] on Disney+; *Saved by the Bell, Punky Brewster* [2021] and *Bel-Air* [2022] on NBCUniversal's Peacock). The "streaming wars" may as well be redubbed "the nostalgia wars," or, the battle for eyeballs that depends upon which media conglomerate can leverage nostalgia most effectively for transgenerational appeal.

Like a critical Swiss Army Knife, the series does different kinds of "nostalgia work" to articulate the complexities and subtleties of what media nostalgias can do when viewers constantly "nostalgize" along with the characters and cultures represented onscreen. Described most prominently by Svetlana Boym, nostalgia can be *restorative* and *reflective*, and the two frameworks are not necessarily distinct. While *restorative nostalgia* aims to rebuild the lost home to recreate a more desirable past, *reflective nostalgia* is a longing via personal or popular memory for other places and times and can be a space for irony and critique (Boym 41, 49–50). Such nostalgias are peppered throughout *Cobra Kai* in relation to masculinity, from Lawrence and LaRusso rebuilding their respective surrogate fathers/senseis' dojos, to the constant recycling of film footage as "memories" for them to reflect upon—both romantic and traumatic—to cope with the present. However, while individual textual triggers of nostalgia abound for both characters and audience members, whether "personal" (experienced firsthand) or "historical" (experienced imaginatively) (Stern 14), the nostalgia programming of *Cobra Kai* has an overarching strategy of transgenerational appeal. Economically beneficial, the successful blending of the parent—child demographic has been examined as a powerful nostalgia marketing tool (Lizardi 2–3). However, in the case of *Cobra Kai*, understandings of transgenerational "co-viewership" is extended from "children's" to specifically "teen" programming, as it targets Gen Z and the parent generation of Gen X (Johnson 7).

Michael Pickering and Emily Keightley's description of nostalgia's potentialities also illuminate *Cobra Kai's* particular brand of transgenerational nostalgia:

> we should perhaps reconfigure it [nostalgia] in terms of a distinction between the desire to return to an earlier state or idealized past, and the desire not to return but to recognize aspects of the past as the basis for renewal and satisfaction in the future. Nostalgia can then be seen as not only a search for ontological security in the past, but also as a means of taking one's bearings for the road ahead in the uncertainties of the present. This opens up a positive dimension in nostalgia, one associated with a desire for engagement with difference, with aspiration and critique, and with the identification of ways of living lacking in modernity. Nostalgia can be both melancholic and utopian [921].

This is of course, highly subjective in *Cobra Kai*, where one man's heavenly home of a dojo is another one's hell. The pliability in the meanings and effects of nostalgia also resides in *Cobra Kai's* hybrid generic format, which extends to teen dramedy. This allows for different onscreen articulations of masculinities at different life phases marked by crisis: adolescence (Gen Z) and mid-life (Gen X). Similar to the creators' descriptions of the show's investigation of the "gray" areas, or binary categorical differences between good/bad, defense/offense, masculine/feminine, Miyagi-Do/ Cobra Kai, young/old, which are cheekily played with, so too are nostalgia's polarizations explored across lines of personal/historical, authentic/ fantastic, melancholic/utopic, restorative/reflective, conservative/progressive, romantic/traumatic, and therapeutic/harmful.

"Waxing" and "Sweeping" Nostalgic in the Time of Gen Z

To understand the critiques and ripple effects of the intersections of media nostalgias and masculinities in *Cobra Kai*, hypermasculinity in 1980s Hollywood blockbusters must be quickly addressed first.[3] According to Susan Jeffords, the "hard body" hypermasculine films and franchises (e.g., *Rambo, Indiana Jones* [1981, 1984, 1989], *RoboCop* [1987], *The Terminator*) directly reflect the decade's national identity, values, and politics as determined by the larger ideological recuperation of masculinity by America's favorite cowboy-president, Ronald Reagan (13–15). She argues that Reagan's New Right political agenda to control sick and unwanted bodies (e.g., patients suffering from AIDS, drug addicts, women seeking abortions), etched a divide between the undesirable weak and desirable strong American (white, male, heterosexual) body that dominated the silver screen. This is achieved not only through the spectacle of muscular physique and skill, but by the wielding of violent force to dominate and or/conquer an enemy. Jeffords also laid the groundwork for hypermasculinity as distinctly tied to "father-son" issues and the importance of a father figure to constructions of masculinity (67). However, aside from the pumped-up bodies of Stallone and Schwarzenegger, such "hard bodies" were also featured in American martial arts film of the 1980s starring iconic tough-guys such as Chuck Norris, Steven Seagal, and Jean-Claude Van Damme. Whether a black-belted special ops war hero or cyborg with bulging pecs, the hypermasculine Hollywood representation is excessive to the point of camp, with each heroic caricature only further exaggerated by his crowd-pleasing one-liners.

From the very beginning, the first *Karate Kid* distinctly plays with depictions of 1980s hypermasculinity as tied to race, muscular physique, and the American obsession over winners versus losers. Against the grain of Hollywood hypermasculinity, the "heroes" are LaRusso and Mr. Miyagi. While embodied by the franchise's younger bully characters such as Lawrence, hypermasculinity is at its most robust in the authoritarian

Kreese, the head of Cobra Kai's hypermasculine hydra. This performance is later amplified by Silver, Cobra Kai's maniacally corrupt corporate owner in *The Karate Kid Part III*. The original franchise establishes a firm polarization of masculinities between the two karate schools, and *Cobra Kai* plays with this binary formula. Codified as "good," the traditional Okinawan karate of Miyagi-Do is aligned with morality, balance, focus, (self-) defense, and individualized training, and it is symbolized by the Bonsai tree and white uniform. On the other hand, the "bad boys" of Cobra Kai practice an Americanized brand of karate, symbolized by the striking cobra and black uniform. It is the hypermasculine karate style of the films' villains (Lawrence, Kreese, and Silver), which translates to contemporary popular conceptions of toxic masculinity, predatory capitalism, as well as fascism (Ku and Wu). First under the tutelage of "Sensei Kreese," the militarized pack mentality of Cobra Kai encourages excessive aggression, violence, winning at all costs, and a motto of "Strike first. Strike hard. No mercy," whether on the mat or off. Through Silver, who made his fortune illegally dumping toxic waste, the hypermasculinity of Cobra Kai pairs with corporate greed and unethical business practices. Season five reprised the role of Mike Barnes (Sean Kanan), a karate champion that Silver hires to aid in franchising Cobra Kai and terrorizing LaRusso in the third film. As season four ended with yet another return of Chozen Toguchi (Yuji Don Okumoto), no longer an enemy of LaRusso but an ally in preserving Miyagi-Do karate, the themes of an authentic and righteous karate versus a malicious Americanized and hypermasculinized version will continue through its male legacy characters.

While hypermasculinity is seductive, *The Karate Kid* canon clearly denounces it as a sure pathway to "losing." The jock archetype is one of the most prominent staples of the 1980s teen film, which typically demonizes the recurrent figure of the generically handsome, popular, wealthy, often fair-haired and always well-coiffed bully (e.g., *Pretty in Pink*, *Revenge of the Nerds* [1984], *Better Off Dead*, *Some Kind of Wonderful*), with William Zabka typecast as this figure (*Just One of the Guys* [1985], *Back to School* [1986]). The character of LaRusso is also generically conventional as the wimpy slacker/nerd/outsider and the lovable, lower-class, less attractive (but not unattractive), non-blonde loser who ends up being the *real* hero. Kreese, a "hard body" military caricature in the realm of PG-rated films, is the physical and emotional opposite of Mr. Miyagi, who is older, shorter, less brawny, and Japanese. Importantly, Mr. Miyagi easily defeats Kreese and any of his followers on multiple occasions with pure skill. *Cobra Kai* executive producer Hayden Schlossberg remarks on a generational transference of hypermasculinity, "We liked the idea that there is something in these lessons he [Lawrence] learned in the '80s—the G.I. Joe, Rambo, Arnold Schwarzenegger lessons—that could maybe help some of these Gen-Z kids" (Jurgensen). This dualism of masculinities by dojo provides the narrative backbone for *Cobra Kai*, as well as a path for weaving its creative reversals and reinventions, which includes empowering mercilessly bullied Gen Z-ers through Cobra Kai training.

While *Cobra Kai* is not a perfect ideological reflection of the 1980s, nor set in the 1980s, the central conflict of the series is that Lawrence and LaRusso cannot "get over" their 1984 high school drama. An extension of hypermasculine values, these characters (and others) constantly live in the shadow of their senseis as surrogate fathers, while longing for their own lost fathers and/or sons, often at one point supported by a single mother. Lawrence and LaRusso's rivalry is entrenched in their divergent mentors and schools of karate, which is only complicated by Mr. Miyagi's adage that there is "no such thing as bad student, only bad teacher" (*The Karate Kid*). This paints Lawrence's character as potentially redeemable from the start. In this case, nostalgia is not a return to a golden age or simpler time of hypermasculinity, nor a linear narrative. Instead, nostalgias continuously multiply in *Cobra Kai*. Dovetailing with the "narrative complexity" of quality television (Mittell 4), nostalgia is a method for interweaving and entangling the adolescent perspectives and storylines of Gen Z karate kids.

The struggles surrounding coming of age, growing up, growing out of, and moving beyond are thematic linchpins of *Cobra Kai*. Often, the show constitutes a gendered reperformance of pop masculinities in some state of (suspended) adolescence. Lawrence is, of course, more emblematic of this temporal drag as he still exudes the symbols of his 1980s teendom: car (red Pontiac Firebird), offensive language (e.g., *pussy, pansy*, and *nerd*), gendered stereotypes, popular music taste (Guns N' Roses, Ratt, Poison, Dee Snider), and fashion (red "Cobra Kai" jacket with zippers and logo, black headband, rock t-shirts). It is Lawrence's out-of-time-ness and political incorrectness that make him likeable and/or sympathetic, and the continuous butt for social, generational, Internet, and computer technology jokes. Through comedy, space is opened for the audience to reflect upon questions concerning the pros and cons of such technological advances, as well as gender norms and ideals across generations.

Much of the show's humor hinges on oppositional stereotypes and clashing identity politics, pitting the past against the present according to generational identification. Lawrence's macho dismissal of the younger "pussy generation," whom he tells to "leave your asthma and your peanut allergies and all that other made-up bullshit outside," aligns with Kreese's Boomer desire to "melt this whole snowflake generation" (*Cobra Kai*). These "old" prejudices are clearly vilified as sentiments of the show's "bad guy" Kreese, or comically dismissed in their exaggerations and outdatedness by Lawrence, in his attempts to reform and do good. This extends to Lawrence's comical performance of "wokeness" in order to recruit female athletes to Eagle Fang, his hilariously titled spin-off dojo, after the All Valley Committee creates a "separate girls' division" for the Tournament. In episode six of season four, humorously yet problematically titled, "Kicks Get Chicks," Lawrence demonstrates his self-proclaimed "awakeness" with the following pitch to Piper (Selah Austria), a lesbian female athlete:

> Let me tell you why my dojo is perfect for a modern young woman like yourself. We live in a world where you gotta be an alpha to survive. You're either a killer or you're dead meat. You gotta be a man. At Eagle Fang, we confront that phrase and we make it empowering for all. We teach anyone who identifies as female to embrace their queenly strength and tear down the neo-masculine hierarchy to confront internalized sexism [*Cobra Kai*].

When Piper inquires if this includes "non-binary" and "gender fluid" students, Lawrence responds: "Yes, fluids are crucial, if you don't hydrate, it affects performance." Lawrence's conduct amuses his young protégé Miguel Diaz (Xolo Maridueña) and the audience is encouraged, likewise, to laugh right along with him. Diaz, amazed that the young woman agreed to join Eagle Fang, asks his sensei if he fully understood the meanings of the terms used, to which Lawrence retorts, "Do I look like I pee sitting down?" Despite a rally to "tear down the neo-masculine hierarchy and to confront internalized sexism" the scene and snippet of dialogue is filled with sexism and ideologies of hegemonic masculinity, even if presented as ridiculous and out of touch. Through such comedic maneuvers, the show slyly straddles political lines, and is at once offensive and progressive, and remains politically non-committal or "fluid" for the purpose of a good laugh. Furthermore, as proved by numerous YouTube video compilations, Lawrence also clearly holds the record for most memorable and quotable one-liners in the show, a tried-and-true tactic of 1980s hypermasculinity.

While comic, this attitude and language is also learned and adopted by their students in ways that clearly have a negative impact. This influence manifests in the dramatic transformation of Eli "Hawk" Moskowitz (Jacob Bertrand) from a shy nerd who is pushed around because of his cleft lip scar to a dangerous bully after being indoctrinated into Cobra Kai. Aside from utilizing sexist language to intentionally insult people, calling boys "girls," and girls "princesses," and even calling Lawrence "soft," Hawk shows a great awareness of generational stereotypes and expectations. When pushed by Samantha LaRusso (Mary Mouser) in the school cafeteria after destroying his ex-best friend's Lego science project, a teacher asks him, "Did she enter your personal bubble without your consent?" To get Samantha LaRusso in trouble Hawk sheepishly feigns a stereotypical response, "Yes, she definitely triggered me in my safe space," only to turn around moments later to snicker with his guy pals. While the show does not entirely let such behavior off the hook, as Hawk is eventually punished and humiliated by his Cobra Kai classmates in season four, it remains open to forgiveness and change as Hawk later joins Miyagi-Do and reunites with his best friend, Demetri Alexopoulos (Gianni DeCenzo). However, the show never forgoes comedic opportunities to capitalize on a good joke, pitting the culturally sensitive against the insensitive, at the expense of Gen X or Gen Z.

Lawrence's vindication as *Cobra Kai's* "comeback kid" is embedded in his relationship to two teenage "sons" who develop their own dangerous rivalry. His star student/surrogate son Diaz, first affiliated with Cobra Kai and then Lawrence's spin-off dojo Eagle Fang, is at odds with Lawrence's estranged birth son Robby Keene (Tanner Buchanan). Keene is initially mentored in Miyagi-Do as a student/surrogate son by LaRusso for the first two seasons, only to switch sides to Cobra Kai and the "grandfather" figure of Kreese. Replicating the past, this karate kid rivalry 2.0 between Keene and Diaz also revolves around a love triangle with LaRusso's daughter, Samantha. *Cobra Kai* deftly revives *The Karate Kid's* love triangle formula and uses nostalgia for heightened teen melodramatic ends. It both plays and indulgently preys upon histories and role reversals to reboot them for Gen Z, who, under Lawrence's wing, also go on dates at Golf N' Stuff to a soundtrack of "Young Hearts" by Commuter, just like the teens in *The Karate Kid* film. Via the vehicle of Diaz versus Keene, the opposing dojos initially divide the bullied in high school (e.g., Diaz, Hawk), from the juvenile delinquent "bad boy" of Keene. Classically handsome, white, and "hard bodied" (like his father), Keene first works at LaRussso Auto Group in season one only to "piss off" his dad. Yet, Keene's change of heart and character transformation only revert again, as he joins Cobra Kai at the end of season three and then existentially questions that path at the end of season four. These ceaseless reversals and switches of roles, sides, loves, allegiances, and alliances remind viewers that the only constant is change; all the while history goes on repeating itself, whether to positive or negative ends—and what could be more high school or adolescent than that: the stability of instability?

As a thematic through-line, all characters, regardless of age, have difficulty "adulting." For LaRusso and Lawrence, this translates not only to their inability to let go of the past, but to their own accountability for failures in parenting and mentoring. At the end of the second season, their "toxic nostalgia" transfers into teenage performances of "toxic masculinity" (whether the characters are male or female identified) and culminates in a school-wide karate riot. While narratively centered on two heterosexual teenage love triangles, with Samantha taking part in both configurations, the eruption of high school chaos and violence echoes the all too real tragic history of high school shootings in the United States. Even though the scene is gun-free and non-graphic in nature, it demonstrates untapped teenage rage, unleashed by the return of repressed 1980s hypermasculinity. There are multiple pairings of male once-best-friends now mortal enemies fighting to join in a battle royal of rivals. This also provides comedic relief in the form of the youngest and most diminutive male rivalry of the minor characters, Bert (Owen Morgan) and Nathaniel (Nathaniel Oh). While Diaz's critical injury at the hands of Keene is a cliff hanger for an anticipated entry into the third season, the sequence also reveals the adoption of hypermasculinity by Tory Nichols (Peyton List), the female rival to Samantha over the attention of Diaz. Not only does Nichols incite the riot, but, in a true tribute to the 1980s, she commandeers the intercom system to begin her quest for revenge by delivering one of the show's most memorable yet misogynistic "hard body" one-liners: "I'm coming for you, bitch." In classic *Cobra Kai* reversal, Samantha utters the very same threat to Nichols when she is finally pardoned and allowed to return to school in season four. As young women can now participate in the once exclusively male space of the dojo, they too can reperform 1980s hypermasculinity.

Cobra Kai: *Pop Cultural Comfort Food for the Wounded American Soul?*

Cobra Kai's critical uses of nostalgia, which are deeply tied to a constant rehashing of *Karate Kid's* 1980s hegemonic masculine values and stereotypes, pit "original" versus "next-gen" representations against one another to depict the crisis of American masculinity in a post-#MeToo and post PC-backlash digital era. However, such narrative, technological, and temporal moves ultimately expand *The Karate Kid's* story universe to seal the deal on the text's transgenerational and thereby popular appeal. From a 2021 Emmy nomination for Outstanding Comedy Series to William Zabka's "Greatest of All Time (GOAT): Zero to Hero" 2020 MTV Movie & TV Award (received immediately after a special performance of *The Karate Kid's* soundtrack's power ballad, "You're the Best Around," by Joe Esposito), *Cobra Kai* has been thoroughly embraced and celebrated. While there are both pleasures and dangers to being "stuck on" or "stuck in" the hypermasculine popular cultures of the 1980s, *Cobra Kai's* spectrum of representations also corresponds to the divisiveness of American life, culture, and politics moving further into the twenty-first century.

While this essay examines *Cobra Kai's* nuanced "nostalgizing," humanizing, and recentering of 1980s hypermasculinity, the show has also been interpreted as an allegorical solution to the searing hyperconflict of political partisanship in the United States. In 2018, The *International Business Times* (UK) ran an essay with its title and tag line summing up its main argument: "Donald Trump Meets the Karate Kid: A Social Parable for Our Times; Thirty Years after the Original Karate Kid, Cobra Kai Tells the Story of an America Doing Battle with Itself" (Owen et al.). Pushing the idea further, Gustavo Arellano of *The Los Angeles Times* claims that a national binge-watch of *Cobra Kai* may ameliorate the dangerous rift caused by Donald Trump's presidency in the wake of the storming of the United States Capitol on January 6, 2021. Arellano equates the destructiveness of Kreese with Trump (understood as a translation of hypermasculinity into toxic masculinity, which extends to season four's predatory capitalist, Silver); Lawrence with a Republican Party that is unable to adapt; and LaRusso with Democrats, who are too concerned with punishing their old GOP bully than with effecting real change (Arellano). He suggests that only with balance, conversation, and understanding can we rescue American democracy and facilitate collective change for the public good (cue Mr. Miyagi's final "look of approval" shot in *The Karate Kid*). At the end of season three, this hope is reflected by LaRusso of Miyagi-Do and Lawrence of Eagle Fang combining their dojos in an alliance against Kreese's Cobra Kai. While their partnership is tested and short-lived in season four, it is only through the combination of styles, comically alluded to as "Miyagi-Fang or whatever," that their students can beat Cobra Kai at the All-Valley winner-take-all-dojos tournament. To this end, the karate kids of Gen Z must be fluent across styles (and by extension political agendas), to see which move lands and not, so that they (democracy) can survive each round and ultimately win the tournament.

Cobra Kai has certainly struck hard, and it has struck a timely chord. The series creates a flexible nostalgic lens to constantly reframe the reperformances and reconstitutions of hypermasculinity. Through its "updated" depictions of winners/losers, father figures, and phases of age, it has found broader resonance beyond just romanticizing the "awesomeness" of the 1980s. By reactivating the past, the text does not just speak to a regressive, conservative, or indulgent longing for the cultures of the "Big '80s," but proposes a way through the "new" American culture wars, via an All-Valley Karate Tournament to "get along" and "get through" the mounting difficulties of the 2020s.

NOTES

1. This quote references the title of a recent documentary film on Avildsen's film career. See Wayne, Johnson D. *John G. Avildsen: The King of the Underdogs*, Kanopy Streaming, Cahssy Media, 2018.

2. Technically, *The Karate Kid* franchise consists of four films and the 2010 remake starring Jackie Chan and Jaden Smith. What is called the "original franchise" and "canon" (created thus far by *Cobra Kai*) are the 1980s films by Avildsen that star both Macchio and Morita in their leading roles: *The Karate Kid* (1984); *The Karate Kid Part II* (1986); and *The Karate Kid Part III* (1989).

3. While hypermasculine representations certainly extend to popular 1980s televisual texts (e.g. *Miami Vice, Magnum P.I., A-Team*), for purposes of this essay and contextualization of the urtext of *The Karate Kid*, film is only referenced here.

WORKS CITED

Allmark, Panizza, "Cobra Kai, Bill & Ted: Comebacks Redefine Middle-Aged Masculinity, but Where Are the Women?" *The Conversation*, 13 October 2020.

Arellano, Gustavo. "What Netflix's 'Cobra Kai' teaches us about how to deal with Trump," *Los Angeles Times*, 18 January 2021.

Boym, Svetlana. *The Future of Nostalgia*. Basic Books, 2001.

De Dauw, Esther, and Daniel James Connell. *Toxic Masculinity: Mapping the Monstrous in Our Heroes*. University Press of Mississippi, 2020.

Jeffords, Susan. *Hard Bodies: Masculinity in the Reagan Era*. Rutgers University Press, 1994.

Johnson, Derek. *Transgenerational Media Industries. Adults, Children, and the Reproduction of Culture*. The University of Michigan Press, 2020.

Jurgensen, John, "How Netflix's 'Cobra Kai' Turned an 'Artifact of the '80s' Into a Star," The Wall Street Journal, 6 January 2021.

Kibby, Marjorie D. "Nostalgia for The Masculine: Onward to the Past in the Sports Films of the Eighties." *Revue Canadienne D'Études Cinématographiques / Canadian Journal of Film Studies*, vol. 7, no. 1, 1998, pp. 16–28.

Ku, Michelle, and Albert Wu. "Cobra Kai, the Twilight of American Empire, and the Allure of Paramilitary Violence," *Los Angeles Review of Books*, 8 June, 2021.

Lizardi, Ryan. *Nostalgic Generations and Media: Perception of Time and Available Meaning*. Lexington Books, 2017.

Maas, Jennifer. "Netflix Top 10: 'Cobra Kai' Season 4 Takes Lead After Just Three Days of Viewing," *Variety*, 4 January 2022.

Mittell, Jason. *Complex TV: The Poetics of Contemporary Television Storytelling*. NYU Press, 2015

Owen, Craig, Alex Channon, and George Jennings. "Donald Trump Meets the Karate Kid: A Social Parable for Our Times; Thirty Years after the Original Karate Kid, Cobra Kai Tells the Story of an America Doing Battle with Itself." *International Business Times: United Kingdom Edition (UK)*, 7 Sept. 2018.

Pallister, Kathryn. *Netflix Nostalgia: Streaming the Past on Demand*. Lexington Books, 2019.

Pickering, Michael, and Emily Keightley. "The Modalities of Nostalgia." *Current Sociology*, vol. 54, no. 6, Nov. 2006, pp. 919–941.

Stern, Barbara B. "Historical and Personal Nostalgia in Advertising Text: The Fin De Siècle Effect." *Journal of Advertising*, vol. 21, no. 4, 1992, pp. 11–22.

Tragic Masculinities
and Craig Mazin's *Chernobyl*

JOHN QUINN

Craig Mazin's 2019 television miniseries *Chernobyl* portrays masculinist culture as a critical source of the tragic incompetence that led to the nuclear catastrophe at the Vladimir Ilyich Lenin Nuclear Plant in 1986. This melancholic depiction of "toxic masculinity" in the 1980s Soviet Union functions as a nexus between the contemporary "crisis" of masculine representation in Western popular culture (see Kimmel; Robinson; Savran) and the hypermasculine valorizations of individualism, liberty and the male body as articulated by the popular film and television of the Reagan decade (see Marlin; Jeffords; Jordan). At the core of this interchange lies a renegotiation of the actuality of hegemonic masculinity in the 1980s. The narrative aesthetics of *Chernobyl* disrupt Reaganite depictions of how the dominant position of men is negotiated, legitimized, and reinforced.

In *Chernobyl*, the performance of masculine hierarchical power relations reveals a social organization that perpetrates failure, where capable but subordinated identities are unable to "break through" and effect change in the face of crisis. This dynamic constitutes a stark contrast to the popular narratives of the Reagan decade in which hyper-capable individuals disrupt ineffective hierarchical power relations to resolve crises in a celebration of hypermasculine triumph. It is to this intersection of failure, triumph, and hegemonic masculinity that this essay first turns its attention. By contrasting *Chernobyl* with action television series of the 1980s, such as *The A-Team* (1983–1987), *Knight Rider* (1982–1986), and *MacGyver* (1985–1992), Mazin's revisiting of the Reagan decade can be situated as a purposeful and pragmatic recodification of the past that demonstrates the representational flux between how the 1980s articulated themselves and how they are now rearticulated for a contemporary audience.

It is notable, however, that, in *Chernobyl*, this contemporary rearticulation is specifically located away from the West and is directly connected to the defunct social and political apparatus of the Soviet Union. Consequently, the second focus of this essay conducts an exploration of how this distance enables an antithetical relationship with other televisual returns to the 1980s. In this context, the tragic nexus of masculine incompetence of *Chernobyl* is positioned as a cautionary nostalgia, or nostalgia in the reflective mode, where the past is used not as simple retrogression, but as a lens through which to examine the present (see Boym; Bevan; Loveday). Conversely, in other 1980s themed television series, such as *The Goldbergs* and *Young Sheldon* (2017–present), representations of the Reagan decade are associated with nostalgia in the restorative mode, where idealized monuments to the past are (re)constructed to commoditize feelings of temporal dislocation in the viewer via the restoration of the familiar (see Boym; Davis; May). As such, the role of Mazin's *Chernobyl* in the recent wave of popular television explorations of the people, politics, power-structures, and pretentions of the 1980s is one of disruption. *Chernobyl* contributes a stark dose of realism to the rich seam of horror texts exploiting the latent unease derived from revisiting the cultural situations of the Reagan decade (e.g., *Stranger Things, It: Chapter One, American Horror Story 1984* [2019]). Moreover, *Chernobyl* resists the frivolous in its return to the 1980s, providing a cautionary counterpoint to the imagined past as a site of comfort.

Failure, Triumph, and Hegemonic Masculinity

In a striking foreshadow of the human tragedy to follow, Mazin's *Chernobyl* opens with the suicide of its "hero" Valery Legasov (Jared Harris), the first deputy director of the Kurchatov Institute of Atomic Energy and chief of the Soviet commission investigating the Chernobyl disaster. From the outset, Legasov's suicide frames *Chernobyl* as a narrative exploration of the inability of the individual to effect change. The viewer is invited to join Legasov as he struggles to mitigate the consequences of the disaster, not as a celebration of his success in the face of extreme adversity, but as an examination of why his contributions to the averting of a nuclear holocaust have resulted in his suicide.

Legasov's journey in *Chernobyl* functions, therefore, as a jarring counter-narrative to the triumphalist exploits of the television heroes of the Reagan decade. Iconic figures of the 1980s, such as the titular Mac (Richard Dean Anderson) of *MacGyver* or Michael (David Hasselhoff) of *Knight Rider*, represent prominent examples of heroic masculinity as articulated by the popular television programming of the Reagan era. Framed as modern heroes who avoid violence where possible and who only resort to lethal action when forced to do so, Mac and Michael are men who use their superior intellect, ingenuity, grit, and physicality to fight crime and corruption in the name of social and environmental justice. Just like his 1980s counterparts, Legasov, too, while lacking in physical athleticism, is initially presented as a highly intelligent problem solver and innovator who stands up to corruption within the Soviet Union in the name of scientific truth and social justice. Of course, in *Chernobyl*, unlike *MacGyver* or *Knight Rider*, the latter of these qualities, the pursuit of truth and justice, leads, as the opening sequence establishes, not to the triumph of the individual over the system, but instead to Legasov's death.

Accordingly, it is via a forlorn symmetry that Legasov makes his entrance proper into the narrative of *Chernobyl*. At the conclusion of the first episode, "1:23:45," we are taken back to the start of Legasov's involvement with the disaster. Recruited by Boris Shcherbina (Stellan Skarsgård), a deputy chairman of the Council of Ministers, Legasov is appointed as a scientific advisor to the committee managing the response to the accident. Legasov's agency as a scientist is, however, immediately limited by the rigid hierarchy of the Soviet apparatus in which he operates. On learning of the nature of the accident from Shcherbina, Legasov offers unsolicited advice and asks why the committee is not meeting earlier than planned. In response, Shcherbina informs Legasov that he is "on this committee to answer direct questions about the function of an RBMK reactor, if they should happen to arise. Nothing else. Certainly not policy." Frustrated, Legasov nonetheless capitulates.

Appearing next in episode two, "Please Remain Calm," Legasov joins the committee in session at the Kremlin. Again, Legasov initially appears to align with the libertarian ideals of the Reaganite action hero, who so often sees the apparatus of the state as "an impediment to getting things done" (Jeffords 142). Unable to contain himself as Mikhail Gorbachev (David Denick), the General Secretary of the Communist Party of the Soviet Union, moves to adjourn the committee under the illusion that the situation is under control, Legasov interrupts the Soviet Premier. His interjection, in which he lays out the reality of the situation at Chernobyl, does not however result in immediate change, or the validation of Legasov as a beacon of truth amidst a fog of misinformation. Instead, Legasov earns a rebuke from Gorbachev for voicing his dissent: "All I hear is a man I don't know engaging in conjecture—in direct contradiction of what has been reported by Party officials."

Whereas Michael Knight and Mac MacGyver would repeatedly stand resolute in their convictions in the face of adversity, not giving ground to restore and reinforce the mystique of masculine individualism (see Kimmel 174–191), Legasov is forced into a humble apology: "I apologize. I didn't mean—may I express my concern as calmly and respectfully as I can?" Allowed to continue now that he has demonstrated the required deference, Legasov does manage to persuade Gorbachev that further investigation is required. Still, he is not rewarded. Rather, he is sent to Chernobyl with Shcherbina. It is here, where the action heroes of the Reagan decade would step bravely into the breach, that Legasov becomes a reluctant hero, forced to take action he did not intend to take by the very system he dared to challenge.

This repeated failure of brave stands becomes a hallmark of Legasov's efforts throughout the remainder of the narrative of *Chernobyl*. Legasov does take risks in an attempt to effect change, but he is never rewarded. In fact, as the narrative progresses, rather than growing as a great hero, Legasov is revealed to be part of the problem. In episode four, "The Happiness of All Mankind," it is revealed that he knew about, and was complicit in the suppression of information about, the fatal defect within the RBMK reactors. In episode five, "Vichnaya Pamyat," when afforded the opportunity to right this wrong at a special meeting of the International Atomic Energy Agency in Vienna, Legasov lies, revealing enough information to give the appearance of truth, but holding back the full extent of the catastrophe.

Legosov fails even in his final and most public stand, where, at the trial of plant managers Victor Bryukhanov (Con O'Neill), Nikolai Fomin (Adrian Rawlins) and Anatoly Dyatlov (Paul Ritter), he blames the disaster not only on the negligence of the management and operators of the No. 4 reactor, but more so, on the suppression of information within the Soviet state. At the conclusion of the trial, he is promptly detained by the KGB and informed that his testimony will be suppressed. Moreover, he is informed that his role in averting wider disaster will also be concealed and that his status within the Academy of Sciences of the U.S.S.R. will be revoked. Thus, Legasov becomes simultaneously a hero and a villain in the narrative of *Chernobyl*. Rather than a transcendent masculinity rising in the face of adversity, Legasov's final stand is likened by the actor who plays him, Jarred Harris (in Part Six of the *Chernobyl* Podcast), to a balloon losing air, where only through his death is there any insinuation of success.

This tragic representation of masculinity is not, however, restricted to the level of the individual alone. The modes of masculine cooperation within *Chernobyl*, openly built on foundations of reciprocal insecurity, are shown too to be inherently defective in solving problems. This is in direct contrast to the popular television depictions of teamwork in the 1980s. The popular television series *The A-Team,* for example, where the collective ability of Hannibal (George Peppard), Face (Dirk Benedict), Murdock (Dwight Schultz) and B.A. (Mr. T) enables the heroes to solve problems that no one else can, clearly articulates the "Reagan-era success ethic that distinguishes itself from the idle elite above and the immoral poor below on the basis of moral merit and self-made status" (Jordan 3). In the *A-Team,* differing masculinities come together to form a transcendent sum greater than their parts, solving problems for the deserving middle by protecting them from the criminal underground, while the heroes themselves evade and outsmart the corrupt forces of government. By contrast, in *Chernobyl,* rather than a productive meshing together, there is instead a destructive grating of masculinities, bound together by a tyranny of insecurity.

The relationship between deputy chief engineer Anatoly Dyatlov and his subordinates in the control room of the No. 4 reactor demonstrates this incongruity of *Chernobyl* with the success ethic of the Reagan decade. In the first and fifth episodes, the happenings in the control room on the night of the 26th of April 1986, are presented as a rigidly hierarchical antithesis of teamwork, where two intersecting frameworks of masculinity collide with disastrous effect.

The first such framework consists of the plant management: director Bryukhanov, chief engineer Fomin, and Dyatlov. Needing to complete an overdue safety test on the No. 4 reactor, the three decide to conduct the test under suboptimal conditions to secure speculative promotions, with Bryukhanov moving up and out of the plant, and Fomin and Dyatlov each stepping up to fill the gap. Rather, however, than working together to ensure the success of the test, Bryukhanov and Fomin, articulating the very essence of the idle elite, leave Dyatlov to oversee the test alone, which, due to further delay, would now be conducted by the inexperienced night shift.

Thus, motivated by self-interest, Dyatlov joins the context of the second framework: the culture of the night shift control room workers. Obsessed with completing the test irrespective of the difficulties, Dyatlov enters a state of denial about the severity of the accident. When the control room technicians present Dyatlov with evidence that the No. 4 reactor has exploded, Dyatlov ignores them. Berating them as fools, he orders his subordinates to continue operating the non-existent reactor. It is here that Dyatlov's insecurity about the potential personal repercussions of having overseen an accident cause him to construct a delusion that downplays the scale of the disaster. Fearing a loss of control, Dyatlov starts to use that same rigid social hierarchy, of which he imagines himself a victim, to force compliance with his instructions. Going as far as sending night shift supervisor Aleksandr Akimov (Sam Troughton) and senior engineer

Leonid Toptunov (Robert Emms) to their deaths by forcing them to manually open the water valves to the absent reactor, Dyatlov's actions function as an inversion of the Regan-era success ethic. Lacking in moral merit, Dyatlov's behaviors constantly undermine the proficiency of the control room team, making them far less than the sum of their parts. Unlike the A-Team, the control room technicians cannot draw on their masculine camaraderie to reinforce their dynamic agency, but rather, they are coerced into compliance with nonsensical instructions via the rigid masculine hierarchy that presses down upon them.

This notion of the ineffective hierarchy continually disrupts the potential success ethic surrounding the disaster and spreads throughout the narrative of *Chernobyl* like the chain reaction that powered the reactors. After being alerted to the accident, Bryukhanov and Fomin return to the plant. Immediately looking to mitigate their involvement with the accident, they accept Dyatlov's account that the reactor has not exploded, despite hearing further personal accounts and evidence to the contrary. When they present this position to the hastily convened Pripyat Communist Party Executive Committee, these insecurities turn to lies that prolong the crisis and cause further problems. Rejecting the notion of evacuating the nearby city of Pripyat in favor of suppressing information by cutting all lines of communication, the committee look to ingratiate themselves with the Soviet Central Committee. The Central Committee, looking to maintain its façade of superiority on the geo-political stage, accelerates this suppression, further complicating the response to the disaster.

Unlike typical action heroes of the Reagan decade, the men of *Chernobyl* discover that they are unable, either working alone or together, to resolve the catastrophic malfunction of the No. 4 reactor. Their masculinities are not capable of transcending the tragic momentum of their narratives. Meanwhile, the real heroes of *Chernobyl* are relegated to the background of the narrative and continually exploited. On the surface, their actions seem to represent teamwork, but, ultimately, these characters are illustrations of forced labor. As an audience, we watch the fire fighters as they give up their lives to extinguish the flames in the exposed core, while Bryukhanov, Fomin, Dyatlov, the Pripyat Communist Party Executive Committee, and the Central Committee deny that the reactor has exploded. We share the horrors of the medical practitioners as they try in vain to save the irradiated first responders, while thousands more are sent into the heart of the disaster. We watch in awe as the liquidators subject themselves to never-before-seen doses of radiation to clear the disaster site, while the Soviet state lies about the levels of contamination to the international community.

Only the miners, sent to dig a tunnel under the core of the No. 4 reactor, come close to the hypermasculine valorizations of individualism, liberty, and the male body that define the action heroes of the Reagan decade. Yet even their actions prove futile: they dig a tunnel that, in the end, is not needed or used for its original purpose before disappearing back to their lives uncompensated for their contribution. In *Chernobyl*, therefore, it is the masculine hierarchies of reciprocal insecurity that cause and complicate the problem. No individuals can operate above the system. Instead, it is the sense of collective responsibility among the ordinary Soviet people that eventually solves the problem. *Chernobyl*, therefore, simultaneously represents both the tragic failure of male cooperation as well as the ultimate necessity of broader social collaboration.

Accordingly, Mazin purposefully and pragmatically recodifies the role of masculinity in the Reagan decade. In *Chernobyl*, heroic males who stand up in the face of adversity and effect change via their exceptionalism are missing from the narrative. Instead, there is only the perpetration of failure and the reduction of ordinary citizens to the status of bio-robots, redefining the contemporary comprehension of the problematic myth of hypermasculine superiority. Yet, in this recodification, there is a distinct and purposeful disconnect from the West. This tragic revisiting of masculinity is by necessity located far from the other contemporary television returns to the 1980s, and it is to the implications of this disconnect that the discussion will now turn.

Restorative and Cautionary Nostalgias

Nostalgia cycles are nothing new in popular culture. They represent what Davis calls "the great dialectical processes of Western civilization: the ceaseless tension of change vs. stability, innovation vs. reaffirmation, new vs. old, utopia vs the golden age" (116). In returning to the Reagan decade, popular television shows such as *The Goldbergs* and *Young Sheldon* do not revisit the past to present it as it was. Instead, they seek to restore a remembered past that is "filtered, selected, arranged, constructed and reconstructed from collective experience" (Davis 116). In continually revisiting a non-specific "1980-something" America, Adam F. Goldberg's personal conservation of his remembered past, *The Goldbergs*, filters out much of the actuality of the Reagan era. By using an exaggerated lens of frivolity to gloss over many of the problematic people, political power structures, and social pretentions of the decade, Goldberg focuses instead on (re)constructing commodifiable monuments, such as the strength of the nuclear family, the utility of traditional gender roles, and the halcyon days of popular film, television, and music. This is nostalgia in the restorative mode.

The resultant sanitizing of the Reaganite 1980s imbues *The Gold-bergs* with an overwhelming sense of youthful optimism, rooted in American middle-class masculinity. Chuck Lorre's *Young Sheldon* activates a similar mode of restoration. Correcting the absence of Sheldon Lee Cooper's (Jim Parsons/Iain Armitage) adulterous and alcohol-abusing father (Lance Barber) from its parent show, *The Big Bang Theory* (2007–2019), *Young Sheldon* uses the Reagan decade to revive its titular protagonist's nuclear family. Reconceived as a loving, if not frustrated, father and family man, George Cooper is sanitized and restored to life in order to symbolically reconstruct the mythic purity "of the lost home" (Boym 41), where, as with *The Goldbergs*, the concerns of an overbearing mother are moderated by the paternal masculinity of a pragmatic father.

Set against this cultural backdrop, Mazin's *Chernobyl* is again the disruptor. As Boym reminds us, reflective nostalgia "loves details, not symbols" (41). So, whereas the narrative aesthetics of *The Goldbergs* and *Young Sheldon* rely upon restoring vague symbols of a lost America that never actually existed, the focus of *Chernobyl* is on revealing the specific details of a disaster that very much did. This clearly positions *Chernobyl* as nostalgia in the reflective mode. Lingering on the "ruins, the patina of time and history, in the dreams of another place and another time" (Boym 41), *Chernobyl* facilitates a cautionary revisiting to that other place, the defunct social and political apparatus of the Soviet Union, where the recovered homeland is not remembered fondly, the nuclear family is practically absent, and the wider sociopolitical context is presented as the antithesis of purity.

It is this purposeful foregrounding of problematic people, politics, power structures, and pretentions that forms the lens through which *Chernobyl* examines the present. By using the othered past, *Chernobyl* becomes a mechanism to safely explore the shared fears and anxieties of its contemporary Western audience. As Legasov asks in the opening monologue of the first episode, "What is the cost of lies? It's not that we'll mistake them for the truth. The real danger is that if we hear enough lies, then we no longer recognize the truth at all. What can we do then?" For Mazin, this concern with the corrosive effects of "fake news" was the key to his revisiting of the Reagan decade, and, as he explains in Part One of *The Chernobyl Podcast*, it constitutes the core thematic explored in *Chernobyl*, which is essentially a show "about the cost of lives [and] the danger of narrative."

In this context, the function of *Chernobyl* is to extol the value of truth over story in the era of alternative facts. The tragic nexus of masculinity as articulated by the narrative of *Chernobyl* reveals a truth that speaks directly to contemporary fears related to masculine power structures in Western politics and popular culture. The failure of Legasov to effect change despite his intellect, position, and willingness to take risks, and the overwhelming insecurity of the political apparatus pushing down upon all of those who attempted, either individually or collectively, to resolve the crisis, provides a stark counterpoint to the hypermasculine valorizations of individualism, liberty, and physical action that were, and still are, commonly articulated by the popular film and television heroes of Western society. As a result, *Chernobyl* purposefully disrupts depictions of how the dominant position of men is negotiated, legitimized, and reinforced, without directly criticizing the West. Ultimately, therefore, Mazin's *Chernobyl* deploys its nostalgia in a way that is simultaneously familiar to, and distant from, the everyday lives of its viewers in order to remind us of the actuality of the past, while positing that those that fail to learn from this tragic past are doomed to repeat it.

Contributor's Note

While Mazin's *Chernobyl* is a work of entertainment, and this essay deconstructs that work as entertainment, I would like to take a moment to recognize the real human and environmental catastrophe that occurred because of the accident at the Vladimir Ilyich Lenin Nuclear Power Plant on the 26th of April 1986.

Works Cited

Bevan, Alex. *The Aesthetics of Nostalgia TV: Production Design and the Boomer Era.* Bloomsbury Academic, 2019.

Boym, Svetlana. *The Future of Nostalgia.* Basic Books, 2001.

Davis, Fred. *Yearning for Yesterday: A Sociology of Nostalgia.* Free Press, 1979.

Jeffords, Susan. *Hard Bodies: Hollywood masculinity in the Reagan era.* Rutgers University Press, 1994.

Jordan, Chris. *Movies and the Reagan Presidency: Success and Ethics.* Praeger, 2003.

Kimmel, Michael S. *Manhood in America: A Cultural History.* Oxford University Press, 2018.

Loveday, Vik. "'Flat-capping it': Memory, Nostalgia and Value in Retroactive Male Working-Class Identification." *European Journal of Cultural Studies*, vol. 17, no. 6, 2014, pp. 721–735.

Marlin, Brenton J. *American Masculinity Under Clinton: Popular Media and the Nineties "Crisis of Masculinity."* P. Lang, 2005.

May, Vanessa. "Belonging from Afar: Nostalgia, Time and Memory." *The Sociological Review*, vol. 65 no. 2, 2017, pp. 401–415.

Part One. *The Chernobyl Podcast.* 7th May 2019, HBO.

Part Six: Bonus Episode with Jared Harris. *The Chernobyl Podcast.* 15th August 2019, HBO.

Robinson, Sally. *Marked Men: White Masculinity in Crisis.* Columbia University Press, 2000.

Savran, David. *Taking It Like a Man: White Masculinity, Masochism, and Contemporary American Culture.* Princeton University Press, 1998.

Safety, Stoneybrook, and the Sitters

Morgan E. Foster

Young adult books of the 1960s and '70s often featured gritty, realistic depictions of young people who were facing large, systemic issues: drugs, poverty, gang violence, sexism, and more. Protagonists were often trying to make their way in a world they didn't understand and where decisions were often made for them by teachers, parents, and other authority figures. In contrast, the 1980s saw a move towards books that were vastly different: books that were almost exclusively written by white authors; books in a series, especially series romance; and books featuring predominantly white protagonists who dealt with the more everyday concerns of being an adolescent. This shift from substance to fluff, content-wise, and the shift from social concerns to individual concerns, led to a great deal of anxiety by librarians, critics, and educators, who lamented the poor quality of books for young people. The hopefulness of President Ronald Reagan's "morning in America" rhetoric was, for some, a welcome respite from the chaotic 1960s and '70s. Culturally, white flight changed city and rural landscapes when families fled to suburban areas, and malls quickly sprang up to become symbols of consumptive excess. Publishers, banking quite literally on the knowledge that youth had disposable income, marketed books to them directly. This helped propel *The Baby-Sitters Club* (*BSC*) books to bestseller lists, which prompted yet another shift in publishing and marketing, empowering girls with purchasing power and opening up a new avenue of revenue for booksellers: the teen paperbacks.

Yet in 1986, amidst a sea of paperback romances, *BSC* emerged as an alternative for preteen girls. Ann M. Martin's series offered a different look at girlhood, one that privileged friendship over romance. For preteens, caught in the liminal space between girlhood and womanhood, the series became instantly popular. Inspired by Martin's own days as a tween babysitter, the BSC series began in 1986 with the publication of the first book in the series, *Kristy's Great Idea*. The series starts off with four protagonists: club president and founder Kristy Thomas, vice president Claudia Kishi, secretary Mary Anne Spier, and treasurer Stacey McGill. Each book tackles the business of running the club, as well as the sitters' homes, families, and interpersonal relationships. All four girls are beginning 7th grade, and they pool their resources into a formal club to ensure that they can make money, serve the neighborhood, and be seen by adults as the responsible, mature, and independent young women they see themselves as. For today's readers, the amount of freedom and agency the babysitters enjoy is shocking—they are often home alone for hours after school, responsible for preparing family meals, and managing their club entirely absent adult supervision. Yet this is by design: in an interview with the *Miami Herald*, Martin says, "I wanted to create this group of friends, girls who were independent, who solved problems on their own, who had their own interests" (Sampson).

Each book focuses on one character's point of view, and every title indicates that book's protagonist: *Mary Anne Saves the Day, Claudia and the New Girl, The Truth About Stacey,* and so on, which meant that readers always knew what to expect. Originally envisioned as a quartet, with one story from each girls' perspective, the books feature standalone plots and conflicts, while still being connected through shared characters, which includes the BSC and the children they sit for. The immediate popularity of the first four books led, over time, the club—and hence the series—to expand to include many narrators and an ever-growing set of perspectives for readers to follow.

Though far less controversial than the romance series fiction I briefly mentioned earlier, the *BSC* is not without its critics. Plots were often predictable and formulaic. In her *Publishers Weekly* review of *Kristy's Great Idea*, Diane Roback wrote, "Martin has written an enjoyable, light-hearted story with much appeal for middle readers. Her characters, especially the four girls, are strongly drawn, and have distinct enough personalities to carry the projected Baby-sitters Club series" (69). In contrast, Adele A. Greenlee, Dianne L. Monson, and Barbara M. Taylor in particular are critical of the *BSC* for what they perceive to be its inattention to current events. They write, "The Baby-Sitters Club series pays little attention to the complex aspects of contemporary society such as AIDS, child abuse, drug addiction, or marital infidelity that have received increasing attention in contemporary recommended literature for children" (218). They critique the way each book "end[s] happily" and the way each problem is one that can be "solved by the characters themselves" (218). While they're not wrong, this view overlooks the social and economic realities of this community and the way those realities impact the lives of preteens in suburban U.S. in three major ways: one, increasing divorce rates, which is reflected by Kristy's, Dawn's, and Stacey's experiences as children of divorced parents; two, the increase of women working outside the home, which leads to increased responsibility for Kristy and Claudia, whose mothers work outside the home; and three, race relations, which Jessi, in particular, faces as part of a new Black family in Stoneybrook.

Friendship is at the heart of the BSC and is perhaps the most enduring theme to emerge from this series. Friendship novels, as Gabrielle Moss dubs them, often "glossed over the very real pain young female friends can cause one another" (Moss 52). I concur; these stories are not without their own shortcomings, but their value is evident in a number of ways. First, the books' emphasis on centering platonic female relationships differentiates the series from the romance-heavy stories of other books marketed to young readers of this era. To be sure, the *BSC* has some romance—Kristy's mother gets remarried, Dawn's mother and Mary Anne's father rekindle their high school romance as adults, and *Logan Likes Mary Anne* (book 10) introduces new character Logan Bruno and his crush on Mary Anne. Characters have infatuations and go on dates, but those are all minor plot points compared to the business of running the club, finishing homework, spending time with family, and, most importantly of all, their friendships with one another. The best way that the *BSC* books separate themselves from other series fiction is their action. Giving her characters some agency and autonomy was part of Martin's plan from the beginning: she told Brooke Hauser of *The New Yorker*, "I didn't want to present one-dimensional girls who only cared about boys and makeup and what to wear to the next dance" (Hauser). These girls are not passive, waiting for parents to make sitting appointments or for their business to be successful. They "actively organized and sought out opportunities" (Moss 146), like wearing sandwich boards to school when a rival babysitter's group threatens to steal their business away. Claudia puts her artistic talent to use by making posters and flyers to hang around town, and they collectively work to maintain professional standards of excellence with every family they sit for. In short, Moss writes, "girls could make something meaningful" (146). I would add that these girls, notably, made something meaningful *with one another*. Their success is not mediated through the male gaze, through male experiences, or really with the help of men at all; it is engineered solely through their own work and ingenuity. When adults do step in, it is often the maternal figures who offer assistance.

The *BSC* was beloved from its inception in part because of its inclusive cast. Claudia, a Japanese American figure, is integral to the series and to the club's survival: it is at her home that the club meets, and she has her own phone and land line for club use. Jessi Martin, a junior officer, is Black, and Stacey's diabetes features prominently in many storylines. While many, including myself, appreciated the various perspectives offered by the series, others were more critical. Mary Bronstein takes issue with Claudia, arguing that Claudia "is construed as a safe Other whose race is not a threat or a concern primarily because of her exoticized appearance and her family's assimilation" (216). She further contends that the inclusion of Jessi is "a brazen stroke of tokenism" that is "outlandish to the point of absurdity in its attempts to fit in signifiers from as many readers' realities as possible. It reeks of corporate marketing decisions to appeal to a wider audience than white girls from traditional families" (225). Bronstein is probably not wrong that including characters with various health issues, religious beliefs, family makeup, and racial backgrounds is a way to sell more books. However, I would point out that Bronstein's critical take of Martin and the *BSC* overlooks the role the books played in readers' ability to identify with the characters and see themselves. While it's difficult to argue that Jessi and Claudia are at best superficially Black and Japanese, their inclusion still marks an important shift in series fiction for girls.

The debate about skin color and its connection to race isn't new. For instance, Ezra Jack Keats was criticized in the '60s by some who argue that nothing about *A Snowy Day* would be different if Peter was white. Arguably, that is true about Jessi and Claudia. Still, I believe representation is important for young readers. Dianne Johnson-Feelings' research, among others, quite explicitly connects the need for children to see themselves and their experiences reflected back to them on the page. Visually, the covers for the *BSC* are integral to this understanding. Claudia is featured on twenty-one of the series' covers, while Jessi has thirteen point-of-view books—one more than Mallory, who joined the club at the same time. For young readers of color, seeing Jessi and Claudia featured in their own point of view stories is important in the whitewashed '80s. Rudine Sims Bishop argues, "Literature transforms human experience and reflects it back to us, and in that reflection we can see our own lives and experiences as part of the larger human experience" (ix). What Bronstein calls "tokenism," I call inclusivity. Furthermore, white readers need to see characters of color. Bishop addresses this as well, writing, "Children from dominant social groups have always found their mirrors in books, but they, too, have suffered from the lack of availability of books about others…. If they see only reflections of themselves, they will grow up with an exaggerated sense of their own importance and value in the world—a dangerous ethnocentrism" (x). It wasn't just Black and Asian readers who needed to see Jessi and Claudia; it was white readers who needed a "sliding glass door" to walk through and become part of a world not their own. For many readers of the *BSC*, the appeal was more than just the friendships; it was also rooted in seeing oneself reflected back on the cover of the book. This representation of diverse perspectives is part of what makes these books so important for readers, explaining their longevity and impact.

Writer and critic Shannon Miller contends that one reason these books resonated with readers is that Martin provided a "taste of what the entertainment landscape could look like if it gave girls and women the opportunity to exist as three-dimensional beings" (Miller). These girls were afforded space to be "community leaders" as well as to "navigate complex relationships and live independently" (Miller). They had to work together for the sake of their friendships, their club, their sitting charges, and their community, which fostered in readers a feeling of responsibility and maturity that the romance series lacked. It is not my intent to pit one genre against another or assign a value to one over the other. Rather, the *BSC* showed readers an alternative way to understand girls, girls' behavior, and girls' interactions with their families, friends, and themselves.

The lasting legacy of the *BSC* is in its willingness to let its young girls be independent. Today's readers may be surprised at the level of freedom the sitters have, but they have earned that trust by demonstrating their reliability, trustworthiness, and dependability at home, at school, and while babysitting. In short, these stories served as more than just fun, fluffy entertainment. They were *necessary*. Meredith Cherland, in her ethnographic essay "Reading Elisabeth's Girlhood," describes her daughter Elisabeth's love for the books, which was predicated on their sameness. Cherland writes, "Scholastic Books made money by meeting her psychological need for predictability" (106). In retrospect, I can see how true that was for myself as a reader and consumer of these books—I too was "comforted by their utter predictability" (Cherland 106). For young people, the mid-late 1980s was a confusing time, when the new 24-hour news cycle showed horror and violence from all over the globe yet was at odds with "the great party known as the 1980s, when the stock market soared, patriotism surged, the Soviet Union crumbled, and America thrived" (Troy 12). Predictability and sameness were a welcome respite from the world. While critics of these books—and there were many—bemoaned the decline of quality and raised concerns about the reading habits of youth, the 176 million copies the *BSC* sold proved that there was an audience for stories about girls. They were not the first series to focus on girls, nor were they the best or longest-running. Still, they are valuable texts because they speak explicitly to and about the experiences of girls on the cusp of their teenage years. The sitters also represent a more multi-dimensional approach to girlhood, one that suggests it's possible—even desirable—to have autonomy and be interested in boys and work all at the same time.

In the conclusion of their research, Greenlee, Monson, and Taylor ask, "What special magic do series books hold for preteen readers?" (223). Their answer confirms what I have already argued: "the special magic is the experience of living the lives of the characters and being engaged in the events in the story" (223). Letting readers have agency over their selections, even if those selections include series books, is unlikely to interfere with "higher quality" literature (224). Furthermore, notions about what constitutes quality are subjective, elitist, and problematic, given that much of the Western canon excludes women writers, writers of color, and contemporary texts. More importantly still, allowing opportunities for young people to choose their own books enhances not only the pleasure of reading, but learning by reading. Catherine Sheldrick Ross, in her qualitative research, provides ample evidence to demonstrate the power of series literature: it encourages reading, it fosters a love of reading, and it often keeps readers interested in reading more. Ross argues that series fiction leads to readers' "discovery of the joy of independent reading" (217), in part because readers, especially struggling or "reluctant" readers, can gain confidence in their skills. She explains, "It is therefore easier for beginning readers to read a series book with a family plot and characters ... than it is for beginning readers to get into a totally new book" (218–19). Series fiction, then, is an important pathway to literacy and to readers' relationship to reading and books in general.

There is something safe in series fiction. In an ever-changing and increasingly disordered world, books provide a safe place to retreat. They also serve as a reminder that violence wasn't always part of a young girl's childhood. In her interview with writer Amanda Woytus, children's literature scholar Margaret Mackey points to gun violence as the primary reason "American kids' lives feel less safe" (Woytus). Mackey explains, "Americans are frightened of each other because you don't know who's the lunatic in the room. That's a lot to wrap your head around as a kid—that you can't trust the people around you. The Baby-Sitters Club wasn't dealing with anything like that" (qtd. in Woytus). Tanner Greenring, cohost of *The Baby-Sitters Club Club* podcast, told Woytus, "Stoneybrook ... just seems like such a place out of time ... it's totally safe. And everyone knows everyone else. And there are no outsiders or danger" (qtd. in Woytus). Given the myriad ways American lives are threatened with gun violence, domestic terrorism, and other safety concerns, there is something soothing about returning to Stoneybrook, even for adults. As Woytus observes, "[T]he past probably wasn't *that* much safer, but I'm pining for the chance to feel that way. I miss believing in a place where nothing bad happened" (Woytus).

Unfortunately, Woytus' "pining" evokes a time that never existed. At a 1991 Georgetown campaign event, presidential candidate Bill Clinton argued, "The 1980s ushered in a gilded age of greed, selfishness, irresponsibility, excess, and neglect" (Clinton). Historian Gil Troy, in his 2005 book *Morning in America*, notes, "Ronald Reagan's two terms were not the eight-year idyll many now recall" (13). Troy points to "social pathologies of crime, drugs, ghettoization, failing schools, family breakdown, and ineffectual immigration policies" (15) as issues Reagan had to contend with, to say nothing of the AIDS crisis and other geopolitical concerns. Nostalgia for the surburban '80s, then, "a place where nothing bad happened," was familiar to many during the summer of 2020. Amidst racial protests, the Covid-19 pandemic, and a contentious presidential campaign, Americans were more eager than ever for seemingly simpler times. Thus, when Netflix dropped all ten episodes of their *BSC* adaptation in July 2020, it quickly became *the* perfect show for a weary nation. Starring a cast of little-known actresses as the sitters and better-known adult actors Alicia Silverstone, Mark Feuerstein, and Marc Evan Jackson as the parents, the adaptation was well-received. *USA Today* reviewer Kelly Lawler notes that the show "is a near-perfect distillation of what made the book series sell millions of copies," and that it is "optimistic but not deluded, youthful but not juvenile and sweet but not mawkish.... It's the rare kids' show that manages to offer just as much for the child as the parent sitting next to them on the couch" (Lawler). For younger viewers, the show speaks to adolescents—and adolescence—as it is experienced in the present day. The mostly white sitters are now more diverse, with Mary Anne reimagined as biracial and Dawn as Latinx. Dawn's father is gay, and one of the club's clients is a trans girl. The sitters use Google Docs to stay organized, while pop culture references to *Game of Thrones* (2011–2019), *Queer Eye* (2003–2007), and, in a nod to Silverstone, *Clueless* (1995) abound. In short, the updates are inclusive, organic, and realistic for the contemporary setting. Reading the books is not a prerequisite for following the show—each character narrates an episode, filling in important details along the way.

Yet I want to focus my discussion on the legions of adult viewers, many of whom reveled in the nostalgia of their childhood brought to life. Previous attempts at adapting the series—a 1990 HBO series and 1995 film—were mixed; reviewer Judy Berman notes that "neither has aged well" (Berman). I, like other adults, was cautiously optimistic about the Netflix version but preparing for disappointment. As Kathryn VanArendonk of *Vulture* writes, "I was dubious about the prospect of adapting the series.... I was worried about an adaptation of *The Baby-Sitters Club* with the same skepticism of anyone who loves something and then learns it's going to be remade" (VanArendonk). Yet to our collective relief, the series is "gentle and adorable" (VanArendonk), "a triumph" (Lawson), "a wonderful surprise" (Berman), and "charming" (Poniewozik). The show rewards its adult viewers, in part because it is lovingly made by Rachel Shukert, a fan of the series herself. She told *Variety* that because the characters "have been 'fully-realized' and 'like friends' to so many kids growing up," there wasn't much she needed to do to make the switch from books to television (Turchiano). As I noted, there is a "broadening out [of] the representation of families in the show" (Turchiano), but Shukert maintained the original spirit of friendship and girlhood which endeared the books to millions of readers.

The show also treated readers to fun visuals lifted right from the books, further connecting adulthood to girlhood and the past. Throughout the books, each sitter writes a summary of her babysitting job. On the printed page, each girl gets her own, personalized font. That typography is used for each episode and rotates, depending on which girl is narrating the episode. It's a small feature, but one that rewards fans with a trip back to their book-reading days. The attention to detail instantly transports adults back to their girlhoods, where those handwriting fonts were as familiar to us as our own. Adult viewers are also rewarded with storylines that speak to who they are now, as parents or burdened adults with work responsibilities. A parent herself, Shukert wanted to focus on the multigenerational aspect by fleshing out the adults as well as the sitters. She notes, "the parents are just these kinds of ciphers to you, and it's like, 'Oh, that's Kristy's mom,' whatever, you don't even know her name" (Zaltzman). The adult viewers, who clearly share more with the parents than the sitters these days, can still find themselves not only engaged in the series, but once again relating to it.

All of the show's elements, from the characters themselves to the fonts to the logo to the setting, invite viewers to be transported to a different place—a place of safety and security, one that indeed seems out of time, as Greenring noted above. Yet watching the show during Covid-19's isolation further emphasized that strange sense of time and unreality: the sitters frequently hug one another and their parents. They sit together at lunch and in Claudia's bedroom for meetings. The girls go to camp and grocery shop with their parents; Mary Anne and Stacey even babysit during a week-long vacation. All of this underscored a feeling of nostalgia for adult viewers' own girlhoods, one that has become as idealized as the Reagan presidency itself: a time of "idealism, of national unity and glory" (Troy 16). For all viewers, though, the Netflix series evoked a different kind of nostalgia, one where we could be together and share experiences with our friends and families. In July 2020, we were only a few months into Covid quarantine—as I write now, one full year of the pandemic has kept the nation segregated and isolated from one another. Rewatching *The Baby-Sitters Club* was a kind of fantasy—a fantasy not of spells and wizards, but of community and togetherness. It was a bittersweet experience that took me—and countless others—back not only to girlhood, but to my adulthood, which has seemed paused during the pandemic.

Series fiction emphasizes the experience of imaginative fantasy in readers. It provided a safe haven for readers, one that was consistent and familiar, despite the turmoil that may have been occurring in their own lives and communities. In many ways, '80s suburbs were the same. Sociologist Mark Baldassare explained in a 1986 *Los Angeles Times* article that while "the suburban *reality* is over—that doesn't necessarily mean the suburban *dream* is over" (McLellan). Sadly, the safety that Stoneybrook offered as a suburban shelter was always that: a dream. Nonetheless, for young readers, the books provided a comfort—they knew what to expect from a *Baby-Sitters Club* book. The books, and the stories and adaptations they have inspired, preserve a nostalgic atmosphere of innocence and safety that is closely associated with the series' roots in the culture of the 1980s. Very few things are at risk in the *BSC*. Fights are resolved, friendships restored, and readers have the pleasant experience of knowing that, almost always, the status quo will be restored by the time they finish. Returning to Stoneybrook time and again shouldn't be a critique. Rather, it should be understood, in part, as a way for girls—and the adults they become—to understand who they are in a rapidly changing world. It should be celebrated as an example of girls exerting agency over their reading habits and learning about other girls whose experiences may be totally unlike their own.

Works Cited

Berman, Judy. "*The Baby-Sitters Club* Is the Only Pure Thing Left in This World." *Time*, 29 June 2020.

Bronstein, Mary. "I Like Sports and You Like Clothes, But We Both Love Babies!" *Girls' Series Fiction and American Popular Culture*, edited by LuElla D'Amico. Lexington Books, 2016, pp. 205–28.

Cherland, Meredith. "Chapter Six: Reading Elisabeth's Girlhood: History and Popular Culture at Work in the Subjectivity of a Tween." *Counterpoints*, vol. 245, 2005, pp. 95–116. JSTOR.

Clinton, Bill. "The New Covenant: Responsibility and Rebuilding the American Community." Remarks, 23 Oct. 1991. Georgetown University, Washington, D.C. Campaign address.

Greenlee, Adele A., Dianne L. Monson, and Barbara M. Taylor. "The Lure of Series Books: Does It Affect Appreciation for Recommended Literature?" *The Reading Teacher* vol. 50, no. 3, 1996, pp. 216–25.

Hauser, Brooke. "The Feminist Legacy of the Baby-Sitters Club." *The New Yorker* 9 Dec. 2016.

Lawler, Kelly. "'The Baby-Sitters Club' On Netflix Will Lift You Out of Quarantine Doldrums." *USA Today*, 4 July 2020.

Lawson, Richard. "Netflix's *Baby-Sitters Club* Series Is Near-Perfect Kids' Television." *Vanity Fair*, 29 June 2020.

Martin, Ann M. *The Baby-Sitters Club*. Scholastic, 1986–2000.

McLellan, Dennis. "Suburbia Changing, but Still Part of the American Dream, Author Says: Urban Realities of the '80s Intruding Upon Idyllic Retreats That Flourished in '50s, '60s." *Los Angeles Times*, 6 July 1986.

Miller, Shannon. "Over 30 Years Ago, *The Baby-Sitters Club* Made Space for Girls From All Backgrounds." *AV Club*, 15 Aug. 2019.

Moss, Gabrielle. *Paperback Crush: The Totally Radical History of '80s and '90s Teen Fiction*. Quirk Books, 2018.

Poniewozik, James. "'The Baby-Sitters Club' Defies and Exceeds Expectations." *The New York Times*, 2 July 2020.

Roback, Diane. "Children's Books—Fiction." *The Publishers Weekly*, vol. 230, no. 18, 31 Oct. 1986, pp. 69.

Sampson, Hannah. "Interview Ann M. Martin, Creator of the Baby-Sitters Club Books." *Miami Herald*, 15 Nov. 2014.

Troy, Gil. "Introduction: Ronald Reagan's Defining Vision for the 1980s—and America." *Morning in America: How Ronald Reagan Invented the 1980s*. Princeton University Press, 2005, pp. 1–23.

Turchiano, Danielle. "'The Baby-Sitters Club' Boss on Adapting Ann M. Martin's Classic Books for the 21st Century." *Variety*, 2 July 2020.

VanArendonk, Kathryn. "*The Baby-Sitters Club* Is a Welcome Surprise and Utter Delight." *Vulture*, 29 June 2020.

Woytus, Amanda. "How the Baby-Sitters Club Reflected Our Dreams of Safety." *JSTOR Daily*, 9 Nov. 2016.

Zaltzman, Lior. "Netflix's Flawless 'The Baby-Sitters Club' Is Brought to You by This Amazing Jewish Mom." *Kveller*, 24 July 2020.

The Cutest Doll at the Arcade

Technology and (American) Girl Power

MYRNA MORETTI

It's 1986 and nine-year-old Courtney Moore is the best *Pac-Man* player at the Smiley's Arcade at Orange Valley Mall. In the lead up to the *Challenger* launch, her teacher Mr. Garcia assigns a class presentation project for each student to explain their personal passion. Courtney decides to design a video game. When her friends suggest that she doesn't know how to program a computer game, she clarifies that "I'm not going to actually *make* a computer game.... I'm going to think up the characters, and the world and the rules, and then explain the game in my presentation" (Hertz 20). Released in September 2020, Courtney 1986! is the latest American Girl historical doll with accompanying accessories, website, and book: *Courtney Changes the Game*. Across this collection of texts and paratexts, 1980s-ness is reinforced through aesthetic codes and narrative details. Neon colors, scan lines, and phrases like "rad" and "grody" abound. However, this emphasis on the 1980s obscures the ongoing relevance of the ambivalent relationship between girlhood and technology in the Courtney-verse.

In *Our Aesthetic Categories*, Sianne Ngai describes "cute(ness)" as an intensification of commodity fetishism that hinges on the dialectical repetition of power and powerlessness. As a minor aesthetic category, Ngai notes how the *cute*'s combined ubiquity and seeming unimportance makes it a vital mode of understanding twentieth- and twenty-first-century American culture. Often associated with children's toys, *cuteness* evokes a sense of helplessness that is often infantile, feminine, and unthreatening (59). However, this perceived "powerlessness" is oftentimes the site of aggressive affective or intellectual demands. This in turn shifts the *cute* object or text into an affectively, if not physically, powerful object. Rather than a tension to be resolved, Ngai writes that this paradoxical relation is

111

inherent to *cuteness*. Often in making an appeal in one way or another, the *cute* object also reveals how persuasive (and hence powerful) it can be.

Ngai's argument is more extensive than this summary and centers around how cuteness in poetry and avant-garde art expresses a relationship to commodity culture. However, her argument helps frame my analysis of the expensive and lauded American Girl toys. Through its merchandise, American Girl/Pleasant Company (AG/PC, purchased by Mattel in 1998) repeatedly expresses a dialectic of power/powerlessness that is embedded in both feminist and capitalist pursuits (Zaslow 6). Dolls have historically been tools for conditioning particular types of girlhood behaviors. They function as powerless objects that prompt girls to demonstrate their power over them through practicing maternal or domestic skills or even making appropriate fashion choices. (Hilu 7; Seiter 61–67) Through their momentary physical power over the dolls, girls are reinscribed into dominant gendered expectations. In the 1980s, as expectations of girls increasingly shifted to include things like higher education and careers, dolls and modes of doll play also evolved to reflect changing definitions of female identity (Hilu 11; Spigel 328).

Founded in 1986, AG/PC presented an educational and empowered alternative to other less "feminist" toys on the market (DeLaCruz 215–218). With accompanying historical books, narratives of girl power, various self-help books for girls, and dolls that anatomically resemble young girls, AG/PC positioned itself as the company of idealized girlhood—for the current low cost of $110 a doll (Deanda et al. 974; Diamond et al. 123; Susina 132). The founder, Pleasant Rowland, was an educator and textbook writer before she established the company in 1986 (Schalk 165). While the historical collections follow the general cultural shift in the 1980s toward "girl power," they are also only available to (American) girls who meet a particular class requirement (McRobbie 135–136; Osei-Kofi 1; Deanda et al. 979). While different book series take on racism, class, and universal social struggles around family and friendship, this "struggle" is always commodified as a desirable, playable, and/or collectible *cute* object (Deanda et al. 982, Susina 133; Zaslow 110). Each American Girl doll's fictional persona presents a narrative of self-empowerment in the face of adversity. However, this also implies that some aspect of their age, gender, or circumstance has rendered them powerless (Gill and Kanai 323). Courtney's collection re-tools these types of contradictions for the 1980s—and for the 21st century.

As Courtney designs her video game and demonstrates her own video game skills, the books bring multiple tensions between girls and technology to the surface. These tensions all suggest modes of power/powerlessness wrapped up in the *cute* AG/PC package. They emphasize the power of feminism, but they also rely on a capitalist neoliberal paradigm that wants girls (and everyone else) to be good laborers and consumers above all else—both by purchasing the dolls and by emulating the doll persona's behaviors (Rottenberg 419; Sherry 200; Story 87–89). This neoliberal mode of feminism is extended through the collection's individualized emphasis on "girl power" and "self-confidence" rather than on ideas of social transformation (Gill 324). To understand the different aspects of girls and gaming in the Courtney collection, I have included cultural histories of girls' media and technology, computer education studies, literary analyses, and sociological surveys—in addition to adapting Ngai's political aesthetic (Kearney 91).

This approach helps to explain how a cute commodity like the Courtney doll presents multiple ambivalent perspectives about girls and their relationship with technology—both in the 1980s and now. In the first section of this essay I draw comparisons between the Courtney version of the 1980s and primary source material for and about girls *in* the 1980s. This comparison reveals how AG/PC presents a version of the material girl decade that emphasizes girls' play in a vitally accurate way while downplaying some of the ways that technological skills might extend into professionalization. In the second section, I analyze the relationship between Courtney and educational entertainment software (or *edutainment*) from the 1980s through to today. Both the game that Courtney designs and the Courtney collection suggest the ongoing role that gendered narratives and thematic preferences play in girls cultivation of technological skills. Throughout, one of the key tensions is whether or not Courtney's disinterest in programming is a sign of powerlessness or whether it holds space for other dynamic possibilities for girls.

Courtney in Context

Across the Courtney book, paratexts, and collection, there are extensive accounts of the embodied experience of gaming, with asides like, "nonstop electronic sounds pelted Courtney Moore's ears as she leaned into the PAC-MAN," and "Courtney tucked a loose curl into her scrunchie without letting up on the joystick. She'd been playing for nearly an hour. Her feet were sore and her eyes were starting to swim" (Hertz 1). The Courtney music video shows Courtney *in* her video game sliding down 16-bit words like "strength" and "confidence." Both in the book and the stop-motion film, Courtney pictures herself *in* the video game as a way to process stressful situations. For girls themselves, the virtual D'Amico's Electronics in the Mall on the Courtney website includes quiz questions about the cost of a VCR in 1986. The Courtney collection involves doll-sized replicas of a boom box, Walkman, TV with a VCR and VHS tape, and a *Pac-Man* arcade game. The extensive range of these options suggests that AG/PC are not in any way averse to close technological encounters. While arcade games certainly opened the door for more widespread technological experience, they were largely on the decline even by 1986 (Donovan 167; Ernkvist 184; Kent 116, 455). Indeed, appeals were made across numerous media for girls (children and teenagers) to become gamers and computer users. This makes it all the more curious that Courtney does not interface with a personal computer at any point or seemingly have any interest in actually programming her game. The exclusion of other modes of gaming or computing technology opens up a tension between Courtney as a historically accurate yet often overlooked gamer (powerful) and a historically inaccurate non-computer user (powerless).

Many contemporary scholars who study video game culture in the 1980s lament the ways that men and boys are emphasized as the central video game and electronics market both at the time and in histories written since (Newman 120; Kocurek 163; Cote 83). Compared to these sources, the representations of Courtney as a skilled video gamer, as interested in video game design, and as a community member at her local arcade seem like they present a unique and *powerful* little lady who is subverting the game establishment. However, current scholarship of video game history often overlooks primary sources that might reveal girls as gamers, users, or, at the very least, interested parties. Close attention to 1980s magazines and television shows for young women shows that Courtney 1986! is indeed not a revisionist history. Her interest in design over programming bears a marked similarity to famed early video game pioneer Roberta Williams, the co-founder and lead designer of Sierra On-Line (Nooney). As Jennifer S. Light suggests, "Courtney 1986!" is writing "women back into the history they were always a part of" (483).

In their November 1982 issue, *Seventeen* magazine ran the results of their first ever "Mini Mag Poll: Are Video Games Here to Stay?" From over 5500 responses—most of which are presumed to be from young women—they found that 62 percent of readers regularly played video games. Seventy-four percent of respondents reported having had a good experience, regardless of play frequency. Various reasons were given for the popularity of video games, including the observations that "playing help's coordination, it's fun, and it's something girls can do just as well as boys" ("Results" 82). While the average respondents were likely a few years older than Courtney, popular media for girls and teenagers can offer unique insight into how young women in the 1980s perceived their relationship to video games and electronic technology.

As early as 1981, Atari aired commercials featuring young girls using a home computer to do their homework and quiz their Mom. The 1982 *Consumer Guide* book, *How to Win Video Games*, found that numerous arcade games had a comparable number of male and female players, with women actually outnumbering men as *Pac-Man* players (87). In multiple episodes of *The Facts of Life* (1979–1988), teenagers Jo and Blair used a computer to resolve interpersonal differences (Clair). On *Family Ties* (1982–1989), it's the youngest preteen sister, Jennifer, who introduces a computer into the family home in 1987 ("Matchmaker"). In the *Family Ties* episode, the family rents a computer for a week, and, in that time, Jennifer uses it for schoolwork, for playing video games, and ultimately convinces her parents to purchase one. In addition to their poll, *Seventeen* ran the short-lived "Game Plan" column in the early 1980s, as well as articles like "Get Ready for the Computer Revolution" and "Computer Friendly" (Maeroff 147; Lee 58). In 1983, they ran an article that stated, "both Sirius and Atari are eager to accept a marketable video game by a teen girl" (Yordan 69). The hypothetical designer could send away for a submission package that requested various technological information and a diskette or cassette with a copy of the program on it. Across all of these examples, girls are presented as capable and confident computer users, gamers, and even programmers.

Many children in 1986 would not have had access to a home computer (indeed many still don't have reliable access in the 2020s), and so perhaps the lack of personal computing in the Courtney-verse reflects AG/PC's reluctance to overstate how Courtney's class status privileges her with access to technology (Bayus et al. 201). Whether or not a girl like Courtney would have had access to a home computer, she might have had school or library access, living in the seemingly affluent fictional town of Orange Valley. When Courtney tells her friend Kip that she's going to design a video game, his response includes an immediate terminology slippage as he asks, "But do you know how to program a computer game?" Courtney responds that she does not plan to *program* a computer game but rather to imagine and to draw one. Video game conceptualization and design is certainly an important and highly skilled path. But in comparison to the actual computing girls of the era, Courtney's arcade gaming acumen falls short of the computing potential that young female gamers were already thought to have cultivated in the 1980s.

This discrepancy speaks to the ongoing cultural tensions that informed the significant backlash faced by Mattel in the early 2010s around their "Computer Engineer Barbie" ("After Backlash"). While "Computer Engineer Barbie" was initially met with excitement and widespread support, the release of the accompanying book, *Barbie: I can be.... A Computer Engineer* prompted even more widespread criticism. In the book,

Barbie is designing a video game, but, in a narrative detail that recalls Courtney's lack of computing skills, she requires the programming assistance of Steven and Brian to turn it into a real game. Then, Barbie crashes her computer, and the boys once again save the day. Since then, Mattel has released "Robotics Engineer" Barbie and partnered with Tynker to offer integrated Barbie-themed programming games across the two companies' websites (Mauk et al. 395). The parallels between Courtney 1986! And Computer Engineer Barbie demonstrate how corporate efforts to encourage young women to cultivate computing skills are still beset by cultural contradictions.

Barbie's ability to suggest careers that girls might one day have contrasts with the AG/PC model of celebrating the culture of girlhood for its own sake. The distinction between AG/PC's emphasis on childhood pursuits and Barbie's focus on long-term career prospects is representative of the tension between Courtney's interest in imagining and playing video games and her seeming disinterest in other kinds of computing skills. The space for creativity and play may serve girls like Courtney better in the long run anyway, since these activities cultivate creative thinking and cultural knowledge. At the same time, the face that Courtney does not have the opportunity to acquire further technical skills threatens to put her behind her peers—a casualty of the so-called computer revolution.

Girl and Games: Then and Now

The dual concerns raised at the conclusion of the previous section attune us to inquiries raised in relation to girls and games across the last thirty years: narrative and game design, skill building, and career enhancement in girls gaming for education (Cassell and Jenkins 4; Newman 154). Since the 1990s, gaming and computing have in many ways become more gender-segregated realms despite feminist gains made in broader society. Female enrolment in computer science is down, women hold fewer jobs in computing, and "Gamergate" in the early 2010s revealed the virulent misogyny present in some corners of contemporary gaming culture (Sharma et al. 1–2; Mortensen 790; Todd 65). Courtney's collection, including a doll-sized, neon cassette tape and Walkman, a Caboodles accessories kit, and *Pac-Man* thermos and lunchbox, is appealing to both girls and nostalgic adult women who were themselves girls in the 1980s.[1] Under the appearance of pure 1980s-ness, Courtney's collection taps into the rhetoric of girl power (including electronic skill) in the 1980s to address the ongoing tension between the feminist aim for increased girls' technological access, representation, and education for girls and the capitalist aim to have more workers and more consumers for the tech industry (Cassell and Jenkins 4). Setting the collection in the 1980s creates a subtle opening for AG/PC to take on the more expansive and contemporary issues around girls' computing culture without ever explicitly stating that this is what they are doing.

This tension opens another modulation of Ngai's *cuteness* paradigm. In this case, space for girls to pursue and hone their computing abilities might superficially look like a matter of playing games with cutesy characters and accessories, while it is actually an opportunity to cultivate *powerful* computing skills that they will need for various pursuits in later years. However, the likelihood remains that these computing skills will also re-inscribe girls back into a capitalist system that promises neoliberal self-empowerment and fulfillment rather than leading to systemic change (Mauk et al. 398; Banet-Weiser 172). While the initial release of Courtney was accompanied by an emphasis on AG/PC's partnership with "Girls Who Code" (GWC), this affiliation is now only visible in a few places on the AG/PC website. Customers still have the option to read about the work of GWC and donate to them through AG/PC, but this information has been relegated to peripheral locations rather than on the main Courtney doll page. This ambivalence is symptomatic of how Courtney orients young readers, players, and customers to video gaming representation and narrative, computer education, and gender without being overly explicit that these issues are ongoing rather than just historical.

In the 1990s, the "girls game" movement gained steam as a way to encourage more girls to be video gamers and in turn to improve the technological skills that are perceived to accompany regular gaming. This diffuse movement included personal computer games, console-based games, and mobile games like Gameboy and Disney's film-specific electronics. Multiple scholars at the time identified key themes that appealed to girls, including a shift away from good vs. evil plots to more character-centered ones, representations of social relationships, and brighter, more colorful graphics (Cassell and Jenkins 21; Subrahmanyan and Greenfield 53, 57). However, Yasmin B. Kafai's study of video game designs done by third graders also found significant overlap between boys' and girls' video game designs in the use of fantasy and adventure elements (93). That said, she noted that girls had less developed video game skills and that only 25 percent of female participants reported regularly playing video games (which in that case was home console or PC-based). This disparity is not reflective of skill, but rather of access. Given the same opportunities, girls had equivalent technological skills to boys (92–95). However, they were more likely to have computer time at school usurped by their male colleagues and were less willing to fight for it (Cassell and Jenkins 12–13). More recently, scholars across several fields have suggested that one way to encourage girls to identify as programmers is through narrative. This includes producing literature and videos about STEM fields, providing female role models, and building narratives into video games that appeal to the ways girls want to interact with technology—or are perceived to want to interact anyway. These narrative strategies range from hailing girls as would-be computer users to facilitating professionalization from a young age (Sharma et al. 3; Haroldson and Ballard 1; Pinkard 479–481).

In *Courtney Changes the Game*, Courtney's video game incorporates elements that would be appealing across genders, including the fact that the game takes place in outer space and that her leading character, Crystal Starshooter, fights various aliens. The book makes this explicit when Justin, the cool bully in her class, even admits that the game idea is "super cool." However, Courtney's design idea also hits several major "girl preferences" from the studies in *From Barbie to Mortal Kombat*. Crystal Starshooter is inspired by *Challenger* astronaut Christa McAuliffe, whom Courtney feels a strong emotional connection to since she is a teacher and a mom. Crystal wears a sparkly purple space suit and a high ponytail. Finally, the key twist in *Courtney* comes when she decides that, rather than fighting a big alien boss battle, the final level of the video game will involve recruiting all the previously defeated aliens to work together with Crystal Starshooter to solve Earth's climate change disaster. To suggest empowerment and ground-breaking video game design, Courtney combines the broad appeal of a fantasy location in outer space with "girl preferences," including camaraderie with adversaries and working to solve real world social problems. The game also positions the player as an astronaut, creating another avenue to identify with women in STEM.

Unlike the featured literature of recent computer education campaigns, the Courtney collection does not suggest particular computer educational activities or career goals. While this might seem to render her powerless to effect change, the opposite may in fact be true. The Courtney collection encourages girl to take up *gaming* as a diverse field of activities that offers them modes to pursue different interests encompassing play, imagination, and possibly computing skills, rather than limiting them to a particular skill set. Instead of enforcing a set of expectations that aligns with a patriarchal technology culture, the Courtney collection sparks possibilities for a more diffuse set of practices with technology that are also more available to girls regardless of circumstance (Harvey 656). This includes designing game narratives and interfaces for various platforms (since Courtney's game never designates a platform and it's seemingly unimportant) and using publicly available affordable gaming spaces.

Beyond Courtney, the AG/PC website has hosted numerous free games for girls since at least the early 2000s—the Kaya and Molly games were personal favorites. Recently, scholars in communication studies have started to question the push to get girls into coding—largely because in the near future these coding jobs may not exist or are unlikely to offer the same financial rewards that they currently do. If anything, the heavy emphasis on coding rather than holistic skills may relegate future generations of women to computing grunt work (Mauk et al. 397; Charette; Costa). While Courtney's dismissal of the idea to actually program her game on the computer seems to reflect a moment of powerlessness, her disinterest both calls back to an earlier generation of female video game designers and may actually help maintain a dynamic opening to technology for girls. Rather than conditioning particular behaviors, the Courtney collection is creating play contexts in which girls might imaginatively pursue different aspects of gaming, computing, and technology.

Conclusion

The latest American Girl doll collection is a commodification of the deeply ambivalent relationship between girls and technology. Dolls are historically a site of tension between play and the acquisition of labor skills (which continues to include cultivating domestic capabilities). Their seeming powerlessness as cute, inanimate, and feminine playthings belies the powerful ways that they can prompt and condition girls to take part in gendered capitalist labor—while continuing to appear powerless under the childhood whim of the player. Although Courtney 1986! is presented as a historical toy, the inclusion of electronic technology as a key aspect of her texts and objects places her in an ongoing dialogue about the relationship between girls and technology in American culture. This includes the frequent exclusion of girls from computing history and the multiple and ongoing efforts to offer technical training to girls.

Amid Courtney's various narrative encounters with technology, as well as through the numerous replica objects available for purchase, AG/PC avoids prescribing specific modes of technological behavior. As a result, the collection offers multiple entry points for girls to be technological users while ultimately suggesting that the only right way to be a user is to do so with the energy of "girl power." Following AG/PC's ongoing model, specific skills are secondary to helping young girls develop individualized neoliberal attitudes (Gill and Kanai 321; Zaslow 54). Courtney's music video and song show Courtney in the computer game. But rather than offering an "edutainment" model, the video highlights attitudes that

Courtney should cultivate about herself: "Totally discovering, what's so uniquely me! Level up for adventure, no challenge bigger than her, she'll find strength and confidence."

If "powerless" dolls are making "powerful" appeals, the Courtney collection encourages girls to engage in diverse creative and technological pursuits—while still hailing them as girls who might just want to play rather than professionalize themselves at the age of nine. Similarly, the explicit and ambient feminism in the Courtney collection extends the shift—that initially gained steam in the 1980s—away from toys of past generations that helped rehearse maternal, romantic, and domestic skills to the exclusion of all else. That said, factors like race, class, and (dis)ability still impact what kinds of girls have access to American Girl, and, by extension, what kinds of girls have access to "Girl Power" (Banet-Weiser 172; Osei-Kofi 2; Schalk 166). Despite being set in the 1980s, Courtney's emphasis on individualized "Girl Power" and the ongoing resonance of multiple ambivalent narratives about girlhood and technology show how much the game still needs to change.

NOTE

1. Numerous videos, Instagram posts, and a TikTok dance challenge have emerged around the release of Courtney 1986! This includes unboxing videos that marvel at how *cute* her merchandise is and its similarity to items owned by the women as children in the 1980s. The Instagram account "adventuresindollcollecting" has even taken it upon herself to cross the Courtney-verse with *Stranger Things* by making her an appropriately sized t-shirt for the camp that the character Dustin attends.

WORKS CITED

"After Backlash, Computer Engineer Barbie Gets New Set Of Skills" *NPR*, 22 November 2014.

Atari Home Computers. "We've Brought the Computer Age Home (Commercial, 1981)." *Youtube*, uploaded by The Museum of Classic Chicago Television, 20 March 2008.

Banet-Weiser, Sarah, and Kate M. Miltner. "#Masculinitysofragile: Culture, Structure, and Networked Misogyny." *Feminist Media Studies*, vol. 16, no. 1, 2015, pp. 171–174, doi:10.1080/14680777.2016.1120490.

Bayus, Barry L. et al. "The Financial Rewards of New Product Introductions in the Personal Computer Industry." *Management Science*, vol. 49, no. 2, 2003, pp. 197–210, doi:10.1287/mnsc.49.2.197.12741.

Cassell, Justine, and Henry Jenkins. "Chess For Girls? Feminism and Computer Games." *From Barbie to Mortal Kombat: Gender and Computer Games*, edited by Justine Cassell and Henry Jenkins. MIT Press, 1998, pp. 2–45.

Charette, Robert N. "The STEM Crisis is a Myth." *IEEE Spectrum*, 30 August 2013.

Clair, Dick, and Jenna McMahon, creators. *The Facts of Life*. NBC, 1988.

Costa, Daniel. "STEM Labor Shortages?" *Economic Policy Institute*, 19 November 2012.

Cote, Amanda C. *Gaming Sexism: Gender and Identity in the Era of Casual Video Games*. New York University Press, 2020.

Deanda, Michael Anthony et al. ""Families, Friendship, and Feelings": American Girl, Authenticating Experiences, and the Transmediation of Girlhood." *The Journal of Popular Culture*, vol. 51, no. 4, 2018, pp. 972–996.

De La Cruz, Lauren. "Magnetic Memory Things: Children's Toys as Objects of Emotion, Memory, and Femininity in U.S. Popular Culture." 2019. Northwestern University, PhD dissertation.

Diamond, Nina, et al. "American Girl and the Brand Gestalt: Closing the Loop on Sociocultural Branding Research." *Journal of Marketing*, vol. 73, no. 3, 2009, pp. 118–134.

Dillon, Roberto. *The Golden Age of Video Games: The Birth of a Multi-Billion Dollar Industry*. AK Peters/CRC Press, 2011.

Donovan, Tristan. *Replay: The History of Video Games*. Yellow Ant, 2010.

Ernkvist, Mirko "Down Many Times, but Still Playing the Game: Creative Destruction and Industry Crashes in the Early Video Game Industry 1971–1986." Södertörns högskola, 2008, pp. 161–191.

Gary, Kelli M. *How to Win Video Games*. Pocket Books, 1982.

Gill, Rosalind, and Akane Kanai "Mediating Neoliberal Capitalism: Affect, Subjectivity and Inequality." *Journal of Communication*, vol. 68, 2018, pp. 318–326.

Haroldson, Rachelle, and Dave Ballard. "Alignment and Representation in computer science: an analysis of picture books and graphic novels for K-8 students." *Computer Science Education*, 2020, pp. 1–26.

Harvey, Alison, and Stephanie Fisher. "Growing Pains: Feminisms and Intergenerationality in Digital Games." *Feminist Media Studies*, vol. 16, no. 4, 2016, pp. 648–662, doi:10.1080/14680777.2016.1193295.

Hertz, Kellen. *Courtney Changes the Game*. American Girl Publishing, 2020.

Kafai, Yasmin B. "Video Game Designs by Girls and Boys: Variability and Consistency of Gender Differences." *From Barbie to Mortal Kombat: Gender and Computer Games*, edited by Justine Cassell and Henry Jenkins. MIT Press, 1998, pp. 90–114.

Kearney, Mary Celeste "Girls' Media Studies." *Feminist Media Histories*, vol. 4, no. 2, 2018, pp. 90–94.

Kent, Steven L. *The Ultimate History of Video Games: From Pong to Pokémon and Beyond*. Three Rivers Press, 2001.

Kocurek, Carly A. *Coin -Operated Americans: Rebooting Boyhood at the Video Game Arcade*. The University of Minnesota Press, 2015.

Lee, Marie. "Computer-friendly." *Seventeen*, November 1985, pp. 58.

Light, Jennifer S. "When Computers Were Women." *Technology and Culture*, vol. 40, no 3, 1999, pp. 455–483.

Maeroff, Gene. "Get Ready for the Computer Revolution." *Seventeen*, October 1983, pp. 147–148, 162.

"Matchmaker." *Family Ties*, written by Bruce David and Bruce Helford, directed by Barbara Schultz, NBC, 1987.

Mauk, Maureen et al. "The Can-Do Girl Goes to Coding Camp: A Discourse Analysis of News Reports on Coding Initiatives Designed for Girls." *Learning, Media and Technology*, vol. 45, no. 4, 2020, pp. 395–408, doi:10.1080/17439884.2020.1781889.

McRobbie, Angela. "Feminism and Youth Culture from 'Jackie' to 'Just Seventeen.'" Macmillan Education Ltd., 1991.

Mortensen, Torill Elvira. "Anger, Fear, and Games: The Long Event of #Gamergate." *Games and Culture*, vol. 13, no. 8, 2016, pp. 787–806, doi:10.1177/1555412016640408.

Newman, Michael Z. *Atari Age: The Emergence of Video Games in America*. MIT Press, 2017.

Ngai, Sianne. *Our Aesthetic Categories: Zany, Cute, Interesting*. Harvard University Press, 2012.

Nooney, Laine. "A Pedestal, A Table, A Love Letter: Archaeologies of Gender in Videogame History." Game Studies, vol. 13, no. 2, 2013.

Osei-Kofi, Nana. "American Girls: Breaking Free." Feminist Formations, vol. 25, no. 1, 2013, pp. 1–7, doi:10.1353/ff.2013.0003.

Pinkard, Nichole et al. "Digital Youth Divas: Exploring Narrative-Driven Curriculum to

Spark Middle School Girls' Interest in Computational Activities." *Journal of the Learning Sciences*, vol. 26, no. 3, 2017, pp. 477–516, doi:10.1080/10508406.2017.1307199.

"Results: Here's What You Say About Video Games." *Seventeen*, November 1982, 82.

Rottenberg, Catherine. "The Rise of Neoliberal Feminism." *Cultural Studies*, vol. 28, no. 3, 2013, pp. 418–437, doi:10.1080/09502386.2013.857361.

Schalk, Sami. "Beforever?: Disability in American Girl Historical Fiction." *Children's Literature*, vol. 45, no. 1, 2017, pp. 164–187, doi:10.1353/chl.2017.0008.

Seiter, Ellen. *Sold Separately: Parents and Children in Consumer Culture*. Rutgers University Press, 1993.

Sharma, Kshitij et al. "Improving Girls' Perception of Computer Science as a Viable Career Option through Game Playing and Design: Lessons from a Systematic Literature Review." *Entertainment Computing*, vol. 36, 2021, doi:10.1016/j.entcom.2020.100387.

Sherry, John F. "The Work of Play at American Girl Place." *Social Psychology Quarterly*, vol. 72, no. 3, 2009, pp. 199–202.

Spigel, Lynn. *Welcome to the Dreamhouse: Popular Media and Postwar Suburbs*. Duke University Press, 2001.

Story, Nancy Duffey. *Pleasant Company's American Girls Collection: The Corporate Construction of Girlhood*. 2002. University of Georgia, PhD dissertation.

Subrahmanyan, Kaveri and Patricia M. Greenfield. "Computers Games for Girls: What Makes Them Play." *From Barbie to Mortal Kombat: Gender and Computer Games*, edited by Justine Cassell and Henry Jenkins. MIT Press, 1998, pp. 46–71.

Susina, Jan. "American Girls Collection: Barbies with a Sense of History." *Children's Literature Association Quarterly*, vol. 24, no 3, 1999, pp. 130–135.

Todd, Cherie. "Commentary: Gamergate and Resistance to the Diversification of Gaming Culture." *Women's Studies Journal*, vol. 29, no. 1, 2015, pp. 64–67.

Yordan, Carolyn A. "Behind the Screens: Teens Earn Big Bucks Designing Video Games." *Seventeen*, July 1983, pp. 69.

Zaslow, Emilie. *Playing with America's Doll: A Cultural Analysis of the American Girl Collection*. Palgrave Macmillan, 2017.

Back to the (Gendered) Future

Feminist Nostalgia in Netflix's
Stranger Things *and* GLOW

ANN M. CIASULLO

Lately, U.S. pop culture has been characterized by a turn back in time—specifically, back to the decade when Spielberg, shoulder pads, and spandex reigned supreme: the 1980s. From film remakes such as *Ghostbusters* (2016) and *It* (2017) to television reboots and revivals such as *Fuller House* (2016–2020) and *Cobra Kai* (2018–present), it's clear that, as Marc Binder writes in *Medium,* "the '80s are immortal in today's cultural discourse." I came of age in the early 1980s, so I am both drawn to and fascinated by this recent nostalgia boom—for personal reasons, insofar as it addresses the anxieties and aesthetics of my youth, but also for intellectual reasons. Having written about nostalgia in other contexts, I am aware of its complex history as well as its much-maligned reputation among serious thinkers, those who dismiss nostalgic impulses as simplistic, reactionary, and even embarrassing.[1] Indeed, over the past three hundred years, the definition of nostalgia has shifted dramatically; long understood as a physical affliction (first identified as such by Swiss medical student Johannes Hofer in 1688),[2] by the mid-twentieth century the propensity for nostalgia was understood to signal a psychological and emotional form of regression. As Jean Starobinski observes in his influential essay "The Idea of Nostalgia," by the 1960s the term had "taken on a pejorative connotation … impl[ying] the useless yearning for a world or for a way of life from which one has been irrevocably severed" (125).

For those of us both interested and invested in nostalgia, however, all is not lost. While nostalgia can be a problematic representational mode in its twin tendencies of simplifying and sanitizing the past, it also has the capacity to be multifaceted and even progressive. Svetlana Boym, in her landmark study *The Future of Nostalgia*, identifies two distinct strands of nostalgia: restorative and reflective. While the former sees the past as a "perfect snapshot," a "prelapsarian moment" to which we should return (49), the latter aims at "narrat[ing] the relationship between past, present and future," thereby "open[ing] up a multitude of potentialities, non-teleological possibilities of historical development" (50). Janelle L. Wilson likewise asserts in her essay "Here and Now, Then and There: Nostalgia as a Time and Space Phenomenon" that nostalgia "is not a mere passive longing for the past, but a potentially dynamic vehicle for (re)envisioning and (re)creating various pasts and futures" (490). Taking my cue from both Boym and Wilson, I will examine two of the more popular 1980s-throwbacks to emerge in the past few years, both Netflix original programs: *Stranger Things* (2016–present) and *GLOW* (2017–2019). These shows share many commonalities: they both take place within the same timeframe (the early- to mid–1980s); they both feature ensemble casts; and, most important for the purposes of my study, they both foreground issues of gender as part of their narrative arcs. In this essay, I argue that these shows present us with a reflective, feminist nostalgia in their narratives in two ways: through an engagement with and subversion of standard 1980s gender tropes, and through complex character development, particularly in relation to the image of the 1980s working girl/mother. Taken together, *Stranger Things* and *GLOW* bring different but equally striking variations of a feminist future to the past.

"I look forward to you never doubting me again"[3]: *Feminist Nostalgia in* Stranger Things

Of the two shows considered herein, *Stranger Things* has garnered far more media attention for various reasons, not the least of which is its narrative foundation in adolescent culture—a foundation that, more than any other aspect of the show, calls upon nostalgia for its effectiveness. Astute viewers know, for example, that in terms of the show's characters, the kids of *Stranger Things* hearken back to those from the 1980s hit films *E.T.* and *The Goonies*.[4] And while there are many aspects of the kids' relationships worth exploring—including the budding adolescent romance between El and Mike, the initially tense but ultimately touching female friendship between El and Max, and the outsider status of "zombie boy" Will, who is implicitly identified as queer[5]—it is to the teenagers, specifically Nancy Wheeler and Steve Harrington, that I wish to turn my attention. Rose Butler asserts that the teenagers are "the show's most under-explored characters" (73), and I agree. While in its first season the show participates in standards '80s tropes vis-à-vis these characters, in its second and third seasons, a feminist narrative emerges in *Stranger Things*, one that complicates and even turns upside down (pun intended) the show's initial investment in these tropes. Through Steve but especially Nancy, the show participates in reflective nostalgia, bringing contemporary understandings of gender to the past of Hawkins, Indiana.

It makes sense to begin by considering the two characters together, since that is how they first appear in the series, and since they so clearly hearken back to the familiar couples of 1980s teen films. Nancy is the strait-laced, studious, proper middle-class suburban girl; Steve is the rich, athletic bad boy with amazing hair, a "one-dimensional jerk of a boyfriend with a penchant for shotgunning beers" (Wanshel). We don't know exactly why they're attracted to each other, but for the purposes of the nostalgic narrative, it doesn't matter; they are types, tropes, ready-made characters whose simplicity is the point. At school, Nancy walks alongside Steve, hugging her Trapper Keeper, while Steve imitates Tom Cruise's character Joel from *Risky Business*, singing "Old Time Rock and Roll" to amuse her. "You are a cliché" ("Chapter Two," *ST*), she says to him, and she is right. While deviations in this stereotypical relationship begin to emerge toward the end of Season 1—with Nancy wielding a gun, showing off impressive shooting skills ("Chapter Five," *ST*), and buying a bear trap for her "monster hunting" ("Chapter Six," *ST*), and Steve showing remorse by helping to remove the slur against Nancy that his friends spray-painted on the movie theater marquee ("Chapter Seven," *ST*)—the series nevertheless wraps up with the couple intact, hanging out at Nancy's house at Christmas. There's the suggestion that her sweetness has had a softening effect on Steve— he wears a cheesy holiday sweater and acts decently to Jonathan, whom he earlier had bullied—but even this feels like a familiar trope, akin to Andie and Blane in the '80s classic *Pretty in Pink*, thereby suggesting that the good girl's role is to help reform the bad boy. In this way, the gender politics of Season 1 felt both familiar and conservative, with the typical gender roles of '80s films replaying in this twenty-first-century nostalgic production.

But then along comes Season 2: after a quick break-up ("Chapter Two," *ST2*), Nancy drops her Trapper Keeper and her boyfriend and becomes a kick-ass heroine, "going on a monster slayin' revenge spree all in the name of her dead best friend" (Kakadelis). Steve's character, too, takes an almost 180-degree turn, from embodying the Tom Cruise swagger of the '80s to embracing the role of mentor and protector à la *Adventures in Babysitting* (1987), a role that has earned him the nickname of "Dad Steve" on the internet.[6] Interestingly, these character developments stemmed in part from criticism of Season 1's gender representation and its repetition of tired tropes, critiques that the creators of the show, the Duffer

Brothers, took seriously. The result is that viewers have the pleasure of seeing Nancy breaking out of her safe suburban life and assuming a role as a fearless agent of change, using her smarts to get at the truth about Barb. When she and Jonathan are briefly held captive in Hawkins Lab, traditionally feminine Nancy yells at the security camera: "Hey asshole! Let us out of here!" She secretly tapes the conversation they have with Dr. Owens so as to expose the government's secrets, telling Jonathan that she wants to "burn that lab to the ground" ("Chapter Four," *ST2*). And when Hopper asks Jonathan if he knows how to use a gun and Jonathan hesitates, Nancy steps up and says, "I can," catching the weapon as Hopper tosses it to her. While Nancy hunts for monsters and the truth, Steve abandons his prior douchebag persona and assumes the role of protector ("Chapter Six," "Chapter Eight," *ST2*). "The little shits are real trouble, you know?" he says to Nancy jokingly ("Chapter Eight," *ST2*), but this statement also underscores his affection for them—an affection highlighted by Robin in Season 3, when she asks, "How many kids are you friends with?" ("Chapter One," *ST3*). While it could certainly be argued that Kick-Ass Nancy and Dad Steve aren't "accurate" '80s characters, it could also be argued that '80s films, with their own inherently conservative bent, didn't allow for the possibility or space for such characters.[7] In his essay "Branding Netflix with Nostalgia," Matthias Stephan describes such a narrative move as a "reconsideration of the past" (31), one that suggests that nostalgia can engage in storytelling strategies that are feminist in their challenge to conventional gender roles.

To my mind, the most progressive gender development in Season 3 (alongside the addition of the funny, dynamic Robin and her reveal to Steve that she is a lesbian ["Chapter Seven," *ST3*]) is the transition of, or possibly merging of, Nancy from the Final Girl—a term coined by Carol Clover to describe the "last girl standing" in horror films[8]—to the Working Girl. One of the first images of Nancy in Season 3 features her walking quickly to work, the office of the *Hawkins Post*, with Huey Lewis and the News' 1982 hit "Workin' for a Livin'" playing non-diegetically over the scene ("Chapter One," *ST3*). Thus, from the start of this season, Nancy is situated within the workplace (fig. 1). In doing this, the series calls upon another familiar 1980s trope: that of the feminist working woman, exemplified in the films *9 to 5* (1980) and *Working Girl* (1988). Still a teenager but no longer interested in the frivolities of high school, Nancy emerges as an ambitious, inquisitive employee who aspires to be a reporter for the paper, but who is continually "put in her place" by the sexist male reporters who just want her to smile and deliver their lunch. They laugh at her, play practical jokes on her, and demean her on a daily basis. In this way, Nancy is not unlike the women in *9 to 5* who want simply to be taken seriously

Fig. 1: Nancy Wheeler (Natalia Dyer) as Nancy Drew, detective and working girl, finding answers to the mysteries of Hawkins (*Stranger Things*, 21 Laps Entertainment, 2016–present).

but whose male boss calls them "honey" and condescends to them. And she is not unlike women in 2021 who want simply to be taken seriously but whose male bosses even now continue to treat them dismissively. As Sarah Halle Corey notes, "Nancy's storyline, unfortunately, could just as easily take place today as it does in the 1980s." When Nancy expresses her frustration over this sexism to Jonathan, saying, "It's humiliating.... You don't know what it's like" ("Chapter Four," *ST3*), she's speaking for herself and for any woman, past or present, who's experienced workplace sexism. With this expansion of the spaces in which Nancy moves—spaces that are dominated primarily by men who won't listen to her, much less take her seriously—*Stranger Things* resists the urge for a "perfect snapshot" of the past by showing the uncomfortable parallels between then and now.

In the face of the patriarchal forces working against her, Nancy digs in her heels (or rather, ballerina slippers—she is both fashionable and practical) and disobeys her boss' orders to stop investigating the rat poisoning problem, telling a nervous Jonathan, "Ask for forgiveness, not permission" ("Chapter Two," *ST3*). Her dogged pursuit of the truth comes as the expense of her comfort in the workplace and her safety in the world, as the very men who harassed her in the office become the Flayed who hunt her in the hospital ("Chapter Five," *ST3*). Mocking her for her drive and curiosity, the male reporters at the *Hawkins Post* diminish Nancy by calling her "Nancy Drew"—but in fact, they are accurate to identify her as such, since Nancy is the only person in the newsroom to take seriously the threats emerging via the rat poisoning in Hawkins (fig. 1). Smart, fearless, and stubborn, Nancy is determined to solve the mystery presented to her by Mrs. Driscoll, who calls Nancy a "little detective" ("Chapter Two," *ST3*)—and she does. In Season 1, Nancy says of Barb's disappearance, "No one is listening to me" ("Chapter Four," *ST*). In Season 3, her male bosses' failure to listen to her results in their becoming the Flayed and ultimately (and satisfyingly) being destroyed by El. In this way, Season 3 most clearly positions Nancy as a feminist heroine, collaborating with but not dependent upon her male peers for success. And interestingly, the person who encourages Nancy to pursue her career is her mother, Karen, who tells her, "You're a fighter…. If you believe in this story … finish it" ("Chapter Four," *ST3*). By situating Nancy as the Working Girl, Season 3 of *Stranger Things* presents us with an '80s heroine whose goal is not to win the boy (*Sixteen Candles, Pretty in Pink*) or simply to kill the monster (*Nightmare on Elm Street*), but who imagines, in the words of her mother, having her story published in the *Indianapolis Star*. The triumph of the Working Girl: it's a story of the present as much as of the past.

"Fuck polite and comatose"[9]*: Feminist Nostalgia in GLOW*

GLOW and *Stranger Things* share much in common, most obviously a nostalgic impulse realized in large part through the aesthetics of the show. Like *Stranger Things*, *GLOW* indulges in '80s music (its theme is "The Warrior" by Scandal), fashion (big hair, neon, and spandex), and of course pop culture references (the show itself is based on an actual mid–80s show, *Gorgeous Ladies of Wrestling* [1986–1989]). What sets *GLOW* apart from *Stranger Things*, however, is that almost all of the characters are adult women. This female ensemble cast perhaps comes as no surprise upon learning that *GLOW*'s executive producer is Jenji Kohan, best known for creating one of Netflix's biggest hits, *Orange Is the New Black* (2013–2019). But the result is that the relationship between nostalgia and gender is always at the forefront of *GLOW* because issues of gender are at the forefront of so many of the female characters' experiences on the show. And as a result of its concept—a nostalgic show based on an actual 1980s show in which the female wrestlers took on stereotypical roles vis-à-vis gender, race, and ethnicity—*GLOW* engages with '80s tropes by necessity. Sophie Gilbert, writing for *The Atlantic*, observes that *GLOW* "has fun with the fact that the characters are literally grappling with female stereotypes in the ring while proving how much more complex and interesting the real women are."

The women are indeed complex, and through their sophisticated characterization, they become far more than any of '80s types they represent in the ring. The show's central protagonist, Ruth Wilder, most explicitly espouses feminist ideals, at one point singing the theme to *The Mary Tyler Moore Show* to rally her co-workers ("Viking Funeral"). She also sleeps with her best friend's husband; becomes pregnant by him and gets an abortion; tries to insert herself into positions of authority in the production of the show and is routinely foiled; takes on the wrestling persona of the most hated type in the Cold War era of the 1980s, the Commie Russian Zoya the Destroyer; and falls in love with her much-older boss, Sam Sylvia. Arthie Premkumar, whose alter ego is the Beirut Bomber, figuratively wrestles with the racist hatred directed at her by the audience and, toward the end of Season 2, with her feelings for Yolanda, who plays Junk Chain. Their same-sex desire is both represented and validated in the series, and as such, the narrative allows their relationship to flourish in a way that would have been nearly impossible in an actual 1980s film or TV show, thereby providing contemporary viewers with a (re)envisioning of the past. Tammé Dawson, whose stage name is Welfare Queen, likewise wrestles with the ethics of her alter ego: a woman based on a mythical character very much of the era, repeatedly identified by then-President Ronald Reagan as a shiftless social parasite. In one of the most poignant episodes, Tammé's son Ernest, who attends Stanford, comes to a performance and sees his mother enact the worst stereotypes of the black welfare mother. Rather than reject her, though, he comes to terms with his mother's choices—choices that make *his* life possible ("Mother of All Matches"). All of these storylines are emblematic of the characterization that occurs on *GLOW*: in calling upon the '80s trope, it establishes and maintains its commitment to nostalgia. But in shattering those tropes, it brings to the show's past a feminist future, one that insists we look beyond and challenge racist, sexist, and classist stereotypes.[10] Put another way, these tropes function paradoxically not to simplify or stereotype the women but to serve as the backdrop against which their characterization unfolds.[11]

While there is more to say about all of these characters, and while Ruth might be the most obvious point of analysis given her feminist ideals, I wish to focus the remainder of this section on the character whose development differently but equally engages in progressive reflective nostalgia: Debbie Eagan. At the opening of the series, no one seems more like a 1980s stereotype of conventional womanhood than Debbie. Blonde, beautiful, and confident, Debbie exudes authority among her female peers because, unlike the other women in the ring, she has had an acting career on *Paradise Cove*, a popular soap opera. The quintessential popular girl, Debbie gets what she wants when she wants it. As a result, I would argue that she represents the female character about whom viewers are invited to feel an ongoing ambivalence. Debbie has been wronged by her husband and best friend, and this fact alone makes her sympathetic. But *GLOW* doesn't allow us to settle easily into such sympathy. Indeed, across all three seasons, Debbie is bitchy and snobbish (she initially views the wrestling as stupid and believes herself to be superior to the other women), selfish and self-serving (she steals the character of Liberty Belle from a fellow wrestler, and she uses her smarts to renegotiate a contract but doesn't offer her help to the rest of the cast), and vindictive (she makes Ruth pay for her sins multiple times, including interfering in Ruth's budding romance with Russell and, most notably, breaking Ruth's leg in a match). As Rachel Cote notes, Debbie uses her beauty, whiteness, and social class to her advantage, often at the expense of the other women in the entourage. She is the adult version of Caroline, Jake's girlfriend from *Sixteen Candles*: the popular mean girl to watch out for. But *GLOW* allows Debbie to be more than that. In the first episode, she tells Ruth how happy she is to be at home with her baby, but we know early on that the domestic life is not enough for Debbie. Her desire to reject this life is exemplified in the episode in which she sells every item in her home in an effort to rid herself of her life with Mike, her cheating husband ("Mother of All Matches"). When she complains to Sam about her job, saying, "I could be at home with my baby," Sam replies in a way that strikes a chord with Debbie: "You love this shit…. If you were sitting at home with that kid, your life would become just anger and resentment" ("This is One"). And he is right. In one of the most satisfying and hilarious moments of *GLOW*, Debbie, in character as Liberty Belle, announces to the audience, "I've been

Fig. 2: Debbie Eagan (Betty Gilpin) imagines life outside the ring and in the driver's seat as a producer and woman in charge (*GLOW*, Tilted Productions, 2017–2019).

baking pies at home. PIES OF RAGE!" ("Every Potato"). She speaks a truth about what life solely in the domestic realm would have meant to her. In these moments, Debbie emerges as more than the trope of the bitchy popular girl; she gives voice to the ways in which she has felt trapped, both physically and emotionally, by her expected gender roles, and how she aspires to free herself from them (fig. 2).

The life she does want, however, is not a simple one, especially for a woman in the 1980s, because what she wants is to be in charge of GLOW *and* to be a present mother for her baby Randy. If Nancy is the Working Girl, Debbie is the Working Mother—ambitious in her career, conflicted about the relationship between motherhood and a professional life, and frustrated by the ways in which Bash and Sam routinely exclude her from the decision-making process. Like Nancy in the newsroom, Debbie is routinely "dismissed, ignored and patronized by the men she works with" (Poniewozik). When the show has an opportunity to grow, Debbie suggests that Bash and Sam—the two male producers—come over for dinner so together they can all strategize on how best to proceed ("Candy of the Year"). She is stood up by them and joined instead by Tammé, who commiserates with her about the challenges of womanhood and motherhood. A few episodes later, Bash and Sam storm the office of network head Tom Grant without her, telling her afterwards that it was a "guy thing." When she expresses frustration, Sam chastises her, "Don't get back up on your feminist high horse" ("Work the Leg"). By Season 3, when she begins to come into her own as a producer, she feels at once a deep satisfaction in her successes and a real ambivalence about motherhood. Getting high with Cherry, she confesses: "Look, I love Randy. But sometimes ... oh god, sometimes, I think about how much easier it would be if I'd never had a baby" ("Say Yes"). Only six years earlier, the magazine *Working Mother* began publication; by the mid-1980s, the tension between home and career became a defining feature of the middle-class working woman's life. Through Debbie, GLOW engages in a nostalgia that is at once familiar and painful: familiar to those who lived through it then, and painful for those who continue to live in those tensions now.

The show's engagement with and expansion of the trope of the Working Mother emerges most explicitly—and to my mind, thrillingly—in its third season, when Debbie more fully steps into her role as producer (fig. 2). She is mentored (if only slightly) by a high-powered businesswoman in Las Vegas, Sandy. Sandy figures as both an aspirational and a cautionary character: a woman who has put her career at the center of her life but has seen that the payoffs are few and far between. When Debbie tells Sam that she doesn't like Sandy, Sam replies, "Nobody likes the ghost of Christmas future" ("Up, Up, Up"). Nevertheless, she and Sandy eventually bond, with Sandy encouraging Debbie to step away from the ring and into the position of producer: "You would be amazed at how much more is possible once you let that part [acting] go and pick up the reigns" ("Hot Tub Club"). At the same time, Debbie captures the interest and heart of a wealthy businessman, Tex, who appreciates her smarts and business savvy—to a point. When she tries to help him seal a high-stakes business deal—the purchase of a television network—he tells her he wants to keep his work and his personal life, and potential future wife, separate. "So I'm here to look pretty and make dinners less painful?" she asks him. The implicit answer is yes. "You're my girlfriend, not my partner," he tells her ("A Very GLOW Christmas"). This moment serves as a reminder to Debbie that despite the affection she and Tex feel for each other, he is, like all the men before him, a man who seriously underestimates her ambition, frustration, and rage. But then comes the coup: as Christopher Rosen notes, "when an opportunity for Debbie to grab her agency back presents itself during the season-three finale … she strikes," stealing Tex's deal out from under him. Encouraging Bash to stay closeted and in his marriage for business purposes, the two team up to buy the company before Tex can negotiate his way through the deal. When asked by Bash's lawyers where she got the information about the network, she simply states, "It's my boyfriend's deal. We're swooping in and pulling it out from under him" ("A Very GLOW Christmas").

The season ends with Debbie fully ensconced in the role of the Working Mother, but it refuses to resolve that narrative in the typical '80s manner. Debbie most certainly will not end up with her man, since she is betraying him. And when faced with having to choose between the Vegas show and her son, she does not leave the show, but instead, at the encouragement of her fellow wrestlers, brings her son to her. She is neither Tess in *Working Girl* (who wins both the job and the man in the end) nor J.D. in 1987's *Baby Boom* (who leaves her high-powered corporate world to start a baby food business in rural Vermont), but instead emerges as a character beyond the trope, inviting her former best friend to join her in victory. Chasing Ruth through the airport to share the news of the network deal with her, Debbie excitedly tells her, "I'm going to build us an Eden. Where we run the show. You and me. No more auditions, no more being at the mercy of these fucking idiots. We'll call the shots" ("A Very GLOW Christmas"). Debbie is not a proponent of sisterhood in the same way that Ruth is: she doesn't talk about "feminist principles" ("Perverts are People, Too"); she typically doesn't accompany her peers on outings; she insists on her own space; and when negotiating her contract, she said, "I have to look out for myself now" ("Viking Funeral"). But the season ends with the promise that she will finally be recognized for the producer that she is. There's an implicit through-line from Nancy the Working Girl of *Stranger Things* to Debbie the Working Mother of *GLOW*: both are ambitious, both are ignored by men in power, and in the end, both find their voice and receive validation that their instincts are right. Sean Scanlan observes that "[r]ather than an end reaction to yearning," nostalgia can be a "technique for provoking a secondary reaction" (4). In the case of Debbie Eagan, the "secondary reaction," I would argue, is anger and frustration—both past and present. Indeed, Philip Gauthier identifies *GLOW* as an "important popular culture vehicle for decrying the pervasiveness of sexism in the United States in the 1980s and for confronting it with the present day" (83).[12] Or, as Sara Tatyana Bernstein succinctly and eloquently notes, *GLOW* "offer[s] stories we should have told then but didn't." One of those stories is the story of rage and silence—and insisting upon being heard; an especially important story in the era of #MeToo. At the start of Season 3, Debbie says about her role as a producer, "No one knows who the fuck I am" ("Up, Up, Up"). But the season ends with the promise that she will be known, finally, for the producer that she is. As Debbie yells at Bash after Sam has left Vegas and the two men have screwed her over multiple times: "I am still here and I brought my fucking kid, so there's not a single day I will not be in your face, and I have VERY STRONG vocal cords" ("Hollywood Homecoming"). Through Debbie, the show resists the pull of restorative nostalgia. Rather than inviting us to go back to a time when things were better—because clearly in terms of gender, they were not—it asks us to revisit a time when things were as they still are now. The gendered past is the gendered future, one in which women demand to be heard.[13]

Conclusion: Looking Back, Looking Ahead

In his landmark study *Yearning for Yesterday: A Sociology of Nostalgia*, Fred Davis makes the simple observation that "the material of nostalgic experience is the past" (8). But what is *done* with that material—that is, how we are asked to imagine and interact with the past—determines whether a text's nostalgia is conservative or progressive. Journalist Brian Lowry suggests that whereas *Stranger Things* "mostly revels in the cultural artifacts of those years.... *GLOW* dispenses with the rose-colored glasses, casting a much less flattering light on the era." I agree with Lowry that *Stranger Things* lends itself to a more indulgent, even restorative nostalgia at times, but the past of Hawkins, Indiana, is not always gratifying: homophobia and sexism rear their ugly heads in every season, thereby interrupting the restorative goal of establishing an unequivocally wistful and "positively toned evocation of a lived past" (Davis 18). Rather, both shows, to different degrees, re-envision and re-create the past with the future in mind. The title of my essay suggests as much through it allusion to one of the most enduring films of the 1980s, *Back to the Future*. Not surprisingly, both shows make reference to this film at least once, situating it as a minor part of the episodes.[14] Their references to this pop culture touchstone underscore how *Stranger Things* and *GLOW* bring the future to the past and vice versa, reflecting a gendered past that is at once painfully accurate and hopefully future-looking. While *GLOW* has been canceled by Netflix, *Stranger Things* will return for another season, and, as we watch it, we should heed the words of Sheila from *GLOW* as she snaps a photograph of her fellow wrestlers: "It's history. Keep your eyes open" ("Viking Funeral").

Notes

1. For one of the strongest critiques of nostalgia in these terms, see Christopher Lasch's 1984 essay "The Politics of Nostalgia." For one of the most important explorations and histories of nostalgia, see Fred Davis's 1979 study *Yearning for Yesterday: A Sociology of Nostalgia*.

2. Hofer used the term to describe the ailments of "displaced soldiers, domestic workers and students who developed symptoms in response to their profound homesickness" (Pallister 2).

3. After several episodes in which Jonathan has expressed worry and skepticism over Nancy's investigations into the rat poison, Nancy says this to him after she's been proven right ("Chapter Five," *ST3*).

4. For an excellent overview of the many 1980s allusions employed in the show, see Sam Adams, "*Stranger Things*: How Netflix's Retro Hit Resurrects the Eighties."

5. In my estimation, the development of the kids as characters is far more fraught than that of the teenagers, inasmuch as the show follows the kids through puberty and the awkwardness that characterizes the experience of grappling with the emergence of sexual desire and sexual identity. On the one hand, the show presents a sympathetic portrayal of Will, the outsider among his friends as puberty sets in, and he—and others—recognize his queerness. On the other hand, the plot trajectory directs us away from Will's sexuality and toward the transformation of El from androgynous to traditionally feminine and almost all of the kids paired in heterosexual couplings, exemplified in the dance scene at the Snow Ball in the end of Season 2 (2.10). As Alison Willmore observes, Season 2 concludes with "a blithely happy ending that also came depressingly close to presenting romance as recompense for its characters' heroism." For further discussion of the muting of queerness and nontraditional gender expression in the kids, see Willmore; Lauren Rearick, "The 'Stranger Things' Showrunners Are Being Called Out for Having Sadie Sink Kiss Caleb McLaughlin"; and especially the excellent analysis by Aviva Briefel, "Familiar Things: Snow Ball '84 and Straight Nostalgia." As Briefel observes, "While the end of the first season sustains the characters' queer difference by drawing on the trope of the closet—Will conceals his secret identity in the bathroom, Eleven hides out in the woods—the conclusion to the second season celebrates their initiation into sexual and gender conformity." For an essay that offers a more sympathetic reading of the gender development of the female kids, see Ashley Reed, "Girls Feel Stranger Things, Too."

6. For a heartfelt discussion of how Steve functions as a surrogate father to the kids, especially Dustin, see Lizzy Francis, "Steve Harrington, Babysitter Extraordinaire, is the True Hero of *Stranger Things*." Parallel to my argument, Francis notes in brief that "the Duffer Brother's [sic] whole thing is upending tropes." Butler also provides an insightful

discussion of the changes in Steve, noting that he "subverts expectations created by teen movie archetypes" (77).

7. Through these changes, *Stranger Things* "breaks with the conservatism of teen movies of the decade" (Butler 78).

8. The Final Girl, according to Clover in her book *Men, Women, and Chainsaws*, is also typically a virginal female protagonist who is "intelligent and resourceful in a pinch" (39). While there are some ways in which Nancy does not conform to the characteristics of the Final Girl (most notably in that she is sexually active but not punished for being so), in most ways she embodies the spirit of the character. For further discussion of Nancy as the Final Girl, see Butler 80–81.

9. In the second episode of the series, Sam says this to Debbie so as to describe the life path she's currently on as a soon-to-be-divorced, stay-at-home mom ("Slouch. Submit.").

10. For an excellent discussion of how the characters, particularly the women of color, "tackle the porous boundary between entertainment and exploitation," see Vikram Muthri, "*GLOW*'s Radical Message about Loving Problematic Art."

11. Unfortunately for fans of the series, *GLOW*'s fourth season was cancelled by Netflix, reportedly due to COVID. Particularly disappointing is that viewers will not have the opportunity to see how the show responds to the demands of the actresses of color on the show. In late 2020, Sunita Mani, who plays Arthie, revealed that she and five other actresses on *GLOW* wrote to the showrunners and producers to demand more sophisticated characterization and more visibility. They note how the show tended to "be brief with our story development to serve the in-depth white storylines" (qtd. in Zornosa). The whiteness of the *GLOW*'s central narratives has been noted by some critics of the show as well; Rachel Cote, writing for *The New Republic*, observes that "[d]espite the showrunners' evident—and crucial—concern with diverse racial and sexual dynamics, these two women [Ruth and Debbie] remain planted at the narrative center." The response the actresses of color received was overwhelmingly positive, and the show's creators planned to implement many of the changes recommended by the six actresses. Sadly, these changes will not be realized. But as Mani asserted, "I'd like our voice and behind-the-scenes narrative of representation to be the last word. Not Covid." For more on this issue, see Laura Zornosa, "Before *GLOW* Got Canceled, Its Actresses of Color Felt 'Disempowered' By Their Roles."

12. Gauthier likewise explores the interplay between nostalgia and the narratives of *GLOW*, focusing on how "the different kinds of nostalgia present in *GLOW* make it possible not only to initiate new ways of interpreting and understanding history but also to invest the past and to place it in service of the present" (76)—which, I would argue, is exactly what Debbie's storyline as the Working Mother is doing in the present moment.

13. In an interview in *Entertainment Weekly*, the showrunners themselves discuss how "the constraints of being a woman in 1980s Hollywood" were front-and-center in their minds when writing Season 3, especially its cliffhanger. Underscoring the ways in which their nostalgia is reflective, they also assert that "[w]omen's relationships to a position of power, it hasn't gotten less complicated with time" (Bucksbaum).

14. References to *Back to the Future* appear in *Stranger Things 3*, "Chapter Seven," and *GLOW*, "Money's in the Chase" and "Nothing Shattered."

Works Cited

Adams, Sam. "*Stranger Things*: How Netflix's Retro Hit Resurrects the Eighties" *Rolling Stone* 21 July 2016.

Bernstein, Sara Tatyana. "TV Reboots Aren't Really About Nostalgia." *Buzzfeed News* 21 Aug. 2018.

Binder, Marc. "Why 1980s Nostalgia is Everything." *Medium* 29 Mar. 2000.

Boym, Svetlana. *The Future of Nostalgia*. Basic Books, 2001.

Briefel, Aviva. "Familiar Things: Snow Ball '84 and Straight Nostalgia." *Post45* 4 July 2019.

Bucksbaum, Sydney. "*GLOW* Showrunners Break Down That 'Game-Changing' Season 3 Cliffhanger Ending." *Entertainment Weekly* 9 Aug. 2019.

Butler, Rose. "The Eaten-for-Breakfast Club: Teenage Nightmares in *Stranger Things*." In *Uncovering* Stranger Things: *Essays on Eighties Nostalgia, Cynicism and Innocence in the Series*. Ed. Kevin J. Wetmore, Jr. McFarland, 2018. 72–83.

Clover, Carol. *Men, Women, and Chainsaws: Gender in the Modern Horror Film*. Princeton University Press, 1992.

Corey, Sarah Halle. "Nancy's Workplace Storyline on *Stranger Things 3* is Way Ahead of Its Time." *Elite Daily* 5 July 2019.

Cote, Rachel. "On *GLOW*, Who Gets To Be Empowered?" *The New Republic* 28 June 2018.

Davis, Fred. *Yearning for Yesterday: A Sociology of Nostalgia*. The Free Press, 1979.

Francis, Lizzy. "Steve Harrington, Babysitter Extraordinaire, Is the True Hero of *Stranger Things*." *Fatherly* 2 Nov. 2017.

Gauthier, Phillipe. "Nostalgia as a Problematic Cultural Space: The Example of the Original Netflix Series *GLOW* (2017)." In *Netflix Nostalgia: Streaming the Past on Demand*. Ed. Kathryn Pallister. Lexington Books, 2019. 75–90.

Gilbert, Sophie. "*GLOW* is a Total Delight." *The Atlantic* 23 June 2017.

Kakadelis, Tina. "Stranger Things, Nancy Wheeler and the Female Hero We Needed." *Medium* 2 Nov. 2017.

Lasch, Christopher. "The Politics of Nostalgia." *Harper's* Nov. 1984: 65–70.

Lowry, Brian. "*GLOW* Shines a Less Flattering Light on Life During the 80s." *CNN Online* 8 Aug. 2019.

Muthri, Vikram. "*GLOW*'s Radical Message about Loving Problematic Art." *Vulture* 23 July 2019.

Pallister, Kathryn. "Introduction." *Netflix Nostalgia: Streaming the Past on Demand*. Ed. Kathryn Pallister. Lanham: Lexington Books, 2019. 1–8.

Poniewozik, James. "*GLOW* Brings #MeToo to the 1980s." *The New York Times* 3 July 2018.

Rearick, Lauren. "The 'Stranger Things' Showrunners Are Being Called Out for Having Sadie Sink Kiss Caleb McLaughlin." *Teen Vogue* 2 Nov. 2017.

Reed, Ashley. "Girls Feel Stranger Things, Too." *Avidly* 19 Aug. 2016.

Rosen, Christopher. "The Final Scene of *GLOW* Season Three Was Betty Gilpin's Shining Moment." *Vanity Fair* 8 July 2020.

Scanlan, Sean. "Introduction: Nostalgia." *Iowa Journal of Cultural Studies* 5.1 (2004): 3–9.

Starobinski, Jean. "The Idea of Nostalgia." *Diogenes* 54 (1966): 81–103.

Stephan, Matthias. "Branding Netflix with Nostalgia." *Netflix Nostalgia: Streaming the Past on Demand*. Ed. Kathryn Pallister. Lexington Books, 2019. 25–39.

Wanshel, Elyse. "People are Worried about Steve Harrington's Fate on *Stranger Things*." *Huffington Post* 20 Mar. 2019.

Willmore, Alison. "*Stranger Things* is Nostalgic for a Time Before Nerds Were Toxic." *Buzzfeed News*. 9 Nov. 2017.

Wilson, Janelle L. "Here and Now, Then and There: Nostalgia as a Time and Space Phenomenon," *Symbolic Interaction* 38.4 (November 2015): 478–92.

Zornosa, Laura. "Before *GLOW* Got Canceled, Its Actresses of Color Felt 'Disempowered' By Their Roles." *LA Times* 20 Oct. 2021.

A Very '80s Love Affair

Joanna Hogg's Formalist Feminism in The Souvenir I

Helena I. Gurfinkel

In *The Souvenir*, Joanna Hogg's partially autobiographical 2019 film, Julie (Honor Swinton Byrne), an earnest upper-class twenty-something film student in the 1980s London, and Anthony (Tom Burke), an older, drug addicted (alleged) employee of the Foreign Office, initially bond over a work of art. As one of his seduction strategies, Anthony shows Julie a Fragonard painting that gives the title to the film. In the painting, a young woman (a character in Rousseau's novel *Julie*) carves the initials of her lover into a tree. While Julie calls the young woman "determined," Anthony opines that "[s]he is very much in love," and his future partner agrees. The lovers' dialogue intimates the aesthetic and formal, rather than psychological or moral, underpinnings of their relationship. Fragonard's/Rousseau's/Julie's act of carving (that is, immortalizing her lover through creativity, which is precisely what happens in the film) suggests that Hogg in effect empowers *her* Julie by means of a uniquely formalist feminism. She curates the cypher that is Anthony as an object of art. Not only does the film refuse to depict Julie as powerless or co-dependent, but it also resists a predictable dive into the psychology of addiction.

While Hogg is not apolitical, her philosophical, feminist, and cinematic response to her 1980s youth is aesthetic. The film does not erase or downplay the social and political touchstones of the Thatcher era. *The Souvenir* puts a spotlight on the economic disparities and unemployment of the early 1980s; the Irish Republican Army and the "Troubles," as well as, through the character of Julie, the struggle for women's empowerment. As John Kirk notes, the (mostly male) British directors of the 1980s depict "the politics of Thatcherism," namely "the ideological constructions of a national ... identity and representations of class" (353). However, Hogg, and her younger self, Julie, also answer the question posed by Teresa de Lauretis and crucial to the feminist filmmakers of the 1970s and 1980s: "What formal, stylistic, or thematic markers point to a female presence behind the camera?" (144). Having made the audience aware of the burning issues of the day, the director turns her attention to Julie's artist's toolbox; both the first and the final shots show her as a filmmaker, in command of her tools, first tentatively, then more fully, with men more or less incidental to her mastery. The film's answer to de Lauretis' question is to create an aesthetic whereby the social issues come to the fore all the more poignantly because the art depicting them takes precedence.

One of the underlying thematic threads of the film is a debate about authenticity and artifice. Two dialogues between Julie and male characters critically interrogate the opposition. Anthony helps Julie write her film-school personal statement. Her intention is to represent an "authentic" self and to characterize filmmaking as a therapeutic pursuit that reveals and heals that self (similar to the soon-to-be-rejected realist strategy of psychologizing relationships and addiction). Anthony the aesthete makes fun of authenticity; subsequently, Julie, sitting in front of middle-aged bearded white male members of the film-school admissions committee, defends the authenticity of a young, upper-class director's effort to make a film about the crumbling Northern working-class town of Sunderland. In both sequences, older male figures visually dominate/surround Julie, while, thematically, also putting her on defense. As she develops as an artist, she does not create conditions whereby authenticity, therapeutics, or realist characterization wins out. Instead, she gets to invent her own formalism and own her artifice.

* * *

Early in the film, Julie encounters Anthony at a party at her comfortable Knightsbridge flat. Throughout the festivities, she holds a camera and snaps pictures of the revelers. The film's first depiction of Julie and Anthony's relationship establishes Julie's predominant identity as an artist and Anthony's as an object. Julie takes a picture of the back of his head. She gazes at him, empowered by a camera; correspondingly, his position with his back to her effectively erases his own gaze. The location of the future couple in the sequence runs counter to the surface interpretation of their relationship: an experienced, decadent older man seducing a younger woman and taking her away from her life's work. For a time, Anthony becomes her life's work: not in the sense of selfless dedication, but, rather, in the sense of honing her creativity and skill.

Anthony is a work of art, both for Joanna Hogg and for Julie. His aesthetic antecedents seem to be the Yellow 1890s and the turn-of-the-twentieth-century dandified decadence.[1] His good looks are sickly, vampire-like, ageless; his sexiness icy. He limns a certain decadent Dorian-Gray-like aesthetic, long before the audience (and Julie) learn about his heroin addiction. Like Wilde's Prince Charming, Julie's is also ageless.[2] We know that he is older than Julie, but, while she turns twenty-five towards the end of the film (and the relationship), we never learn his age. He dresses with an affectation, all Victorian-gentleman cloaked in colonialist mystique. For example, presumably to reveal more of his life to Julie, he produces an Orientalist-looking photograph, taken, he says, "in Afghanistan, in 1973." His questionable affiliation with the Foreign Office purports to explain the unavailability of further information.

In the first in the series of love letters to Julie (writing being part of both his courtship and self-fashioning), he avows that he had been born in 1980 (the year in which the beginning of the film is set), because that is the year he had fallen in love with her. The point is precisely that aesthetics, such as writing and photography, rather than facts of birth and history, gestures at his elusive identity. Parenthetically, the photograph is preserved inside an old edition of Ernest Temple Thurston's mostly forgotten Edwardian novel *The City of Beautiful Nonsense*, from which Julie reads aloud. The novelistic and photographic origins of Anthony's story meld with the mysterious origins and behavior of the novel's protagonist, John Grey (echoing Wilde's lover, John Gray, and Dorian Gray), as well as with Anthony's (and Julie's) obsession with the aesthetics of Venice, which I will discuss below.

The dark decadent language of aesthetics that writes, or films, Anthony into being also includes the opera soundtrack that plays when Julie and Anthony are together in the Knightsbridge apartment. It is Belá Bartók's 1911 *Bluebeard's Castle*, the artistic antecedents of which harken back to Richard Strauss and Nietzsche. We may get literal with the libretto and think about Judith, the sinister Duke's latest wife and victim, as Julie, but the budding filmmaker is more akin to her Fragonard/Rousseau namesake than to Bartók's hero. She actively resists destruction and participates in the molding of Anthony's character. The opera's origins in turn-of-the-twentieth-century philosophy and aesthetics could be interpreted as a Symbolist guide to understanding Anthony.

In fact, the film is never literal. One of its formalist strategies is to evade, explicitly, a realist psychologizing of the pair of lovers. The film's formalist approach to characterization gives us no realist(ic) explanation either for addiction or for co-dependence. Julie and Anthony have functional parents, whose warm, welcoming homes provide the young lovers with food, drink, and attention. Desperate phone calls to Julie from Anthony's mother, Barbara (Barbara Peirson), puncture the film, and

Julie's mother (Tilda Swinton) nurtures her daughter's relationship and ambitions, despite the precarious nature of both. A woman who speaks at an AA meeting, which Julie attends in an effort to help Anthony, is saved by her father. We may speculate about the class-related underpinnings of the characters' psyches, or their Oedipal struggles, but we know as much about them as we do about Anthony's adventures "in Afghanistan, in 1973." A stylized object teaches us more about Anthony than a visit to his welcoming family of origin. The strength of film's artist-protagonist is a stubborn adherence to the surface, rather than to the content, of Anthony. The same refusal to explain and psychologize empowers Julie as an artist, because, to paraphrase Oscar Wilde's aphorism, it "reveals[s] art and conceal[s] the artist" (3). Throughout the film, she is often hunched over a typewriter or film-editing equipment. Hogg reveals both the literal and figurative tools of her art.

* * *

In particular, the Venice trip, appearing squarely in the middle of film, illustrates Julie's (and Hogg's) feminist formalist aesthetics. Prior to the trip, Anthony puts on a show, pretending that Julie's apartment has been robbed, while, in fact, he has stolen her possessions, and presumably, sold them for heroin. Julie undergoes humiliation and a violation of relational trust and authenticity. This is not the first appearance of money in the film. After the first date, the well-to-do Julie foots the bill for her lavish outings with Anthony. The film has a complex view of female empowerment: Julie's control of the finances both underscores her power and hints at her enabling behavior.

While Anthony might be behind the Venice theatrics, Julie subsidizes them. Anthony creates the atmosphere of dark Venetian erotica and its uncanny—and customary—ability to link sex and death. When we think of Venice, we do not merely sing, as Anthony does, badly, inside the expensive and nostalgic London-Venice express train, Charles Aznavour's "How Sad Venice Can Be." Venice is a necessary scenic backdrop of romantic coupledom, but it is also a scene of unconsummated desire and devastation. Over a Harrods lunch, Anthony brings up a former girlfriend who had committed suicide while with him in Venice. Mann's *Death in Venice* comes to mind, as does the legendary suicide of Constance Fenimore Woolson, hopelessly in love with Henry James. Incidentally, both examples bring us back to the decadent turn-of the-twentieth-century antecedents of Anthony's performance of the self.

Anthony grounds Venice, as, indeed, he does everything, in the Eros-Thanatos dynamic. Yet it is not entirely clear who masterminds the sumptuous train setting, the exquisite costumes that could have been worn at least half a century earlier, the darkly romantic sequence of a sprint through the streets of Venice to the opera; and the luxurious hotel room with a canal view. The sequence is such a clichéd reproduction of a Venice love affair that it is almost a self-conscious parody. As noted earlier, Julie does much of her screenwriting work on a typewriter. She writes scripts for the film school; similarly, she types up the to-do list for the Venice trip. The similarity suggests that she has a hand in staging it and revels in its staginess.

* * *

The sequence is a turning point at which Julie transitions from attempting to extract authenticity from the situation ("You stole my stuff," she cries to Anthony, hoping, in vain, for remorse in return). Instead, she learns to perform, stage, direct, and enact the decadent romance that she underwrites, thus, against all romantic conventions, exhibiting power. Two conversations (one in the Knightsbridge flat post-robbery, and the other on the train to Venice) position the two lovers precisely across from one another, indicating equality and Julie's refusal to be dominated. It is a far cry from Julie's physical and intellectual encirclement by middle-aged bearded film professors questioning her authenticity and credentials.

Hogg is masterful at creating mirror-image sex scenes that indicate the transition of power from men to Julie. For example, the scene of Julie and Anthony's first sexual encounter is the reverse of a scene in which, Julie, temporarily broken up with Anthony, has sex with a man her age. In the first scene, Julie dons underwear that Anthony has brought "from Paris" (all locations that Anthony mentions must be in quotation marks) and becomes subject to his desiring gaze. The scene subtly plays with power even at this early stage: unexpectedly, Julie starts by performing oral sex on Anthony, which like her payments at restaurants, constitutes a clever game of alternating power and submission. Subsequently, Anthony performs oral sex on Julie, indicating that the power dynamic continues to be in flux, and that Julie has learned to enjoy her sexuality. While separated from Anthony, Julie takes up with a fellow student. Their encounter is the precise reversal of the earlier one with Anthony. Ensconced in bed, Julie gazes at the nude young man, who is about to become a casual partner. By immersing herself in the artistic experiment with Anthony, Julie learns to direct, to gaze, and to satisfy her desire in the way she sees fit. She effectively stages the scene of seduction with the younger lover.

The film's power of sexual observation extends to Julie's attire. Always modestly dressed, she prefers innocently pink pajamas and robes at home. Towards the end of the film, she is dressed in a flowery, red robe with a pattern reminiscent of decadent designs of the late nineteenth and early twentieth century. While the brighter color signals more forward and confident sexuality, the aesthetics of the pattern bring her closer to Anthony's performance of the self.

The possession of the hopelessly addicted Anthony as a beloved art object, to which she holds just as tenaciously as her Enlightenment namesake does to the tree, leads her, against any conventional narrative of empowerment, to hold on to the relationship, instead of abandoning it. Paradoxically, Anthony is at his most honest when the self is erased. During a dehumanizing bout of heroin withdrawal, Anthony delivers a performance of impending death. As a budding director, Julie is the camera. She weeps and watches the signs. When she gets the news of Anthony's overdose, she is relatively calm. Her mother, who sleeps over in Julie's flat on that tragic night, cries instead, with her head to the wall, and Julie comforts her, as if the mother-daughter roles become reversed. It is an unusual reversal, but, Hogg suggests, as a consummate artist, Julie absorbs and observes the experience, in order to inform her art with it.

An "authentically" emotional reaction to death is not an artist's fate. After Anthony's demise, Julie directs a scene in a film-school hangar. The young woman whom she films recites Christina Rossetti's poem "Song [When I Am Dead, My Dearest]." Tragedy is absorbed through a poem by a woman, who, like Julie, had struggled to acquire a voice in a male-dominated artistic community. This community, the pre–Raphaelites, had, significantly, laid the foundation for aestheticism and decadence that had inspired the dead man's self-image. The film constantly cuts between film-school scenes and relationship scenes, but, as a transition, Julie always calls Anthony. Now, with Anthony gone, there is no link, or border, or a shot that sutures the personal and the artistic, the authentic and the artificial, life and art, and Julie can dedicate herself to the latter. In the final shot of the film, Julie opens the door of the dark hangar in which the shooting had occurred and sees the light and nature outside. Obviously, the natural light contrasts with, and replaces, the darkness of the studio; having experienced loss, Julie steps from the darkness into the light. The experience of curating Anthony and the relationship into a treasured work of art (a souvenir) empowers and transforms the young filmmaker. Opening the studio door into nature need not be construed as a triumph of nature, or authenticity, over art, however. Instead, the viewer easily recognizes the setting of a lawn and hedges outside of the film school. This is the background, against which Anthony's voiceover had read the love letters to Julie; in other words, it is the setting of her consumption of those letters. In the end, Julie masters and appropriates the landscape and Anthony's language.

The sequel, *The Souvenir Part II* (2021), confirms, and brings to the fore more explicitly, Hogg's formalist/aesthetic feminist philosophy. While the first film starts with Julie's abandonment of the socially conscious Sunderland film and devoting herself to loving Anthony, the sequel centers on her work on a screenplay and production of a film. In the process, she acquires her own voice by contending with familial and educational authority. In other words, the second part ensures that Julie's *künstlerroman* becomes more about the *künst* (art) than the *roman* (in the combined German and French senses of the novel and romance) which, even today, is quite uncommon for women artists.

∗ ∗ ∗

Like the written, sartorial, and painting languages, music holds a special place in the film's formalist sensibilities. Compared to older popular songs and opera, 1980s pop is omnipresent. It is not a mere consequence of the film's setting, but, instead, a language that aesthetically brings this setting into being. Just prior to the beginning of Julie and Anthony's romance, Joe Jackson's 1979 track "Is She Really Going out with Him?" plays in the background. Its date kicks off the 1980s, and its music and lyrics convey the doomed nature of the relationship. Twice, songs serve to introduce Christmas and postcard-like shots of festive London, which the film uses to mark the passing of years. The two iconic 1980s tracks are Jona Lewie's "Stop the Cavalry" (1980) and Chrissie Hynde's "Two Thousand Miles" (1983).

In W.H. Auden's words, "Time ... [w]orships language" (83); the language of song sets in motion the chronology of the plot. While Hynde's hit is appropriately elegiac, Lewie's seemingly lighthearted Christmas ditty evokes "Mr. Churchill," presumably the political predecessor of Mrs. Thatcher, as well as expressing an anti-nuclear-war sentiment. Yet another example of the 1980s political pop is Bronski Beat's "Smalltown Boy" (1984). In the early days of AIDS, the iconic song and video condemned homophobia. The song accompanies Julie's return to her work and friends at the film school during a separation from Anthony. The political tenor of the song intimates Julie's social consciousness, shown earlier with her Sunderland film. Jimmy Somerville's advocacy of a freedom to love may also gesture at Julie's own attainment of sexual freedom outside of a monogamous relationship.

Some of the songs on the soundtrack remind us of the sociopolitical strife of the 1980s. Similarly, Anthony's (most likely) fraudulent claim that he is a Foreign Office employee that is involved in the Irish Troubles seemingly counters the preceding argument that the film's overarching concern is aesthetic and formalist. Joanna Hogg states in a *Vulture* interview that two events of the 1980s, the bombing of the Harrods and of the Iranian embassy, are at least hinted at ("Joanna Hogg Is Having Trouble"). On two occasions, Julie and Anthony drive to a location that appears to be affected by a bombing; Anthony claims to have to go there "for work." The audience is aware of the addiction at least by the second visit; the plausibility that Anthony's dealer is at the location increases.

During a comically proper visit to Julie's parents' country estate, Anthony and the hosts debate the IRA and the Troubles. Anthony supports the IRA, to the consternation of Julie's conservative father, who believes that such cannot be a stated position of a Foreign Office employee, and to the encouragement of Julie's more liberal mother. Anthony haltingly confirms that it is his personal position. Somehow, there is no doubt that the film's politics favors the IRA, yet Anthony's identity is fragile, and his speech is uncharacteristically halting. Anthony is a film-school dropout, who comes from a family of artists of working-class origins. The views on the IRA are his, yet he poses as someone else.

By the same token, Julie's (and the film's, or director's) concerns with the early–80s economic disparities plaguing places like Sunderland, about which she strives to create a film, are undoubtable. Yet, much like the IRA conversation, the unfinished documentary becomes not a complete and true reflection of the social and economic problems of the day, but, instead, the crucible of the film's philosophical debate about authenticity vs. artifice. The Sunderland project disappears early in the film. *The Souvenir* is more philosophically interested in the aesthetics of performance than in politics. More precisely, it is interested in representing the politics through an innovative feminist aesthetic lens.

As Ciara Barrett notes in her feminist reading of Hogg's *oeuvre*,

> Critical analysis of her films has thus far largely been concerned with ontextualizing Hogg's representation of upper-middle-class Britons within a history of class-conscious British auteur filmmaking, with comparing her style as a filmmaker to that of a range of European arthouse auteurs … and with distinguishing her work from mainstream genre filmmaking. I argue that this three-pronged critical approach has ultimately worked against an appreciation of Joanna Hogg as a subversive feminist filmmaker, despite Hogg's frequent assertion in interviews that she is interested in exploring uniquely female experiences on film through various strategies of performance and representation [2].

Barrett's critique of the perception of Hogg as strictly a social critic is in line with my analysis of the director's latest film. Indeed, journalistic responses to the 2019 film reveal class as the reviewers' predominant interest.[3] The uncomfortable binaries, such as continental/British and aesthetic/social, pigeonhole Hogg into a narrow, male-centric framework of a national cinematic tradition. They potentially blind the audience to the distinct feminist artistic techniques that, indeed, perhaps unexpectedly, center on "performance and representation."

Andrew Emerson notes that Hogg subverts the viewers' expectations precisely through the formalist experiments with the point of view, in which she aligns herself with Laura Mulvey's foundational "Visual Pleasure and Narrative Cinema."[4] It is not clear, however, why Hogg's feminism is "unexpected" ("The Unexpected Feminism"). One explanation is, perhaps, that her feminism, as Barrett also contends, comes from her formalist innovation, rather than from a social and psychological realist approach expected from her as a British director of a certain generation. Critics expect Hogg to emulate Mike Leigh or Stephen Frears, but her work is more akin to the cinema of Derek Jarman, with whom she worked and communicated as a young filmmaker. A feminist director identifies with a queer one: while it is impossible to accuse Jarman of a lack of social conscience, his statements of sexual liberation and class critique are, above all, formally innovative.

When they first meet, Anthony describes Julie (to her face) as a "freak," to which Julie, unexpectedly indeed, replies "Thank you." Julie is unfazed by a seeming putdown by a condescending man; she also sees "freakishness," or difference, as an advantage. As an artist, she risks standing out from a crowd. This exchange serves as a metaphor to the expected reception of this film as a straightforward sentimental autobiography, or a direct statement on class in the 1980s United Kingdom. This is an expectation that Hogg is prepared to turn upside down by her "freakish" aesthetic.

NOTES

1. It is important to define decadence and aestheticism from the outset. By Hogg's formalism, I mean attention to form, broadly defined (cinematic technique, aesthetics) that not only supersedes a focus on content but also actually creates innovative content. One of the historical and philosophical antecedents of this approach is the decadent/aesthetic/Symbolist movement of the turn of the twentieth century, with which Anthony identifies, and which Hogg deploys to create him as an object of art. In a recent essay on decadence and disco (which brings together two similar chronological periods), William Rees notes that decadence is "a broad and slippery term" (127). Nonetheless, he defines it rather crisply: "Decadent artists rejected bourgeois Victorian values of industriousness and moral conviction, instead emphasizing apathy, overindulgence, aristocratic refinement, and Victorian notions of perversity including unconventional sexuality" (127). Of course, Anthony's defiance extends to the values of Thatcher's England, while Hogg's own aesthetic approach defies the expectations of "doing" socially conscious feminist art a certain way.

2. In her review of the film in the May 13, 2019 (online), issue of *The New Yorker*, Rebecca Mead reveals the biographical details of Hogg's real-life model for Anthony:

> Her companion, who had studied art history at Cambridge University and at the Courtauld Institute, in London, struck her as immensely more knowledgeable. Nine years her senior, he was brimming with the confident, ironical charm bestowed by élite English schools. He wore double-breasted pin-striped suits

and bow ties, and he had pronounced aesthetic preferences: Symbolist opera, the movies of Powell and Pressburger, a brand of Turkish cigarette with an elliptical shape ["Joanna Hogg's Self-Portrait of a Lady"]

The film is widely acknowledged as a thinly veiled autobiography, which necessitates supplying this information. In addition, according to Mead, the interests and inclinations of the Anthony prototype clearly position him within the decadent aesthetic that precedes the setting of the film by decades.

3. See, for example, Guy Lodge's "*The Souvenir*: How Joanna Hogg Humanizes 'Middle-Class Problems'" from May 15, 2019, or Peter Bradshaw's "*The Souvenir* Review—sumptuous class study puts Joanna Hogg in the limelight," from August 29, 2019. The latter title is particularly unsettling, since Joanna Hogg had been "in the limelight" as a director for decades. The (male) reviewer seems to suggest that it is only by adhering to a certain male-dominated British realist tradition that a female director can find herself "in the limelight."

4. When I reference the male gaze earlier in the essay, of course, I also draw on Mulvey's formulation.

Works Cited

Auden, W.H. "In Memory of W.B. Yeats." *Selected Poems*, Vintage Books, 1979, pp. 80–83.

Aznavour, Charles and Françoise Dorin. "How Sad Venice Can Be." 1967. YouTube.com, 30 Nov. 2009 Charles Aznavour—How sad Venice can be (1967) - YouTube.

Barrett, Ciera. "The Feminist Cinema of Joanna Hogg: Melodrama, Female Space, and the Subversion of Phallogocentric Metanarrative." *Alphaville: Journal of Film and Screen Media*, issue 10, 2015 https://doi.org/10.33178/alpha.

Bradshaw, Peter. "*The Souvenir* Review—Sumptuous Class Study Puts Joanna Hogg in the Limelight." *The Guardian*, 29 Aug. 2019, The Souvenir review—sumptuous class study puts Joanna Hogg in the limelight | Film | The Guardian.

De Lauretis, Teresa. "Rethinking Women's Cinema: Aesthetics and Feminist Theory." *Multiple Voices in Feminist Film Criticism*, edited by Diane Carson and Janice R. Welsch, The University of Minnesota Press, 1994, pp. 140–161.

Emerson, Andrew. "The Unexpected Feminism of *The Souvenir*." *The Film Watcher: Ruminations on the Movies*, 30 May 2019, The Unexpected Feminism of The Souvenir—The FilmWatcher.

Jones, Nate. "Joanna Hogg Is Having Trouble Telling Where Her Memories End and *The Souvenir* Begins." *Vulture*, 14 May 2019, Joanna Hogg 'The Souvenir' Interview (vulture.com).

Kirk, John. "Urban Narratives: Contesting Space and Place in Some British Cinema from the 1980s." *Journal of Narrative Theory*, vo. 31, no. 3, Fall 2011, pp. 353–379, DOI: https://doi.org/10.1353/jnt.2011.0071.

Lodge, Guy. "The Souvenir: How Joanna Hogg Humanizes 'Middle-Class Problems,'" *The Guardian*, 19 May 2019, The Souvenir: how Joanna Hogg humanises 'middle-class problems' | Film | The Guardian.

Mann, Thomas. *Death in Venice*. Dover, 2010.

Mead, Rebecca. "Joanna Hogg's Self-Portrait of a Lady." *The New Yorker*, 13 May, 2019, Joanna Hogg's Self-Portrait of a Lady | The New Yorker.

Mulvey, Laura. "Visual Pleasure and Narrative Cinema." *Screen*, vo. 16, no. 3, 1975, pp. 6–18.

Rees, William. "'Le Freak, c'est Chic': Decadence and Disco." *Volupté: Interdisciplinary Journal of Decadence Studies*, vo. 3, no. 2, 2020, pp. 126–142, DOI: 10.25602/GOLD.v.v3i2.1456.g1569.

Rossetti, Christina. "Song [When I Am Dead, My Dearest]." *The Complete Poems*, Penguin, 1999, p.126.

Temple Thurston, Ernest. *The City of Beautiful Nonsense*. Chapman and Hall, 1909.

Wilde, Oscar. "The Preface to *The Picture of Dorian Gray*." *The Picture of Dorian Gray*, edited by Michael Patrick Gillespie, Norton, 2007, pp. 3–4.

Fight the Power
Social Justice

Jem, She-Ra, and My Little Pony

Combating Misogyny, Homophobia, and Racism in Girl-Centered Reboots

Melanie Hurley

In the 1980s, *Jem and the Holograms* (1985–1988), *She-Ra: Princess of Power* (1985–1987), and the *My Little Pony* television specials (1984 & 1985), film (1986), and cartoon (1986–1987) all featured powerful, successful, and adventurous female characters, expanding the possibilities for female identity[1] and combating the dominant backlash discourses of the Regan era (Faludi). In the 2010s, the era of Trumpism and Brexit, reboots of these series, namely, IDW's *Jem and the Holograms* comics (2015–2018), Netflix's *She-Ra and the Princesses of Power* (2018–2020), and Discovery Family's *My Little Pony: Friendship is Magic* (2010–2019; hereafter *MLP: FiM*) revisit the imaginative terrain of the 1980s to rewrite and extend that space in ways that promote inclusion and togetherness at a time when such progressive world-building is once again sorely needed.

The heroines of *Jem*, *She-Ra*, and *My Little Pony* prove their prowess in the stereotypically masculine roles of rock stars and heroes. *Jem* contests the belief that girls suffer from technophobia, and its ethnically diverse cast incorporates both white, American women and women of color and of other nationalities into the rock world. With her immense physical strength, healing powers, and the ability to talk to animals, the eponymous heroine of *She-Ra* challenged both the masculine (super)hero ideal and the feminine princess ideal. Finally, *My Little Pony* subverted the androcentric nature of fantasy, cartoons, and American equine literature through its gynocentric Ponyland and its characterization of Megan, a brave young girl who acts as the ponies' primary human helper. In the face of backlash, these series subverted gender paradigms.

The reboots all expand on the worlds and narratives of the originals to continue their depiction of impressive heroines and to become even more inclusive. IDW's *Jem* depicts queer characters and diverse bodies; *She-Ra's* planet Etheria is now a place where LGBTQ+ characters thrive, and *MLP: FiM* includes episodes that combat anti–Black racism and promote body positivity. The reboots all showcase the beauty of diversity, endorsing progressive social and cultural politics and new ways of approaching the world.

Subverting the Backlash in "Outrageous" Style: 1980s Heroine Cartoons

In the 1980s, backlash discourses dominated the mainstream media. Depictions of ambitious, powerful career women frequently were negative, with *Fatal Attraction* (1987) outright villainizing the career woman and *Baby Boom* (1987) placing her in a "downshifting narrative," a story in which she elects to work less and reign in her ambitions for the sake of a romantic partner and family (Parkins 66). Heroine cartoons defy this trend. Jem, She-Ra, and Megan are strong, pretty, autonomous, and caring; in short, they combine feminist identity with the stereotypically feminine. While mainstream media was excluding such possibilities for female identity, children's media[2] was keeping them alive, contesting the backlash by circulating opposing ideas about female identity.

Jem and the Holograms entices and encourages girls to define themselves as multidimensional agents. The show centers on Jerrica, whose holographic AI computer Synergy allows her to become Jem. The heroine struggles to balance her roles as a record executive (as Jerrica), a mysterious frontwoman (as Jem), and the head of Starlight House, a foster home for girls (as Jerrica). However, the series never suggests that she ought to scale down her career in favor of her caretaking role; in fact, the narrative makes Jerrica's career necessary to her caretaking position, as she and her sisters (the other members of the Holograms) use the profits from their music to fund Starlight House. The Holograms' careers are intensely exciting, leading them on worldwide adventures and into intrigue and romantic dramas. They travel to exciting locales, such as Hawaii and the mythical Shangri-La (season 1, episode 18, "Hot Time in Hawaii"; season 2, episode 22, "Journey to Shangri-La"), and they must contend with The Misfits, a rival girl band that continually attempts to sabotage them. On top of it all, Jerrica's long-time boyfriend, Rio Pacheco, does not know that she is Jem, and he begins to pursue the pink-haired singer, causing Jerrica to become jealous of her other identity and believe that Jem is more loved than she is (season 1, episode 6, "Starbright, Part 1—Falling Star"; season 1, episode 26, "Glitter and Gold"; and season 3, episode 6, "Midsummer

Night's Madness"). No matter how hectic their lives become, though, the Holograms are always there for one another, enjoying the fun times and giving each other support through the difficult ones.[3] The show suggests that women can be both nurturing and successful, while having friends, fun, and adventure.

As it is primarily a series about young women who use advanced technologies to make and disseminate music, *Jem* strongly opposes the stereotype of female technophobia.[4] North American and British society genders technology as male, encouraging boys to experiment with it, but teaching girls to fear it "unless it is associated with cooking, cleaning, communicating, or beautifying themselves and their surroundings" (Kearney, "Pink Technology" 8). In *Jem*, however, not only does Jerrica operate Synergy, but a host of female youth prove themselves to be tech-savvy. The Holograms and The Misfits have only young female members, and two of the three members of The Stingers are female, and all of them play electric instruments, such as electric guitar, keytar, and keyboard. Minx, The Stingers' synthesist, is particularly technologically-able, as she knows how to play *and* build synthesizers, as well as how to assemble other complicated gadgets. *Jem* portrays a gynocentric high-tech music world, validating girls' interest in rock music, electric instruments, and advanced technology.

Jem is equally progressive for its ethnically diverse cast of female characters whom it integrates into the world of rock. Among the main characters, Shana, a fashion designer, and the original drummer for the Holograms and later the bass guitarist, is African American; Aja, the Holograms' lead guitarist, is Chinese American; Raya, the Holograms' second drummer, is Mexican American; Jetta, The Misfits' saxophonist, is British; and, Minx is German. Supporting characters further extend *Jem's* inclusivity: Krissie and Ba Nee, two Starlight girls, are African American and Vietnamese American, respectively, and the choreographer Danse, although born in America, is the daughter of a Yugoslavian dancer, Nadia Dvorak. Almost all these characters are active in making music, as even the Starlight girls get to sing their own songs (season 1, episode 23, "The Jem Jam, Part 1"; season 1, episode 24, "The Jem Jam, Part 2"), and others contribute to rock through dance and fashion. *Jem* certainly does not shy away from representation and inclusion, and it never implies that anyone is less important, talented, or worthy than anybody else because of their heritage.

She-Ra: Princess of Power likewise upsets gender stereotypes, but it disrupts norms of representation in princess and superhero narratives by combining them: Princess Adora/She-Ra is no damsel in distress, but a self-assured princess who looks after herself, her friends, and her world. In both of her forms, this princess is alluring, a depiction that draws on the image of the "Glamazon." *Merriam-Webster* defines a "Glamazon" as "an exceptionally glamorous, tall, and self-assured woman." The word also refers to a 1980s women's fashion ideal. Often, Glamazons had gelled, slicked hair, and wore masculine suits and perhaps glittering accessories or otherwise ostentatious clothing and jewelry (e.g., gilt earrings, shoulder pads, and overly large buttons) (Dyhouse 136–138). It was a kind of glamor that "could suggest aggression, as well as self-assertion" and "associated glamour with the female warrior" (138). She-Ra does not wear these specific fashions, but she is both tall and self-assured, and more importantly, she literally embodies the glamor of the female warrior. As Adora, she is a leader in Etheria's rebellion against the Horde, and as She-Ra she is the amazingly powerful hero the planet needs. *She-Ra* thus promotes ideals of women's strength and independence rather than their passivity.

She-Ra is a caregiving princess yet, like Jem, she does not downshift, living both literally and figuratively as a "superwoman" and expanding the options for female identity. She-Ra can heal wounds and talk to animals, abilities that associate her with nurturance and nature; still, the series does not suggest that a woman ought to abandon power for family or domesticity. She-Ra sometimes receives visits and help from her twin brother, He-Man (*He-Man and the Masters of the Universe*, 1983–1985), maintaining a connection to her family, but first and foremost, she contributes to the Rebellion. She-Ra occasionally encounters children on her travels and acts as a good role model for them, but she does not abandon her mission to care for them, simply helping while she is present and then moving on (season 1, episode 6, "Duel at Devlan"; season 1, episode 11, "The Peril of Whispering Woods"). Her interactions with animals are similar, for she helps them or they help her, and then she sends them on their way (season 1, episode 14, "Friendship"; season 1, episode 16, "The Return of the Sea Hawk"). *She-Ra* therefore upholds rather than undermines feminist gains through her choices and actions.

My Little Pony features neither rock bands nor superheroes, but still challenges stereotypical gender roles and behaviors because it counters the androcentric norms of the fantasy genre through its gynocentric magical world. Fantasy narratives often double as hero narratives, and, historically, Western narratives have constructed heroism as masculine (Jones & Watkins 1–2). Many fantasies have male protagonists, including J.R.R. Tolkien's *The Hobbit* (1937) and *The Lord of the Rings* trilogy (1954–1955), and J.K. Rowling's *Harry Potter* series (1997–2007). *My Little Pony*, which takes place in the magical Ponyland, by contrast, features a large cast of female characters. In its television specials and the theatrical release *My Little Pony: The Movie* (1986), it inserts these female characters into high fantasy adventures. For example, in *Rescue at Midnight Castle* (1984), the ponies thwart the plans of the evil centaur-like Tirac, using the Rainbow of Light to destroy his Rainbow of Darkness, and the 1986 film requires them to stop the Smooze, a sentient purple sludge, from destroying Ponyland. *My Little Pony* is, then, a refreshing girl-centered fantasy.

The ponies' friend and helper, Megan, challenges the established patterns of both hero and American equine narratives because of her gender, increasing the possibilities for girl-centered stories. Alison Haymonds (2000) argues that girls in "pony books" (that is, stories "in a British setting, generally rural, with a young hero, nearly always female, whose relationship with her pony is central to the action" [54]) are "transformed by their association with ponies into physically adept, brave riders, tackling their own problems, and getting some measure of control of their lives" (51). Megan similarly proves herself a courageous and able hero for the inhabitants of Ponyland. In *Rescue at Midnight Castle*, she becomes the keeper of the Rainbow of Light, one of the more powerful magical items in the series, and she rides Firefly, a pegasus, in a direct attack on Tirac. Unlike the pony stories that Haymonds discusses, however, *My Little Pony* is American, and the placement of a girl in an American equine narrative is strange: the American tales are usually boys' coming-of-age stories that are "inextricably bound up with the story of the Wild West" (Haymonds 57). Since Megan lives on a ranch and has a horse named TJ, she is not too far removed from this story, but she joins it to a feminized world of colorful, magical ponies. Megan upsets expectations of fantasy and equine narrative and is consequently a welcome figure in children's media.

Jem and the Holograms, *She-Ra*, and *My Little Pony* display many possibilities for female identity through their autonomous, strong, and compassionate heroines, and they encourage girls to aspire to stimulating careers, creative expression, and leadership positions. Their reboots in the 2010s develop the possibilities further, recreating these 1980s worlds to promote new progressive perspectives.

Beautiful Bodies and Lesbian Love: Subversive Reboots in the 2010s

The nostalgia industry has been big business in recent years. Disney has remade many of its classic animations, including *Cinderella* (1950 & 2015), *Beauty and the Beast* (1991 & 2017), *Aladdin* (1992 & 2019), and *Mulan* (1998 & 2020), and likewise there have been reboots of several television series, from *Murphy Brown* (1988–1998 & 2018) to *Walker, Texas Ranger* (1993–2001; rebooted as *Walker*, 2021–). 1980s cartoons have also received reboots, including *Jem*, *She-Ra*, and *My Little Pony*, revivals of their fictional worlds that are true to their spirits and push their inclusivity and progressive politics further by openly opposing unrealistic beauty norms, bodily shame, and anti–Black racism, and improving their representativeness by introducing queer characters. In an era of anti-migration and isolationist rhetoric and violence against the Black community, and when the "Bury Your Gays" trope (the killing of queer characters) is still relatively common in media,[5] such series are crucial for mounting an opposition to such rhetoric and behavior.

IDW's *Jem and the Holograms* comic series expands on the cartoon's inclusivity to feature a lesbian romance, with the first volume displacing Jerrica/Jem and Rio in favor of Kimber and Stormer (a Misfit). In the cartoon, even though other characters have relationships, the ironic Rio, Jerrica, Jem triangle is the central romance and the source of most of the romantic drama. However, it is the relationship between Kimber and Stormer that is crucial to *Showtime*'s (the comic's first volume's) plot arc.[6] Their relationship causes a great deal of tension within The Misfits, as Pizzazz becomes extremely unhappy that Stormer is dating a member of the competition, and, with the support of the other Misfits, she threatens to kick Stormer out of the band if she continues seeing Kimber (52, 74–75). The threat frightens Stormer because, as she tells Kimber, her music is everything to her (75), so the pair then decide to date secretly, causing stress for Kimber. *Showtime*'s focus on Kimber and Stormer thus allows a lesbian romance to have the significance usually reserved for heterosexual relationships.

Through Stormer, the *Jem* comics show that mainstream beauty ideals are far too narrow and exclusive and create a strong argument against fat-phobia and fat-shaming. Voluptuous Stormer is not stereotypically beautiful and sometimes suffers for it. In the second volume of *The Misfits: Our Songs Are Better* (2017), a flashback to Stormer's childhood reveals that other children in her school told her that she would never succeed on stage because of her weight (36). Pizzazz, however, admires her talent and passion and accepts her for who she is (38): a subsequent flashback to an early Misfits performance even shows Pizzazz attacking an audience member for calling Stormer a whale (39–40).

Furthermore, when the comic presents Stormer from Kimber's perspective, it broadens ideas of sexual desirability. In the first volume, Kimber is walking along and eating a slice of pizza at The Battle of the Bands festival, but suddenly stops and says "Whoa," her eyes sparkling. The next image is Stormer dressed in a cute orange dress and heels and surrounded by stars, followed by an image of Kimber kissing her (106). Stormer is a beautiful woman inside and out, and society needs ideas of beauty that include women like her.

Netflix's *She-Ra and the Princesses of Power* goes further than *Jem* with its depictions of queer characters, for it presents a completely non-heteronormative world that subtly normalizes sexual and gender diversity. Many characters either openly belong or appear to belong to the LGBTQ+ community. Two princesses, Netossa and Spinnerella, are a married couple. George and Lance, a couple who run a library and share a passion for history, have raised thirteen children, including Bow, one of the members of "The Best Friend Squad" (the other two are Adora and Glimmer, the princess and later queen of Bright Moon). Scorpia's appearance and behavior suggests a queer identity: she has short white hair, shaved on the back and sides, and a muscular physique, and she desperately tries to impress Catra, another member of the Horde, over the course of seasons one, two, and three. She even takes Catra to the Princess Prom as her date (season 1, episode 8, "Princess Prom," fig. 1), a choice that does not receive comment, signaling Etheria's acceptance of diverse sexualities. The third season introduces a non-binary character, a shapeshifter named Double Trouble. While Double Trouble's status as a self-serving villain is less than ideal given the rarity of non-binary characters in popular culture, the other characters' consistent and unquestioning use of the pronouns "they/them" whenever referencing the shapeshifter is nonetheless significant progress in representation. In Etheria, homophobia and enbyphobia do not exist; it is an amazingly inclusive place.

Fig. 1. Scorpia takes Catra to the prom in "Princess Prom": *She-Ra and the Princesses of Power,* season 1, episode 8 (DreamWorks Animation Television, 2018).

The series finale reveals lesbian love as an underlying structure of the entire series, and it is an act of that love that saves all of Etheria, giving lesbian love a role that is usually given to heterosexual love. Catra and Adora's relationship is fundamental to She-Ra. Catra and Adora were best friends when they were growing up in the Horde, but Adora's defection to the Rebellion (season 1, episode 2, "The Sword [Part 2]") resulted in Catra becoming her archenemy, not only because they were now on opposite sides, but also because Catra took Adora's choice to leave the Horde personally. The two come up against each other often, and Catra is clearly bitter. However, Adora never gives up on Catra, and she saves Catra from Horde Prime's (the ultimate's villain's) mind control (episode 5, "Save the Cat"). In animation, final rescues and the accompanying kisses usually occur between heterosexual couples, as occurs in Disney's Snow White and the Seven Dwarfs (1937), Sleeping Beauty (1959), and Beauty and the Beast (1991), but in "Heart (Part 2)" (season 5, episode 13), the final rescue and kiss involve Catra and Adora. Catra recognizes that Adora is dying, and she exclaims, "Don't you get it? I love you. I always have. So please, just this once. Stay!" Adora says she returns Catra's love, they kiss, and Adora transforms into She-Ra and stops Horde Prime once and for all. She-Ra and the Princesses of Power thus queers the usual romantic tropes, giving power and respect to other forms of love.

MLP: FiM does feature a lesbian couple, young pony Scootaloo's guardians, Aunt Holiday and Aunt Lofty, but it is more notable for other features, such as its anti–Black racism episode "Bridle Gossip" (season 1, episode 9), which uses a zebra, Zecora, to illustrate why racism is wrong. The episode codes Zecora as Black: her species, her accent, her golden neck rings, and the masks that decorate her home all come from Africa or have been inspired by African cultures. All five of Twilight Sparkle's best friends fear Zecora; they tell Twilight that she is evil, but they cannot provide any evidence for it. They seem to fear Zecora simply because she is different. Twilight says it's all "gossip and rumors," but she becomes caught up in their beliefs after they all get poisoned with Poison Joke. While "rescuing" Applejack's little sister, Apple Bloom, from Zecora (Apple Bloom followed her out of curiosity), the ponies stand in some blue flowers. Zecora tells them the flowers are dangerous, but they believe she is cursing them. They all awake the next morning with problems; for example, Twilight's unicorn horn is floppy and covered in spots and Rainbow Dash, a pegasus, cannot fly straight. In the end, they learn that Zecora knows how to cure them and is not an evil enchantress after all. The show unequivocally shows that fearing or hating someone because of their appearance, race, or other difference is illogical and causes problems for everyone involved, and, through its specific coding, issues a particularly strong statement against anti–Black racism.[7]

The series' episode "Call of the Cutie" (season 1, episode 12) uses coding equally well to create a positive narrative around puberty, shifting the conversation around the female body from one of menstrual shame to one of the acceptance of nature. The teacher, Cheerilee, explains that ponies receive their cutie marks when they discover their special talent and the direction of their life. The ponies in the class are relatively young, but most of them have their cutie marks already. Apple Bloom, however, does not, and she is embarrassed that she is a "blank flank." Over the course of the episode, Apple Bloom discovers that she cannot force a cutie mark to appear; as her sister says, "These things happen when these things are supposed to happen." She will discover where she belongs in her own time. In addition to being a story about learning and growing at your own pace, the show's design allows the appearance of cutie marks to signify menarche: ponies treat getting their cutie mark as a major life event; all the ponies to whom Apple Bloom speaks are female; and, a young pony named Diamond Tiara is even having a cute-ceañera, a pun on "quinceañera," a Latin American celebration of a girl's fifteenth birthday, her coming-of-age. The show is incredibly positive in its depiction of bodily changes, characterizing them as something to look forward to rather than as something to fear or of which to be ashamed. A comparison to cutie marks could even prove to be a useful way to explain menstruation to children familiar with the show. The episode suggests that female bodies are beautiful and encourages positivity around growth and changes of all kinds, no matter how and when they arrive.

In the 1980s and 2010s, both decades of backlash against progressive politics, *Jem*, *She-Ra*, and *My Little Pony* persisted in representing diverse characters. In these texts, strong, successful girls and women challenge the androcentric nature of rock music, technology use, (super)hero, fantasy, and American equine narratives. Furthermore, the reboots' representations of racial, sexual, gender, and body diversity challenge racism, homophobia, enbyphobia, and fat-phobia, replacing them with the acceptance and the forming of friendships across differences, while their promotion of body positivity expands notions of beauty and opposes menstrual shame. The reboots' return to the fictional and fantastical worlds of 1980s makes them even more inclusive and forward-thinking, showing through their fiction how our future world could be.

NOTES

1. I am using the term "female identity" rather than "feminine identity" here because I believe the word "feminine" carries too many controversial connotations, such as suggesting that girls are passive, kind, and domestic. However, I do not mean for this biology-based term to exclude transwomen. For the duration of this paper, it indicates all persons who identify as women.

2. Even when it becomes massively popular, children's media remains subcultural rather than mainstream because of its youthful target audience whose members are subject to more restrictions than people of the age of majority.

3. Some particularly striking examples of their care for one another are the forgiveness the other Holograms offer Kimber after *Cool Trash*, a fictional celebrity gossip magazine, publishes unflattering descriptions of them from her diary (season 2, episode 3, "Scandal"), and Jerrica's support of Kimber when she wants to marry Jeff, even though she thinks Kimber is making the wrong decision, and Kimber's returned emotional support when Jem does not win the Academy Award for Best Actress (season 2, episode 27, "Hollywood Jem, Part 2—And the Winner Is . . .").

4. I presented a paper on the topic of the *Jem* franchise's depiction of young female media-makers, entitled "'Truly Outrageous': Constructions of Tech-Savvy Young Womanhood in Hasbro's *Jem and the Holograms* Media Franchise," at York University's Humanities Graduate Conference, "Reformatting the World: Conference on Technology and Humanities," which took place from February 23–24, 2018. I thank the organizers of that conference for giving me the opportunity to present my work and to receive feedback on it.

5. Relatively recent examples of the trope include Lexa's death on *The 100* (2014–2020) in "Thirteen" (season 3, episode 7) and Denise Cloyd's death on *The Walking Dead* (2010–) in "Twice as Far" (season 6, episode 14).

6. My references are the volumes of collected issues. These collections do not include page numbers: I am counting from the first page of the volume.

7. Alternatively, a viewer could interpret the use of the zebra as racist itself, given the intensely racist history of coding cartoon animals as Black; examples include *Dumbo*'s (1941) jive-talking crows, *The Jungle Book*'s (1967) King Louie, the swing music-loving King of the Apes, and MGM's depictions of Cab Calloway, Duke Ellington, Fats Waller, Louis Armstrong, and Ethel Waters as frogs (Breaux, 2010; Condis, 2015). However, Zecora lives in a fictional equine-centric world: *MLP: FiM* omits Megan and all human characters, leaving no possibility for the series to introduce a Black human character. Since the ponies exist in all colors and already include fantastical species such as unicorns and pegasi, an entirely different creature is required to make the anti-Black racism argument, and a non-equine creature would run the risk of suggesting that the character coded as black is not equal to the main characters. My interpretation of this episode, as a white viewer and scholar, is therefore positive; however, the use of the zebra is up for debate, especially by Black viewers and scholars.

WORKS CITED

Breaux, Richard M. "After 75 Years of Magic: Disney Answers Its Critics, Rewrites African American History, and Cashes In on Its Racist Past." *Journal of African American Studies*, vol. 14, 2010, pp. 398–416.

Campbell, Sophie, et al. *Jem and the Holograms: Dimensions*, illustrated by Campbell et al. IDW, 2018.

Condis, Megan. "She was a Beautiful Girl and All the Animals Loved Her: Race, the Disney Princesses, and their Animal Friends." *Gender Forum*, vol. 55, 2015.

DiTillio, Larry, and J. Michael Straczynski, creators. *She-Ra: Princess of Power*. Filmation, 1987.

Dyhouse, Carol. *Glamour: Women, History, Feminism*. Zed Books, 2010.

Faludi, Susan. *Backlash: The Undeclared War Against American Women*. Crown, 1991.

Faust, Lauren, creator. *My Little Pony: Friendship is Magic*. Allspark Animation, Studio B Productions, and DHX Studios, 2019.

"Glamazon." *Merriam-Webster*, www.merriam-webster.com/dictionary/glamazon.

Haymonds, Alison. "Rides of Passage: Female Heroes in Pony Stories." *A Necessary Fantasy? The Heroic Figure in Children's Popular Culture*, edited by Dudley Jones and Tony Watkins, Garland, 2000, pp. 51–72.

Jones, Dudley, and Tony Watkins. Introduction. *A Necessary Fantasy? The Heroic Figure in Children's Popular Culture*, edited by Jones and Watkins, Garland, 2000, pp. 1–19.

Kearney, Mary Celeste. "Pink Technology: Mediamaking Gear for Girls." *Camera Obscura*, vol. 25. no. 2, 2010, pp. 1–39. *EBSCOhost*, doi: 10.1215/02705346–2010–001.

Parkins, Wendy. "'Shall I Be Mother? Motherhood and Domesticity in Popular Culture.'" *Feminism, Domesticity and Popular Culture*, edited by Stacy Gillis and Joanne Hollows. Routledge, 2009, pp. 65–78.

Rowling, J.K. *Harry Potter and the Chamber of Secrets*. 1998. Raincoast, 2000.

_____. *Harry Potter and the Deathly Hallows*. Raincoast, 2007.

_____. *Harry Potter and the Goblet of Fire*. Raincoast, 2000.

_____. *Harry Potter and the Half-Blood Prince*. Raincoast, 2005.

_____. *Harry Potter and the Order of the Phoenix*. Raincoast, 2003.

_____. *Harry Potter and the Philosopher's Stone*. Scholastic Canada, 1997.

_____. *Harry Potter and the Prisoner of Azkaban*. Raincoast, 1999.

Thompson, Kelly. *Dark Jem*, illustrated by Sophie Campbells. *Jem and the Holograms*, vol. 3, IDW, 2016.

_____. *Enter the Stingers*, illustrated by Jen Bartel and Meredith McClaren. *Jem and the Holograms*, vol. 4, IDW, 2017.

_____. *Jem and the Holograms: Infinite*, illustrated by Stacey Lee et el. IDW, 2018.

_____. *Our Songs Are Better*, illustrated Jenn St-Onge. *Jem and the Holograms: The Misfits*, IDW, 2017.

_____. *Showtime*, illustrated by Sophie Campbell. *Jem and the Holograms*, vol. 1, IDW, 2015.

_____. *Truly Outrageous*, illustrated by Gisele Lagace et al. *Jem and the Holograms*, vol. 4, IDW, 2017.

_____. *Viral*, illustrated by Emma Vieceli et al. *Jem and the Holograms*, vol. 2, IDW, 2016.

Tolkien, J.R. R. *The Fellowship of the Ring*. 1954. HarperCollins, 2007.

_____. *The Hobbit, or, There and Back Again*. 1937. Collins Modern Classics, 1998.

_____. *The Return of the King*. 1955. HarperCollins, 2007.

_____. *The Two Towers*. 1954. HarperCollins, 2007.

Nostalgia for What Always Was

Race and American Superheroes
in Television and Film

PATRICK L. HAMILTON *and* ALLAN W. AUSTIN

Thanks to the sustained dominance of the Marvel Cinematic Universe (MCU) and the DC Extended Universe (DCEU) in the twenty-first century, stories about superheroes are more a part of American culture than they ever have been. But while these contemporary adventures eclipse much of what came before them visually and narratively, they remain significantly mired in patterns of racial inclusion and representation stemming from 1980s multiculturalism. Despite the ground-breaking efforts of select films within both oeuvres, racial stereotypes persist, and nonwhite characters still often occupy marginalized and otherwise limited positions vis-à-vis otherwise white mainstays. Consequently, the blockbusters of today remain dangerously superficial in suggesting "progress," revealing how the racial attitudes and understandings inherent in the 1980s have, in fact, never actually gone away. Such continued reliance on models of representation stemming from a Reagan-era model of race might feel "new," but in reality highlights how little has changed in the willingness of Americans to address long-standing problems in race relations between then and now.

The election of Ronald Reagan in 1980 signaled the end of a sustained movement for racial reform that started in earnest following World War II and blossomed in the civil rights era. The new president undermined even the limited goals and programs of his predecessors, attacking affirmative action, packing the Civil Rights and Equal Employment Opportunity Commissions with new members hostile to their very missions, and excluding nonwhites from whatever economic gains his administration mustered (Chafe 453, 456, 459, 467; Austin and Hamilton 177). Multiculturalism developed against this background, stunting its aims and accomplishments. Stemming from a much earlier movement for cultural pluralism, multiculturalism flourished in the 1980s and early 1990s as the result of what David Hollinger describes as its simplicity and generality (Hollinger 92, 96, 2, 98, 100, 101; Austin and Hamilton 178). Similarly, bell hooks demonstrates how the feel-good liberalism of the 1980s commodified nonwhite cultures in ways that hardly portended racial progress (21–22). The practical result reified nonwhite individuals. Anthony Appiah likens multiculturalism's approach to diversity to reductively shelving books by size and shape. Alternatively, Stacy Alaimo compares multiculturalism to the rigid and flattened racial and ethnic caricatures in Disney's "It's a Small World" ride (qtd. in Hollinger 34; Alaimo 163; Austin and Hamilton 179). Such comparisons hardly flatter the accomplishments of multiculturalism.

Beginning with 1977–78's *The All-New Super Friends Hour*, the cartoon exploits of DC heroes very much reflected the less flattering aspects of multiculturalism, as various of its creators later recognized. John Semper, who worked on *Super Friends: The Legendary Super Powers Show* (1984–1985), critiqued what he described as a "ham-fisted" approach that presented "cartoon character versions of ethnicities." Alan Burnett, story editor for the same season, added, "[T]hey really were tokens with a capital 'T.' They didn't have any personality, they weren't in the background, they weren't in DC Comics." Such critiques gesture towards the ways in which the series fell short of anything but the flattened depiction of race Appiah's and Alaimo's metaphors capture.[1] Even those looking at the era through more rose-colored glasses ultimately reveal these same limits. Former DC Publisher Dan Didio describes these additions, in retrospect, as "a huge step in the right direction," arguing—and thus again reflecting a core belief of multiculturalism—that what's important is that "people are making the effort" ("Evolution: New Heroes, Viler Villains and Ethnic Additions: How Super Friends Prefigured the Era of Cultural Diversity in Animation,").

With *The All-New Super Friends Hour* (1977–78), the Saturday morning staple added several nonwhite characters—Black Vulcan, Samurai, Apache Chief, and Rima—to a roster of otherwise white heroes. The various iterations of the *Super Friends* series from 1980 to 1986[2] continued to include the first three alongside two new ethnic additions: first, El Dorado, an original Latino character, in the 1980–82 series and, second, Cyborg, an African American character transplanted from the comics in the 1985–86 series. While both sets of additions diversified the super team, how they did so demonstrates the sharp limits of racial acceptance in the "Age of Reagan." In any number of ways, the racialized newcomers existed in contrast to the more established heroes (particularly Superman, Batman,

Wonder Woman, and Aquaman), differentiating them from and diminishing them in comparison to their supposed peers.

To start, the series' depictions of nonwhite heroes are ultimately stereotypical and reductive. The nature of certain characters' abilities, for instance, is often over-determinedly "exotic." The Japanese character Samurai is one such example. Originally debuting in the late 1970s, he possesses a plethora of exotic abilities. He can turn himself invisible, or into flame, or into a whirlwind simply by uttering what the series narrator repeatedly avers are the Japanese words for these states. Adding to this are such episodes as "Journey into Blackness" and "Termites from Venus," in which Samurai suddenly wields a samurai sword made of pure energy. The Mexican hero El Dorado debuted in the 1981 season and comprises an even more random grab bag of various and even nonsensical abilities, speaking to how the series viewed its ethnic additions as stereotypically and reductively "exotic." By wrapping his cloak around himself, El Dorado can teleport. He is also able to increase his size, communicate telepathically, and project ray blasts from his eyes.

Adding to their depiction as racialized caricatures, these nonwhite

Fig. 1. El Dorado's adventures were often set against and thus reified his Latinx background as in this image from "The Alien Mummy" (*Super Friends*, Worldvision Enterprises, 1981).

superhero characters frequently found themselves involved in plots that reified other aspects of their cultural identities as "exotic." Numerous plots involving these characters revolve around threats emanating from racialized geographies or "homelands." The 1981 episode "The Warrior's Amulet" saw Samurai rushing to save his homeland from the threat of a thirteenth-century Japanese warlord and his army of "demon warriors," who trigger a lava flow from Mt. Fuji. Plots built around El Dorado similarly fetishized his cultural background. His first appearance in "The Alien Mummy" kicks off in a "remote Mexican wilderness"; the adventure that follows is set in what El Dorado notes are "the mysterious ruins of my people" (fig. 1). Similarly, when he and Wonder Woman team up to thwart the art thief Palette, they of course end up protecting "an exhibit of rare Aztec treasures [that] just opened at the Metro Museum" ("Palette's Perils"). Apache Chief joined such stereotypical action. In "Once Upon a Poltergeist," he works with Batman and Robin to investigate a series of earthquakes under the Wayne Building that are ultimately the result of it having been built atop what a ghost mistakes for a Mohawk burial site, leading the trio into conflict with a vengeful spirit. To assuage it, Apache Chief uses smoke signals to draw it to a proper burial site, just as, in an earlier episode, "Colossus," he utilized a shrink ray shaped like a peace pipe against the titular space giant. When an adventure pulls some Super Friends into "the lifeless swamps of darkest Africa," Black Vulcan returns to his ancestors' homeland to battle voodoo vampires ("Voodoo Vampire"). While the white Super Friends travelled freely across the globe, the series more often confined its nonwhite additions to ethnic locales and storylines, hemming in their heroism in revealing ways.

Speech was another means by which the series marked these characters as "different" and "exotic." Samurai's and El Dorado's dialogue, for example, is inflected with words from their native languages. Samurai's various abilities, as noted, are invoked when he utters specific Japanese terms; he likewise makes various exclamations in his native tongue and even exclaims, "By the great pagoda!" during "The Warlord's Amulet." El Dorado similarly says "amigo," "de nada," "bueno," and "gracias," to name but a few Spanish terms and phrases that pepper his dialogue. Perhaps more (in)famously, Apache Chief shouts what the narrator assures us is the Apache word for "big man" whenever he wants to enlarge, drawing on what he describes as his "Indian tribal powers" ("The Man in the Moon"). Samurai, playing into a myriad of racial stereotypes, dispenses a kind of fortune cookie wisdom. He declares in "Termites of Venus" for example, "Strength is not the answer, Superman. Our minds are our only advantage"; and in "The Warlord's Amulet," he similarly avers, "Only practice leads to excellence." Apache Chief speaks in his own more formal and laconic syntax. In "Yuna the Terrible," as he confronts the titular villain, he stiltedly states, "Now it is you who are in need of mercy. But do not fear—I will not harm you." Even more wooden is his taunt at Bulgor the Behemoth in a later episode: "You may be big as a house, but Apache Chief will soon be as big as a mountain" ("Bulgor the Behemoth").

Beside their ethnic identities, the nonwhite Super Friends' roles/functions within the team also contributed to their marginalization. *Super Friends* episodes from 1980 through the 1983 "lost" season comprised three different stories. Generally speaking, one of those three stories would team a nonwhite character up with one or more of the team's white mainstays; thus such characters never appear without a white character by their side. Black Vulcan's role in the "Bazarowurld" episode from 1981 is particularly exemplary of this pattern and its effects. He spends most of the episode cleaning up after Superman, taking the white hero's orders, or otherwise standing around. He also gets trapped in a hall of mirrors, leaving Superman to defeat Bizzaro himself, which he does before Black Vulcan can free himself. As the episode's voiceover narration underlines, Bizarro faced defeat "at the mighty hands of Superman"—and no one else. When nonwhite heroes could play larger roles, it was often only when none of the more established heroes were available. For example, in "The Case of the Dreadful Dolls," El Dorado and Robin are the only heroes left uncontrolled by the villainous Dollmaker, the former only now being allowed to take charge when he's paired with Batman's teen sidekick. In "Uncle Mxyzptlk," Samurai also only has command of junior members, leading the teenage Wonder Twins to help rescue Superman.

The final season of *Super Friends*, which ran from 1985 to 1986, saw the ethnic presence on the team diminished, in spite of Cyborg's addition. Besides this new member, Samurai is the only nonwhite Super Friend to appear, and he plays a much lesser role on the team, perhaps best demonstrated by "The Fear," where he appears but remains silent during a team strategy session and has no dialogue in the entire episode; his one heroic action is to use his whirlwind powers to transport an already-defeated Scarecrow. Even more humiliating, though, is his appearance in "The Case of the Stolen Super Powers," where Samurai is only shown on a news report being humiliatingly defeated by the lowly Penguin.

Cyborg's addition ultimately did not change things much. In hindsight, his inclusion rested on a blithe confidence about how "easy" multiculturalism could be: once individual white team members accepted Cyborg, racial issues were solved. In reality, however, Cyborg—at least after some initial focus on his origin story and uncertainty about being a superhero—was marginalized within the team as a newcomer or rookie. Evidencing this status is how overwhelmed he is in his first episode, where he journeys with the team to Darkseid's Apokolips ("The Seeds of Doom"). He also plays an historically problematic comic role on the team, taking out a giant robot in "The Ghost Ship" with debris his errant blast broke free or, when he learns the team must return to Apokolips in "The Darkseid Deception," exclaiming, "Apokolips? Ah, my favorite place!"[3] That the producers of *Super Friends* could highlight a new hero was clear, as the white newcomer Firestorm was promoted heavily starting in 1984's season; they simply chose not to do the same for Cyborg or, really, any of the seemingly lesser nonwhite heroes that already existed.

Continuing the Limits of Multiculturalism: The Marvel Cinematic Universe and the DC Extended Universe

Freed in the twenty-first century from the technological limits of the twentieth, filmmakers seemed primed to surpass what once was only possible on the comic book page or animated television screen. And certainly, given the Super Friends shows' often ridiculous plots, stilted animation, and one-dimensional characters, the MCU and the DCEU are in many ways quantum leaps beyond what superhero narratives once were. Nonetheless, today's films and television shows have not fully escaped problematic patterns reverberating from the 1980s in their treatments of nonwhite heroes and other characters.

This is not to discount the achievements of certain films. The vision of Wakanda in Marvel's *Black Panther* (2018) eschews the reified homelands of *Super Friends* for a geography that is resoundingly Afrofuturist and effective. *Shang-Chi and the Legend of the Ten Rings* (2021) similarly veers from stereotypes and problematic exoticization in its depiction and, in fact, celebration of Asian culture and settings from the domestic to the otherworldly. *Thor: Ragnarok* (2017), too, makes a subtle, yet trenchant critique of imperialism, revealing Asgard to have been built on savage conquest. More controversial but no less daring was what Marvel did in *Iron Man 3* (2013) to subvert the more often problematic Mandarin. Here, the classic Asian villain—based on what creator Stan Lee himself described as a Fu Manchu knock-off written as "an inscrutable, mystical Asian villain" (Austin and Hamilton 70)—became instead a nightmare vision of a white-created, corporatized terror, a critique that *Shang-Chi* extends as well. *Eternals* (2021) likewise deserves praise for its diverse casting of the lead characters and incorporation of various global locales and cultures, all organically arising from the story that the film tells. Finally, director Patty Jenkins made obvious if limited efforts in *Wonder Woman* (2017) to acknowledge racial injustice, most prominently in an exchange between the Blackfoot character Chief (played by Eugene Brave Rock) and Gal Gadot's Wonder Woman that acknowledges Native American genocide at the hands of white men like Steve Trevor.

But where these films to varying degrees succeed, the MCU and the DCEU overall present a more mixed attempt to move beyond the kinds of racial understandings prominent—and problematic—in Reagan-era multiculturalism. Where the MCU and DCEU are perhaps most successful is in avoiding the pitfalls of that nigh-bygone era's reliance on reductive stereotypes. However, that's not to say they are entirely successful. The character of Mantis, introduced in *Guardians of the Galaxy Vol. 2* (2017) and portrayed by actor Pom Klementieff (who is of Korean descent), replicates a variety of stereotypes associated with Asians and Asian Americans, particularly women. In her naiveté, which often makes her the butt of jokes, she perpetuates elements of the "perpetual foreigner" that casts people of Asian descent as foreign and strange, unable to adapt to and fit in with white society. She also plays into the "yellow peril" type in possessing a mystery that presents a potential threat to her erstwhile teammates in what she knows and keeps hidden about her master Ego and his plans involving Star-Lord/Peter Quill (Austin and Hamilton 155–157). Moreover, she exhibits a stereotypical submissiveness toward Ego as well as the Guardians. If Mantis is an example of such stereotypical representations persisting into the MCU, then the character of Chief in the otherwise-hailed *Wonder Woman* presents a DCEU example. Such problematic representation begins with his moniker, which hails from any number of World War II films and their fictional, multicultural platoons designed to hide racial inequalities from white Americans who didn't want to see them.[4] He likewise inhabits the stereotypical roles of trackers and primitives, but perhaps most grating in his depiction is his use of smoke signals to alert Diana and Steve to their enemy's location.

However, even if the MCU and DCEU are less reliant on reductive stereotypes, to a more significant extent they maintain the superficial forms of inclusion and marginalized positions/roles that were established in the 1980s for nonwhite heroes and characters. From the DCEU, *Justice League* (2017) includes the African American hero Cyborg, formerly played by Ray Fisher, who disappears for rather large stretches of the movie, and Jason Momoa's Aquaman, even if the actor's racial and ethnic identities do not really factor into his character; the 2021 "Snyder Cut" of *Justice League* corrects some of this in its greatly expanded role for Fisher's Cyborg. Similarly, superficial inclusivity permeates *Suicide Squad* (2016), where somewhat nuanced characters like Will Smith's Deadshot and Jay Hernandez's El Diablo are outnumbered by paper-thin characters like Adewale Akinnuoye-Agbaje's Killer Croc, Karen Fukuhara's Katana, and even Viola Davis' one-note badass version of Amanda Waller. 2021's *The Suicide Squad* actually takes steps backwards in terms of representation: it features a much less diverse cast and basically swaps Smith's Deadshot for Elba's Bloodsport—providing similar abilities and motivations for both—implicitly treating the black characters as interchangeable. Other DCEU films such as *Shazam!* (2019) and *Birds of Prey (and the Fantabulous Emancipation of One Harley Quinn* [2020]) feature diverse casts in the Batson family and Birds, respectively; however, they very much serve the white main characters' stories in both films.

Beyond these rather limited "star" turns, nonwhite characters occupy supporting roles. Alongside *Wonder Woman*'s Native American Chief during World War I is the Moroccan Sameer (more commonly called "Sammy"), played by actor Saïd Taghmaoui. The present-day of the DCEU also features several African American supporting characters: Perry White (played by Laurence Fishburne) and General Swanwick (played by Harry Lennix) both debuted in *Man of Steel* (2013), followed by Silas Stone, Cyborg/Victor Stone's scientist father, in *Justice League*, featuring Joe Morton in the role. Populating the "background" with diverse characters matters, of course; *Super Friends* even did so, at times featuring diverse urban citizens and nonwhites as leaders, politicians, astronauts, and others. Doing so acknowledges a diverse America (and, at times, world), but does so in ways that don't always allow such diverse characters to do more than betoken a larger inclusivity.

The more-heralded MCU also betrays a tendency to relegate nonwhite characters to supporting roles. Though it became more significant later, the role of James Rhodes (played initially by Terrence Howard) in the original *Iron Man* (2008) movie was firmly in the supporting/sidekick role, a fact reinforced by the momentary glimpse of a second suit of armor that was, as Rhodes himself states, only potentially for use "next time." The first *Thor* (2011) moved closer to nonwhites in superheroic roles, as the Asgardian and thus otherworldly characters of Heimdall and Hogun were diversified via the casting, respectively, of Idris Elba and Tadanobu Asano. Such superficially race-swapped characters, however, seemed to reveal little commitment to building a multicultural universe in which non-whites assumed equal roles with white superheroes. While the color-blind casting that allowed Elba and Asano to assume their roles in *Thor* can be hailed, it also speaks to how race served only as a kind of window-dressing, as there was nothing more to the characters than a changing of skin color. The angry fan backlash to the race-swapping as well as the ultimate deaths of both characters further points to the limits on racial equality that continue to be carried forward into contemporary America. Marvel's *Ant-Man* (2015) added two more nonwhite supporting characters: Michael

Peña's Luis and Tip "T.I." Harris' Dave. Both play complementary roles, and often for laughs, as does Randall Park's Jimmy Woo in the sequel *Ant-Man and the Wasp* (2018). The first two *Spider-Man* films, *Homecoming* in 2017 and *Far from Home* in 2019 surrounded the titular character with a diverse supporting cast: Zendaya's Michelle and Jacob Batalon's Ned, who do stand out as fully-developed characters. There are, as well, numerous other students representing diverse backgrounds (if a bit superficially) at Peter Parker's school. While such inclusion is not inherently bad, when it goes little further than that, its potential to escape the gravity of 1980s patterns remains at least somewhat compromised.

Moving on from the nonwhite characters in supporting roles to those few who occupy superheroic ones might be expected to yield greater results. And certainly, the fact that Cyborg, War Machine/James Rhodes (subsequently portrayed by Don Cheadle), the Falcon/Sam Wilson (Anthony Mackie), and the late Chadwick Boseman's Black Panther/T'Challa are heroes in their own rights within their respective universes is cause for celebration. And it is fair to say that Boseman's Black Panther—both character and film—are certainly triumphs when it comes to race, even if the villainy of Killmonger rests in part on stereotypes of Black rage and violence tied to the civil rights era. Other limitations impinge, too. Both Rhodes and Wilson are troublesome due to the ways in which their identity is a knock-off of a white hero, War Machine an obvious Iron Man clone and Wilson taking on the Captain America mantle at the end of *Avengers: Endgame* (2019). The Disney+ series *Falcon and the Winter Soldier* (2021) thoughtfully addressed Wilson's struggle in carrying on this legacy, though the rumored continuation of this plot point in an upcoming fourth *Captain America* film starring him again speaks to the difficulty of breaking out of this familiar pattern. While both play important enough roles, to be sure, both also find themselves trapped in roles that continue to feel like those of sidekicks or imitators, even when they are ostensibly doing something more. A more promising debut has been Teyonah Parris' Monica Rambeau in the Disney+ series *WandaVision* (2021), which ended both by suggesting Rambeau's development of superpowers and continuation as a potentially significant player within the MCU.

In addition to such limits for the black "headliners," significant representation for heroes of Asian, indigenous American, Latinx, or other descents remains mixed. *Shang-Chi and the Legend of the Ten Rings*, of course, has done a lot to redress the paucity of prominent Asian heroes, limited to supporting roles like Woo prior to this film. The development of Native American heroes is more limited. Outside the MCU proper, though about as unheralded as the film itself, the arrival of Danielle Moonstar in *The New Mutants* (2020) should perhaps not go unremarked, leastways for how it eschews the stereotypical fringed and buckskin garb of her comic book predecessor's origins for more modern costuming. However, the film's white-washing of characters like the Afro-Brazilian Sunspot and failure to problematize the racism of Illyana Rasputin/Magik towards Moonstar detract significantly from what else it may otherwise accomplish. More promising is the debut of Echo/Maya Lopez (played by Alaqua Cox) in the Disney+ *Hawkeye* series. Native American, deaf, and an amputee, Cox's Lopez was complex and nuanced rather than fetishized and exoticized, as evidenced by the elimination of the warpaint and feathers of her comic book version for an overall modern aesthetic; the character being spun off into her own forthcoming Disney+ series allows (hopefully) what this portrayal accomplished to be bolstered (fig. 2). Further potential highlights in the MCU include a planned *Ms. Marvel* Disney+ series that will feature the Pakistani-American hero, played by Iman Vellani, who will then appear in *The Marvels* alongside Brie Larson's Captain Marvel and Parris's Rambeau, and the debut of Latinx hero America Chavez in *Doctor Strange and the Multiverse of Madness* (2022).

The future slate of the DCEU, on the other hand, is less promising, as the recent films—save perhaps *Black Adam* (2022) featuring Dwayne Johnson in the titular role—remain as predominantly-white as ever; more prominent racial representation can be found, however, on DC's small-screen offerings. DC's "Arrowverse" on the CW network featured four seasons of *Black Lightning* (2018–2021) and currently includes *Batwoman* (2019–present), which, as of the second season, has black American actor Javicia Leslie donning the cape and cowl, and *Naomi* (2022) further marking progress, at least for black heroes. Similarly, the HBOMax series *Peacemaker*, which spun out of *The Suicide Squad*, did well with the character of Leota Adebayo (played by Danielle Brooks), a black lesbian character who is as much a main character as the titular hero.

Despite some significant and promising

Fig. 2. The depiction of Echo (Alaqua Cox) in the Disney+ *Hawkeye* series adopted a more modern aesthetic for the character, eschewing the premodern aspects of her comic book incarnation (from "Ronin," *Hawkeye*, Marvel Studios, 2021).

depictions, it has, overall, been all too easy for the same kind of problematic racial superficiality that plagued the 1980s to carry over into elements of contemporary superhero popular culture. In an era of increasingly widespread awareness of racial violence, police brutality directed disproportionately at nonwhite persons, and the resulting protests crystallized by the Black Lives Matter movement, Americans have sought refuge in fictional narratives that suggest easy "fixes" to race problems in the United States. But that hardly seems a promising remedy. The "Age of Reagan" presented a solution to such issues that was anything but, as superficial inclusion did little to promote a real and broad equality, as evidenced by the tumult that besets Americans as they enter the third decade of the twenty-first century. The American nostalgia for what always was reveals a blind spot that hinders further racial progress in the United States, and the continued reliance on such timeworn and failed "solutions" suggests a failure to honestly confront the racial sins of our founding that continue to confound Americans today. The obsession with 1980s nostalgia precludes the imaginative solutions necessary to do something that might bring real structural change, rather than simply perpetuating superficial images that might make some feel better about, but not address, the deeper issues plaguing our modern world.

Notes

1. Such flatness, it should be pointed out, functions differently for the white heroes, as most viewers have at least some understanding of their back stories; for the new or even lesser-known nonwhite heroes, no such background exists, trapping them in a two-dimensionality that does not threaten or diminish the white heroes in the same way.

2. From 1980–1982, the series was titled *Super Friends* then became *SuperFriends: The Legendary Super Powers Show* from 1984–1985 and, finally, *The Super Powers Team: Galactic Guardians* from 1985–1986.

3. In this comic function, Cyborg evokes the stereotype of the "coon," in which blacks, according to Donald Bogle, appeared only as an "amusement object" or "black buffoon" and thus were "used solely for comic relief" (7).

4. John W. Jeffries describes this phenomenon: "Every squad and every ship's compartment, so it has seemed in memory and the movies, had someone named Kelly, and Goldstein, and Kowalski, and Jones, someone named Tonelli, and Larsen, and Sanchez, and Schmidt, perhaps even an Indian called 'chief'—Americans all, from Brooklyn and Dixie and from all across the land, joined in common cause" (120).

Works Cited

Alaimo, Stacy. "Multiculturalism and Epistemic Rupture: The Vanishing Acts of Guillermo Gómez-Peña and Alfredo Véa, Jr." *MELUS*, vol. 25, no. 2, Summer 2000, pp. 163–185.

Austin, Allan W., and Patrick L. Hamilton. *All New, All Different?: A History of Race and the American Superhero*. University of Texas Press, 2019.

Chafe, William H. *The Unfinished Journey: American Since World War II*. 6th ed., Oxford University Press, 2007.

Hollinger, David. *Postethnic America: Beyond Multiculturalism*. Revised ed., Basic Books, 2005.

hooks, bell. *Black Looks: Race and Representation*. South End Press, 1992.

Jeffries, John W. *Wartime America: The World War II Home Front*. Ivan R. Dee, 1996.

"Dad, every serial killer is somebody's neighbor!"

The Problem of White Supremacy in Summer of '84

ERIKA TIBURCIO MORENO

The 1980s have been frequently represented in popular culture lately, and *Summer of '84*, released in 2018, exemplifies the recent interest in revisiting the social and cultural attitudes of the Reagan era. The filmmakers, producers François Simard, Anouk Whissell, Yoann-Karl Whissell (also known as RKSS), have stated that, along with screenwriters Matt Leslie and Stephen J. Smith, they came up with the idea for the film in 2015, before the retro–'80s style boomed in popularity (Popcorn Talk). Set in Ipswich, Oregon, the film is about a killer on the loose, threatening suburbia. Davey (Graham Verchere), who is obsessed with conspiracy theories, convinces his friends Woody (Caleb Emery), "Eats" (Judah Lewis), Curtis (Cory Gruter-Andrew), and Nikki (Tiera Skovbye), to investigate Wayne Mackey (Rich Sommer), who turns out to be the serial killer. Although the story was conceived in a pre–Trump political climate, the social and political polarization of the Trump era clearly influenced *Summer of '84*, which uses a nostalgic setting to depict a twisted tale of serial murder and a traumatic journey into the adult world.

The slasher and coming-of-age genres are mixed in *Summer of '84* in ways that challenge '80s nostalgia by identifying a kind of anxiety common to both the Reagan and Trump eras. Both presidents addressed masculine national anxieties regarding exterior dangers threatening harm to American identity. During the Reagan years, popular culture, especially film, connected patriotism, violence, and traditional values with muscular male models (Jeffords 24). Similarly, the Trump administration has also been characterized by white, male hostility against social advances by minorities. The Alt-Right, a core subset of traditional Trump supporters, comprises individuals who support a racist hierarchy based on the alleged superiority of Anglo-Saxon males (Marsden 90). In *Summer of '84*, the sinister depiction of a 1980s suburb as an uncanny territory establishes the town itself as an extension of the dreadful acts of the serial killer, a figure who personifies the virus of patriarchal white supremacy that infects conservative discourse, both then and now.

Not Such a Nostalgic Decade!

Ipswich, Oregon. June 1984. This initial text in the opening sequence of *Summer of '84* places the audience in a familiar suburban setting. The camera follows the newspaper boy, Davey, who is covering his route. From the very beginning, the movie displays iconic images of the 1980s, such as modern houses, homestead vinyl mailboxes, kids riding bikes, neighbors gardening in their yards, arcade machines, and walkie-talkies. The film's creators have explained that they wanted to remind viewers of the years when they were children and to evoke popular titles like *Stand by Me* or *Monster Squad* (1987) (Crimmins). In these and other nostalgic representations of American boyhood, young characters have traditionally cherished privacy and personal spaces, taking advantage of gadgets and seeking isolated places that allow them to behave freely and socialize according to their own rules. This tendency is exemplified in *Summer of '84* when the group of teenage friends meets in the treehouse or communicates via walkie-talkies. In particular, the bowling alley where the boys pass the time combines an atmosphere of confidentiality against a background of pop music. In an early scene set in the bowling alley, the soundtrack provokes an ambiguously emotional reaction in the spectator. While this scene enacts a nostalgic representation of young boys looking at girls, the lyrics of the song they are all listening to, "Cruel Summer" by Bananarama, released in 1984, anticipates the dreadful journey the main character is on the verge of undertaking.

Musically, the predominance of synthwave, a soundtrack style that blended electronic elements into action, sci-fi, and horror scores of the 1980s, parallels the "retro 80s" style of similar titles such as *Stranger Things* or *American Horror Story 1984*. As Nicholas Diak states, this stylistic device alludes to John Carpenter's suspenseful film scores and the soundtracks of survival horror videogames, challenging the positive associations of *Summer of '84*'s suburban imagery. Synthwave's deeply unsettling ambiance reveals the fragility of the idealistic memories of those years.

That flimsiness becomes more visible when the youths must confront reality as trouble invades their secure spaces. From a political perspective, television brings the Cold War into Davey's home when his family is having dinner, reminding him of the threat of Mutually Assured Destruction that hangs over his leafy suburban existence. According to *Summer of*

'84 screenwriter Matt Leslied, this reference disputes the optimistic vision held by Reagan supporters while also connecting the past to ongoing geopolitical tensions:

> Davey's father Randall has that line, he says, "The Cold War's never gonna end. Your future is doomed, Davey." That's obviously us pointing at the fact that here we are in 2018, right back in this weird cold war again. As they say, history doesn't repeat itself, but it does rhyme. A lot of the social and economic issues of that era are relevant again, which really goes a long way toward making a film set back in the 80s feel relevant to audiences today [Collier].

The film also tackles other serious social issues ignored in popular inspirational films from the '80s in order to portray a more complex view of the past. The link between conservatism and nostalgia represented by the "Reagan/Bush '84" yard sign in Eats' garden is articulated in different moments, for instance, when Eats jokes about AIDS while they are combing through Mackey's trash can. Furthermore, a crucial aspect that the movie criticizes about the Reagan era is the breakdown of the traditional family, as represented by divorce (Nikki's parents), parental alcoholism (Woody's mother), and parental absence because of long working hours (Davey's father). This lack of structure leaves the children unprotected while a serial killer is on the loose.

Additionally, the unrestrained criminal at large in the community is an omnipresent risk that epitomizes the dark tone of the film. Front-page news, TV reportage, missing-children milk cartons, and even the nickname "the Cape May Slayer" emphasize the ability of the monster to murder undetected while also establishing a dialogue with the moral panic in the 1980s about evil threats to good citizens. The hysterical alarm prevalent in '80s American mass-culture about child abuse exaggerated and misrepresented the real problem. Historically, the tendency towards individualism, the growth of working women, and increasing urbanization triggered the spread of the fear of violence and crime. The dread of "stranger danger" provoked an obsession with surveillance and security alike (Burke ch. 11). The theme of paranoid surveillance played a key role in the construction of the archetype of the serial killer, whose social ambiguity is exemplified by Mr. Mackey's double life as both a homicidal monster and a police officer.

Two Sides of the Same Coin: White Violence and a Serial Killer in Blue

Wayne Mackey is depicted as a charming neighbor and highly respected police officer who secretly kills teenage boys. Real serial murderers such as Ted Bundy and John Wayne Gacy played a crucial role in how RKSS envisioned Mackey's character (Crimmins). Whiteness was an essential component of these criminals' profile that influenced their depiction in popular media. Robert K. Ressler, who coined the term serial killer at the end of the 1970s, stated that most serial killers were white males who were successful in their personal interactions (Ressler and Shachtman ch. 4). Thus, individuality vanished in favor of a discourse that turned these killers into profiles in such a way that different criminals like Jack the Ripper, H.H. Holmes, or Henry Lee Lucas were included in this label and defined by their crimes. The increasing media attention devoted to these criminals, as well as the growing popularization of true crime fiction and talk shows, changed how the public perceived these criminals, resulting in:

> A new cultural image on monstrosity, a powerful tool for emerging forces in politics and society that sought to counter the sexual revolution, second-wave feminism, and the emerging struggle for gay and lesbian rights. Combining a discourse of madness and monstrous evil made the serial killer into a powerful symbolic construction of all that had gone wrong since Woodstock [Poole 152].

It is vital to point out that the spread of this discourse coincided with the slasher movie boom. Both popular journalism and horror movies participated in the shift to dehumanize serial killers, but, in slasher movies, this process turned serial killers into supernatural, unstoppable killing machines. Although the slasher subgenre established a clear division between normalcy and monstrosity, postmodern horror challenged these categories, blurring their boundaries and turning danger to the social order into an endemic condition (Pinedo 93–94). At the same time, however, otherness continued reproducing the same hierarchical structure that conservatism had defended from the '80s onwards. Michael Myers, or Ghostface, as well as other psycho killers such as Patrick Bateman or Hannibal Lecter, were still white men who preserved the power to threaten society.

Wayne Mackey's depiction as a monster follows the same behavioral pattern of previous slasher film killers, but his monstrosity coexists with Mackey's affable outward persona. Mackey can effortlessly balance his private and public life, successfully deceiving his neighbors. From a criminological perspective, he would be labeled as the most dangerous kind of serial killer: an organized killer who is highly intelligent, able to deceive his victims, and good at control as well as adaptation to any situation (Ressler and Shachtman ch. 6). Mackey has lived in the neighborhood for a long time, and nobody mistrusts him. This point is emphasized when Davey talks to his parents after gathering evidence, which, despite its validity, is disregarded. Mackey's public identity as a role-model is based on his outward behavior, which is always friendly and attentive.

Conversely, his portrayal as a monster is produced differently, through a twofold exploration of his evil nature. First, the news media play a key role, disseminating an atmosphere of giddy panic. Front-page news draws attention to the killer's condition as a free individual who can kill whomever he decides. Headlines such as "Cape May Slayer, fifteen confirmed victims and still counting!" or "Fear across Cape May hits fever pitch" spotlight how the killings will continue, suggesting that any boy may be murdered and that no one is safe. Meanwhile, television provides updates on the latest news about the killer. The sheriff on TV informs the public of the Cape May Slayer and the letter he sent claiming responsibility for the deaths of 13 teenage boys and two adults. Afterward, the officer affirms, "We've confirmed the accuracy of these statements. I can now officially label this person as an active serial killer." The presenter profiles him as a white male in his late 40s who lives alone and targets males aged 12 to 16. This scene, including the frightened expression of Davey's mother, connects to the 1980s moral panic regarding a projection of otherness whose evil mirrored external cultural enemies who could endanger suburban lives (Jenkins 112). Unlike physically heinous creatures, these monsters could disguise themselves and continue killing whomever they wanted.

As no murder is shown on screen until the climax of the film, the boys' investigation and the contacts between Mackey and Davey are essential to corroborate Mackey's otherness. Mackey's identity as an organized killer is emphasized through his meticulousness and his well-planned strategy of decomposing corpses with sodium hydroxide and burying them in a distant forest. In the final stage of their investigation, Davey, Woody, and Nikki decide to enter Mackey's house, where they descend into the basement. Mackey's house allegorizes his double nature. While the living room offers a comfortable image, the locked room in the cellar where he tortures, kills, and decomposes his victims represents his bloody impulses. Nevertheless, the clear distinction is called into question after discovering that portraits hanging in the "public" part of his house are actually pictures of his prey, not his relatives.

Throughout Davey's contacts with Mackey, control and surveillance are the outstanding themes explored. Mackey is extremely considerate, tactful, and patient with Davey, reasoning away every accusation and pretending not to worry when he is informed about the boys' investigation. This restraint intertwines with watchfulness, illustrated when both neighbors use binoculars to spy on one another from their respective windows; Davey's surveillance is interrupted when he discovers that Mackey is watching him as well. Mackey's profession as a police officer and his identity as a white male contribute to the lack of suspicion he arouses among his neighbors. The relative impunity with which Mackey carries out his

crimes reflects the status of white men as unquestioned figures of authority, a prevailing attitude that has been culturally normalized (Reburn 51).
The same dynamic is suggested when Mackey kidnaps the boy in the middle of the street.

Monstrosity and power are explored in the only sequence that reveals
Mackey's real dark side. After hiding in Davey's attic, the officer sneaks
into the boy's room, where Woody and Davey are sleeping, to kidnap them.
In the forest where the victims are buried, Wayne Mackey cuts Woody's
throat and threatens Davey, saying that he will return to kill him in the
future. From a filmic perspective, this scene contains the only close-ups
that violate personal space. While Woody is bleeding to death, the camera pedestals up to depict Mackey's pleasure. The killer's dominance is
rooted in his remorseless and persistent position of surveillance, a position affirmed by the threat Mackey makes to Davey in lieu of killing him
outright:

> Sorry? You forced me out of my home! You stole my life! You do not get to be
> sorry. All I wanna do is kill you. That's not enough for you. You have spent so
> much time ... thinking about me. I want you ... to keep thinking ... about me.
> I want you to imagine what I am going to do ... when I come back for you.
>
> And I am going to come back for you. After you have spent your life ... look-
> ing over your shoulder. After you have wondered every single day if that is the
> day that I'm gonna come for you. One day ... you'll be right.

Mackey's ability to menace Davey's life resides in the killer's absolute freedom to move about undetected, camouflaged within the social privileges
he enjoys as a white male authority figure.

Additionally, the bond between lawbreaking and law enforcement
in Mackey weaves the generic attributes of this type of monster together
with the current problem of police violence. The increasing awareness of
police brutality during the Trump administration (January 2017–January 2021) contrasts markedly with the cavalier attitude Trump himself has
endorsed, most notoriously in his 2018 speech to law enforcement officers,
in which he remarked,

> Like when you guys put somebody in the car and you're protecting their head,
> you know, the way you put their hand over? Like, don't hit their head and
> they've just killed somebody—don't hit their head. I said, you can take the
> hand away, O.K.? [Trump]

Following Trump's comments, more people of color were brutalized
by police. Stephon Clark was shot and killed in Sacramento, trigger-
ing social protests. As in the cases of other fatally shot men such as Ter-
ence Crutcher or Eric Harris, those responsible would not be charged for
their deaths. Throughout the Trump presidency, the extreme far right was

strengthened, and structural racism grew increasingly explicit. The Unite the Right Rally that took place in Charlottesville in August 2017, resulting in three deaths, presaged the storming of the Capitol Building in Washington, D.C., by pro–Trump militants on January 6, 2021, which resulted in five deaths. All this irrational violence demonstrated that white people could commit crimes remorselessly and without facing any consequences.

Summer of '84 associates these anxieties about police actions and white hatred with Mackey's hypocrisy, and the complicity on the part of society is exemplified by Davey's parents, who refuse to trust Davey or the evidence he shows, and who expose their son's investigation to Mackey in the interest of avoiding conflict with their white policeman neighbor. Indeed, despite their long-term relationship with Mackey, Davey's parents do not know anything about Mackey's background: they confront their son, saying that Mackey cannot be the killer because he has been a police officer and neighbor since before Davey was born.

The serial murderer in *Summer of '84* represents social anxieties relating to white violence. Mackey's escape at the end of the movie and his promise to return to haunt Davey transform him into the immortal monster of slasher lore, akin to Jason, Freddy, and Michael Myers, in a way that confirms his power, while also allowing him to become a representation of the endemic violence that pervades American culture. Furthermore, masculinity is depicted as a fraught battleground of normalcy and otherness because, while Mackey represents conservative, aggressive white maleness, the protagonists come of age confronting and resisting this model of masculinity, and Davey, in particular, must go through a traumatic experience as the price of entry into the adult world.

Reaching Adulthood Is No Longer Funny

Masculinity is an essential social construction that includes a process of adaptation to gender discourses. Identity and manliness intertwine to establish bonds among all individuals who present themselves to the world in ways that are coded as "masculine." Lately, however, the discourse of masculinity has been affected by a crisis of traditional gender roles. The coming-of-age genre in *Summer of '84* addresses the inherent violence in the construction of white masculinity in such a way that discovering adulthood results in a traumatic experience for the group of young protagonists, 15-year-olds who are struggling between child and adult desires. *Summer of '84* explores two outstanding features that, according to Robin Wood, are common in the horror genre. Firstly, sex is an essential facet through which the characters define themselves as becoming adults. Indeed, Davey receives a new level of confirmation and acceptance from his peers when they believe that he has had sex with Nikki. Secondly, neglectful parenting forces the film's young characters to assume responsibility and face a dangerous killer on the loose (Wood 314, 319). Their parents' flaws—neglect, divorce, workaholism, and general obliviousness—challenge the tone of '80s nostalgia and underscore the sinister atmosphere of the slasher genre. Notably, Wes Craven's *A Nightmare on Elm Street*, a postmodern movie that depicts suburban reality as a nightmarish world whose spectacles of horror destabilize conservative stereotypes, was released in 1984. Like Craven's film, *Summer of '84* suggests that teenagers are meant to assume responsibility for their parents' mistakes and to suffer for their parents' errors.

The teenagers in *Summer of '84* discover themselves to be immersed in the cultural anxieties of their historical moment, and their investigation into the identity of the Cape May Killer becomes a metaphor of the American journey into the darkness of American violence. Davey's bedroom offers a refuge of childhood; his posters and newspaper clippings about conspiracy theories suggest a fantasy world sealed off from adulthood. Similarly, Eats' treehouse symbolizes a similarly protected space, and, as a meeting place, it provides all of the teens with a private bubble where they can exist without parental supervision. This preserve of innocence is destroyed, however, when Davey finds that the world is no longer safe. Both the audience and the main character must confront Woody's death and, consequently, Davey's traumatic initiation into adulthood, which is indistinguishable from his transformation into Mackey's vulnerable prey. Mackey's revelation as a serial killer distorts the happy ending of popular '80s movies, replacing it with a sinister view of a world surrounded by death, violence, and uncertainty, where Davey has failed to comply with the imperative to adopt the values of conventional masculinity or to claim the power to be derived from turning into a superior white man. From a social perspective, the United States faces the same kind of victimhood, facing psychopathic authorities, personified by Donald Trump, who have normalized violence and turned society into an unsafe space whose human relations are mediated by irrationality.

These turbulent times that Davey lives through in 1984, as well as the troubled times that we inhabit in the twenty-first century, are illustrated in the Davey's final voiceover monologue. These lines, which are repeated in a slightly different order from the movie's opening lines, convey an anxious tone that permeates the new world:

> You never know what might be coming around the corner. And that's the thing about this place, it all might seem normal and routine, but the truth is the suburbs are where the craziest shit happens. Just past the manicured lawns and

friendly waves, inside any house, even the one next door, anything could be happening and you'd never know. If I've learned anything, it's that people hardly ever let you know who they really are. Tough pill to swallow, I know, but it's true. Even serial killers live next door to somebody.

Work Cited

Burke, Joanna. *Fear: A Cultural History*, Kindle ed. Virago, 2005.

Crimmins, Deirdre. "Exclusive Interview: RKSS discuss *Summer of 84* and their love of True Crime." *Rue Morgue*, 4 Sep. 2018.

Diak, Nicholas. "Lost Nights and Dangerous Days: Unraveling the Relationship Between Stranger Things and Synthwave." *Uncovering* Stranger Things: *Essays on Eighties Nostalgia, Cynicism and Innocence in the Series*, edited by Kevin J. Wetmore, Jr., Kindle Ed. McFarland, 2018.

Hafner, Josh. "Police killings of black men in the U.S. and what happened to the officers." *USA Today*, 18 March 2018.

Jeffords, Susan. *Hard Bodies: Hollywood Masculinity in Reagan Years*. Rutgers University Press, 1994.

Jenkin, Philip. *Using Murder: The Social Construction of Serial Homicide*. Routledge, 1994.

Marsden, Lee. "Pushing Back the Obama Legacy: Trump's First Year and the Alt-Right-Evangelical-Catholic Coalition." *The Trump Presidency. From Campaign Trail to World Stage*, edited by Mark Oliva and Mark Shanahan, Palgrave Macmillan, 2019. *Springer Links*, DOI: 10.1007/978–3–319–96325–9.

Pinedo, Isabel C. "Postmodern Elements of the Contemporary Horror Film." *The Horror Film*, edited by Stephen Prince. Rutgers University Press, 2004, pp. 85–117.

Poole, W. Scott. *Monsters in America: Our Obsession with the Hideous and the Haunting*. Baylor University Press, 2011.

Popcorn Talk. "Interview with the Directors of 'Summer of 84,' Roadkill Super Star | Horror Movie News Ep 38." *YouTube*, 7 August 2018.

Reburn, Jennifer. *Watching Men: Masculinity and Surveillance in the American Serial Killer Film 1978-2008*. 2012. University of Glasgow, PhD dissertation.

Ressler, Robert K., and Tom Shachtman. *Whoever Fights Monsters*, Kindle ed. St. Martin Press, 2015.

Trump, Donald. "President Trump: Don't be too nice." *YouTube*, uploaded by CNN, 28 July 2017.

Wood, Robin. "Teen, Parties, and Rollercoasters: A Genre of the 90s." *Hollywood from Vietnam to Reagan … And Beyond. Expanded and Revised Edition*. 1986, Columbia University Press, 2003, pp. 309–332.

Dallas Buyers Club

Libertarian American Dreams in the Neoliberal 1980s

CRAIG CLARK

The opening shot of Jean-Marc Vallée's *Dallas Buyers Club* (2013) is of a rodeo arena (fig. 1). A person on horseback circles its dirt floor, moving from screen left to screen right. Held in their right hand, prominently visible in the shot's foreground, is America's "sacred symbol," the Stars and Stripes of the American flag (Mayward 2). Distorted but discernible, a voice sings "O'er the land of the free" to the familiar tune of the American national anthem. The arena's perimeter wall is painted at regular intervals with the flag of Texas, its lone star a symbol of the state's "pronounced individualism" (Hogan 454). This is a story, set in the mid–1980s, of an individualist Texan outlaw cowboy, Ron Woodroof (Matthew McConaughey), and his libertarian American Dreams. This essay explores those American Dreams as they emerge against the backdrop of Reagan-era neoliberalism.

Fig. 1. Sacred symbols: the flags of America and Texas in *Dallas Buyers Club* (Truth Entertainment, 2013).

Libertarian American Dreams

> The libertarian vision is all in Jefferson. Read your Decla-
> ration of Independence: We are all created equal; no one
> ought to have any special rights and privileges in social
> relations with other men. We have, inherently, certain
> rights—to our life, to our freedom, to do what we please in
> order to find happiness.
> —Brian Doherty, *Radicals for Capitalism:*
> *A Freewheeling History of the Modern*
> *American Libertarian Movement* (21)

> A piece of wishful thinking composed in haste, the Dec-
> laration was born and lives as the charter of the American
> Dream. It constitutes us.
> —Jim Cullen, *The American Dream* (58)

Libertarianism is a uniquely American brand of radicalism (Doherty
15) which, like the American Dream, is rooted "in the impulses of America's founding" (Doherty 20). The Declaration of Independence's guarantee
of the right to "Life, Liberty, and the Pursuit of Happiness" stands as the
implicitly libertarian (Doherty 21) charter of the American Dream (Cullen 58). The Declaration formally articulates the Dream in tandem with
another of America's founding documents, the Constitution (Samuel 3).
America's Founding Fathers were, in a sense, prototypically libertarian;
their American Dream was one of freedom (Cullen 41) and freedom is the
philosophy of libertarianism (Doherty 147). The Constitution defines a
role for federal government that is, in its small size and limited mandated
power, characteristically libertarian. Libertarians believe government
should possess, at most, the authority to protect citizens from violence and
larceny. It should not, therefore, impose upon an individual's private sexual affairs, dictate which drugs they can and cannot consume, or interfere
in the economy by way of taxation and regulation. A reduction in the size
of government and the removal of its influence from people's lives would,
libertarians believe, allow the individual to pursue happiness with the
greatest degree of success (Doherty 3–5).

Libertarianism is founded upon the same individualist tradition
(Doherty 37) of freedom, equality, opportunity and private property,
as America is itself (Wright 1–2). The economic component of individualism, the self-regulating market of laissez-faire (Wright 16), is not only
implicit in the age-old American Dream of free enterprise (Cullen 58),
it also forms a cornerstone of libertarian ideology (Doherty 29). Market
individualism is symbolized by the cowboy, a distinctly American character who emerged on the frontier (Wright 1–3), home to those who rejected

government interference (Adams 113) and a breeding ground for individualism (Adams 173). It was there, on the frontier, that the American Dream was kept alive, integrating itself as part of the American psyche (Adams 119).

The American Outlaw

The Western allegorizes, and is underpinned by, its cultural mythology, which is centered around the American Dream (Wallmann et al. 17). *Dallas Buyers Club*, writes Akkadia Ford, uses aspects of the Hollywood Western and its sub-genre the "Rodeo Film" to portray its protagonist Ron Woodroof "as a proudly heterosexual rodeo cowboy" (71). Indeed, this becomes apparent in the opening sequence of the film. It commences not with an image, but with the sound of animalistic grunting and panting. A rodeo arena comes into view, seen through the slats of a bull stall. The source of the noise is not, as the setting implies, a raging bull primed for release, but three people, one man and two women, having sex and sniffing cocaine. One of the three, protagonist Ron Woodroof, is every inch the cowboy in his distinctive hat and checked shirt. He is introduced, prior to the closure of the opening credits, as a criminal anti-hero (Ford 71) and, immediately following their end, he announces himself as a homophobic bigot, saying of Rock Hudson during the film's first exchange of dialogue, "All that fine Hollywood pussy, wasted on a guy who smokes his fucking friends."

During this scene, Woodroof also assumes the role of bookmaker, taking bets on whether his friend, T.J. (Kevin Rankin), can remain on the back of a bucking bull for eight seconds. Most forms of gambling were, and still are, illegal in Texas ("Gambling"). He cajoles T.J. with the promise that he will soon be "getting blown by a hundred-dollar hooker," implying that he has in the past, and will again in the future, engage the services of a prostitute. Solicitation and prostitution are, like gambling, illegal in Texas ("Tex. Pen. Code § 43.02" [1973]). When Woodroof loses the bet, he cuts and runs, ingeniously avoiding the chasing mob of gamblers by punching a policeman friend, forcing his own arrest. Of the illegal activity Woodroof engages in, it is only this theft that would, in a libertarian society, be considered a crime; libertarians seek the abolition of laws restricting private sexual affairs, drug use and freedom of speech (Doherty 3).

Woodroof is, in his own words, "a goddamn rodeo" and this, he believes, should be obvious to everyone (fig. 2). He does not, however, just assume a cowboy's aesthetic. The archetypal cowboy possesses no social rank or lineage, has no immediate family, and earns money doing lowly or illegal work (Wright 21). Woodroof conforms to this description perfectly. Following in his father's footsteps, he is an electrician by trade, a blue-collar bachelor whose lowly status is established by his trailer park home. He supplements his income with petty crimes like gambling, theft, and the sale of small quantities of cocaine. He is a rebellious cowboy who ignores laws that would otherwise infringe upon his personal liberty. Hailing from Texas, the spiritual home of the outlaw folk-hero (Meyer, 95), he is a man whose actions, however crudely self-interested and hedonistic they might be, pose questions about the meaning of justice and freedom.

Heroic Libertarianism in the Neoliberal 1980s

> Pharma companies pay the FDA to push their product.
> —Ron Woodroof in *Dallas Buyers Club*

Ronald Reagan was a self-styled cowboy president (Le Coney and Trodd 168) whose anti-government rhetoric was characteristically libertarian (Doherty 445). As president, however, he facilitated America's turn not to libertarianism, but to neoliberalism (Harvey 9). While it is easy to conflate these two ideologies—like libertarians, proponents of neoliberalism advocate for the free market and believe the role of the state should be minimized (Harvey 2)—they are fundamentally different. Despite its free market pretensions, neoliberalism is, ultimately, an ideology of planning and cronyism that inevitably culminates in crony capitalism (Doherty 588). Crony capitalism occurs whenever state intervention in the market engenders a corruption of the relationship between government and business (Harvey 97) via the enactment of public policies and regulations that favor political actors and political entrepreneurs at the expense of their market counterparts (Khatri 3). In its reliance on cronyism, neoliberalism breaks the meritocratic rules of the free market by rewarding the politically connected at the expense of better-skilled candidates (Alonso Alonso). There is no guarantee the customer will be satisfied by the products and services that emerge from this arrangement. This is contrary to the economics of laissez-faire, which enable the entrepreneur to profit by meeting the needs and desires of their customers (Doherty, 425).

In *Dallas Buyers Club*, the Food and Drug Administration (FDA), National Institute of Health (NIH) and Internal Revenue Service (IRS) form a crony capitalist cabal with Dallas Mercy Hospital and Avinex Industries. Working together, this triumvirate throttles market competition and places undue restrictions on individual freedom, the consequences of which are devastating for the HIV and AIDS patients their endeavors are supposed to help. As the film draws to a close, a judge

Fig. 2. The cowboy Ron Woodroof (Matthew McConaughey) in *Dallas Buyers Club* (Truth Entertainment, 2013).

lectures Richard Barkley (Michael O'Neill) of the FDA on the purpose of the agency. The FDA was not, he explains, formed to prevent people from getting help, but to protect them. This summary encapsulates the film's broader libertarian perspective on government intervention. That is, the FDA's failure to achieve its stated mission reflects the libertarian belief that such interference, regardless of the nobility of its intention, is doomed to failure (Doherty 269).

Early in the film, Ron Woodroof tests positive for HIV and is estimated to have just thirty days to live. He discovers that a drug, AZT, is being tested for its potential to treat the virus. Armed with this information, he returns to the site of his diagnosis, Dallas Mercy Hospital, to purchase a supply. Woodroof is a cowboy, and the cowboy is an American symbol of individualism and market theory. It is thus with a cowboy's belief in America as a market society that he approaches Dr. Saks (Jennifer Garner) with an honest offer to buy AZT. He is disconsolately surprised to discover from Dr. Saks that AZT, and several other drugs being used to treat patients around the world, are unavailable in the U.S. because they have not been approved for use by the FDA. Woodroof is, however, an outlaw, and outlaws are not easily deterred by rules and regulations. Indeed, the outlaw-hero is renowned for confounding and outwitting his nemeses by employing "trickster" style tactics (Meyer 106). Woodroof does just that, and, circumventing the system, he strikes a deal with a hospital janitor to buy AZT on the black market.

Woodroof consumes the drug liberally and without medical supervision until the hospital tightens its security and access to the supply is abruptly terminated. Dying and desperate, he seeks treatment in Mexico from Dr. Vass (Griffin Dunne) who, upon Woodroof's arrival, informs his new patient that AZT is "poison." Like Woodroof, Dr. Vass is an individualist. Practicing medicine in Mexico, he is liberated from the shackles of America's regulatory bureaucracy, leaving him free to design courses of treatment, none of which include AZT, based upon his direct understanding of the scientific literature. The medication he prescribes Woodroof not only saves his life; it extends it. Dr. Vass is not, however, able to return to America to treat patients there because he has had his license to practice in the U.S. revoked. His treatments also include substances not approved by the FDA. There is little, then, to suggest the FDA's regulatory system does anything other than prevent patients, like Woodroof, from receiving the most effective available medication in their battles against HIV and AIDS. AZT, the only drug being trialed in the U.S., not only lacks efficacy, but has the adverse effect of worsening the patient's condition. As Dr. Vass explains, "It kills every cell it comes into contact with."

Woodroof has an epiphany: where Dr. Vass cannot travel, he can. His car trunk filled with supplies, Woodroof returns to Texas to sell Dr. Vass' medication to American AIDS and HIV sufferers who have been abandoned by the establishment medical system. Woodroof's customer base is, in large part, comprised of a community he views with contempt and, unsurprisingly, his initial attempts at salesmanship fail. His desire to make money forces him to reckon with his homophobia and the transformation of character this catalyzes enables him to fully realize his heroic potential. He partners with a transgender woman, Rayon (Jared Leto), who plays an integral role in the business's eventual success. Woodroof's relationship with Rayon evolves as the film progresses, and they develop an intimate friendship which holds profound meaning for Woodroof. While out shopping with Rayon at a grocery store, Woodroof encounters his estranged friend T.J. Unaware the two are acquainted, T.J. begins homophobically mocking Rayon. Woodroof physically imposes himself on T.J. and forces him to greet Rayon with a handshake. Initially, Rayon flinches at this righteous display of outlaw violence but, as the scene draws to a close, she acknowledges Woodroof as an outlaw "people's champion" (Meyer 94), her smile quietly conveying feelings of satisfaction and pride. Rayon subsequently reprises her role as a cipher for the outlaw's "people" when she reciprocates Woodroof's help by showing him support and admiration (Meyer 107). She does so by enduring a difficult encounter with her father to secure the funds needed to rescue the Buyers Club from imminent financial ruin. Woodroof emerges as an outlaw-hero, then, because of his entrepreneurial entry into the free market.

Woodroof reads about a French study, published in the *Lancet* medical journal, that proves the veracity of Dr. Vass' claims about AZT. The researchers describe AZT's efficacy as questionable and highlight concerns about the drug's toxicity. These findings do nothing to halt the

FDA's approval of the drug. On the contrary, AZT is released onto the market after just eight months of testing. This surpasses the expectations of Avinex Industries sales representative Rick Ferris (Jonathan Tabler), who had hoped to bring the drug to market after one year of trials, itself a fast-tracking of the standard drug approval timeline of between eight and twelve years. A joint press release made by Avinex and the NIH makes no mention of the *Lancet* article. The NIH is guilty of, at best, dereliction of duty, or worse, deliberately conspiring to suppress information. Avinex reaps the rewards of AZT's fast track to market, the company's share value increasing by a "whopping 12%" upon approval of the most expensive drug ever marketed. Its price, $10,000 per annum per patient, is vastly higher than the $400 per month Woodroof charges for the medication prescribed by Dr. Vass. Woodroof's Dallas Buyers Club offers the patient a better product at a cheaper price and thus poses a threat to Avinex's monopolization of the market. Rather than outcompete the Buyers Club by developing a superior product, government intervention ensures Avinex's market monopoly is secured.

The assault on free enterprise is led by the FDA's Richard Barkley. Reminiscent of the 1950s organization man, he is the antithesis of Woodroof's individualist cowboy, a bureaucrat who seems intent on destroying the American Dream. Flanked by the police and agents from the DEA, he raids Woodroof's premises, financially penalizing him for "non-compliance and improper labeling." What Woodroof's products do, and how effective they are, is none of his concern; his *raison d'être* is, by his own admission, the prevention of markets for illegal drugs. Woodroof implores him to look at his research but, armed with the inflexible certainty provided by rules and regulations, Barkley bluntly instructs him to follow bureaucratic processes. This is not, however, Woodroof's first encounter with the antagonistic agencies of government, and he has, over time, developed an understanding of the machinations of crony capitalism. The processes to which Barkley refers are, Woodroof claims, "FDA bullshit for pay up." These payments, as Woodroof makes clear in another confrontation with Barkley, this time at a support group for HIV and AIDS patients, determine who can and cannot succeed in the neoliberal marketplace. Small businesses, like his Buyers Club, are denied entry to the crony cabal by the deliberately prohibitive high cost of entry. Grandstanding, he says, "You see, the pharma companies pay the FDA to push their product. So fuck no they don't want to see my research, I don't have enough cash in my pocket to make it worth their while."

Woodroof insinuates that crony capitalism operates on a system of legitimized bribery. The veracity of his claim is manifest in an earlier scene involving two other agents of cronyism, the Dallas Mercy Hospital board, and Avinex's Rick Ferris. The latter promises the former that, should they conduct AZT trials on behalf of Avinex, both the hospital and the physicians who administer the AZT to patients will be "very well compensated" for their efforts. These financial incentives effectively guarantee the approval of AZT. One of the hospital's most prominent physicians, Dr. Sevard (Denis O'Hare), develops a blasé attitude towards AZT and the approval process. He is unperturbed by the drug's release onto the market before the findings of the trial have been finalized and published, and ignores concerns raised by Dr. Saks about its efficacy. He perceives the individualist Dr. Saks as a threat and invites her to resign when he discovers she has distributed Dallas Buyers Club literature throughout the hospital. Dr. Sevard compares unfavorably with his individualist counterparts, Dr. Vass and Dr. Saks. His antipathy towards scientific research is motivated by the corrupting influence of crony capitalism. Financial incentives ensure his fealty to Avinex and its pursuit of market monopoly. His hierarchy of priorities becomes dominated not by a duty of care to his patients, but the needs of Avinex Industries. Market monopoly is secured when the FDA brandishes its legislative power to outlaw the business activities of Buyers Clubs like Woodroof's. This is the culmination of the film's libertarian representation of neoliberal crony capitalism. Woodroof is an exemplar free marketeer, whose business endeavors benefit him and the lives of his customers, while the agents of crony capitalism benefit financially only at the expense of those they purport to help.

Fig. 3. President Ronald Reagan: the cowboy pretender.

Conclusion: The Cowboy Outlaw Dreams of Libertarian Free Markets

The American myth of the cowboy symbolizes the individualist ideas upon which America was founded. Libertarianism, the ideology of laissez-faire, is founded upon this American individualist tradition. Ronald Reagan appealed to the history of American individualism with his cowboy aesthetic and anti-government rhetoric, his image invoking the frontier, home to both the cowboy, the personification of market individualism, and those who sought freedom from government interference (fig. 3). The frontier, which proved a fertile breeding ground for both individualism and the American Dream, is not, however, a concept contained by time and place (Wallmann et al. 3). Reagan's cowboy image and libertarian posturing, then, suggest the re-emergence of the frontier in the 1980s and, with it, a renewal of the market values of individualism expressed by the cowboy myth. Indeed, Reagan's presidency promised much for libertarianism, but this promise was left largely unfulfilled (Doherty 446) as the nation turned not to libertarian laissez-faire, but neoliberalism.

This sense of libertarian disappointment pervades *Dallas Buyers Club's* representation of the Reagan era. The film's protagonist, Ron Woodroof, is a true cowboy who embodies the individualist spirit of America's founding. His American Dream of entrepreneurial freedom from regulation is countered at every turn by government agencies working in service to their crony capitalist collaborators. He is forced to run his Dallas Buyers Club as an outlaw in the libertarian "world of black market countereconomics" (Doherty 400), and it is with an outlaw's resistance to "the established 'system' of his times" (Meyer 94), neoliberalism, that he pursues liberty, ignoring those laws that have no place in a libertarian society. Indeed, the very existence of such laws is a damning indictment of the superficiality of Reagan's libertarian anti-government pretensions.

As an exponent of the cowboy myth of individualism, Woodroof reveals a paradox at the heart of American culture: to live with the freedom guaranteed by America's Founders in the Declaration of Independence (Doherty 21), he must become an outlaw. It is as an outlaw that he joins the generations of ordinary men who have risen up throughout history to save the American Dream (Adams viii). In doing so, he resists the neoliberal crony capitalist forces who seek to destroy the Dream, and with it, his business. In the face of adversity, he pulls himself up by his bootstraps and celebrates his success as a "self-made" individualist by purchasing a symbol of the American Dream, the Cadillac (Samuel 88). He is the libertarian entrepreneur par excellence, profiting fairly from his business endeavors by meeting the needs of his customers. The market enables and catalyzes his transcendence of homophobia by bringing him into contact with a community that, at the outset of the film, he treats with hostile disdain. By contrast, neoliberal crony capitalism not only prevents HIV and AIDS patients from accessing the best possible treatment at the most affordable prices; it incentivizes corruption and negligence. *Dallas Buyers Club* thus condemns Reagan-era neoliberalism for its misappropriation of the American founding principle of individualism, while simultaneously celebrating the potential for libertarianism, the ideology of liberty and free markets, to make the world a better place.

WORKS CITED

Adams, James Truslow. *The Epic of America*. Second edition, Routledge, 1933.
Alonso Alonso, Lucas Juan Manuel. "Crony Capitalism and Neoliberal Paradigm (Part II)." London School of Economics.
Cullen, Jim. *The American Dream*. Oxford University Press, 2003.
Doherty, Brian. *Radicals for Capitalism: A Freewheeling History of the Modern American Libertarian Movement*. Public Affairs, 2007.
Ford, Akkadia. "Whose Club Is It Anyway?: The Problematic of Trans Representation in Mainstream Films--"Rayon" and Dallas Buyers Club." *Screen bodies (Print)*, vol. 1, no. 2, 2016, pp. 64–86, doi:10.3167/screen.2016.010205.
"Gambling." Texas State Law Library.
Harvey, David. *A Brief History of Neoliberalism*. Oxford UP, 2007.
Hogan, William Ransom. "Rampant Individualism in the Republic of Texas." *The Southwestern Historical Quarterly*, vol. 44, no. 4, 1941, pp. 454–480, JSTOR.
Khatri, Naresh. "Definitions of Cronyism, Corruption, and Crony Capitalism." *Crony Capitalism in India: Establishing Robust Counteractive Institutional Frameworks*, edited by Naresh Khatri and Abhoy K. Ojha, Palgrave Macmillan UK, 2016, pp. 3–7. https://doi.org/10.1007/978-1-137-58287-4_1.
Le Coney, Christopher, and Zoe Trodd. "Reagan's Rainbow Rodeos: Queer Challenges to the Cowboy Dreams of Eighties America." *Canadian review of American studies*, vol. 39, no. 2, 2009, pp. 163–183, doi:10.1353/crv.0.0035.
Mayward, Joel. "Profane Parables: Film and the American Dream." *Journal of Religion & Film*, vol. 20, no. 3, 2016.
Meyer, Richard E. "The Outlaw: A Distinctive American Folktype." *Journal of the Folklore Institute*, vol. 17, no. 2/3, 1980, pp. 94–124, JSTOR, doi:10.2307/3813890.
Samuel, Lawrence R. *The American Dream*. Syracuse University Press, 2012.
"Texas Pen. Code" § 43.02 (1973).
Wallmann, J.M. et al. *The Western: Parables of the American Dream*. Texas Tech University Press, 1999.
Wright, W. *The Wild West: The Mythical Cowboy and Social Theory*. SAGE Publications, 2001. *Cultural Icons Series*.

Ryan Murphy's '80s and the Past as Political Postmodern Battleground

Ilaria Biano

Popular culture's fascination with the 1980s appears to have reached a level of pervasiveness that may outstrip any previous wave of nostalgia. Like previous waves of nostalgia, such as nostalgia for the '50s during the late '70s and early '80s, for example, the current wave of '80s retro-chic emphasizes pop-cultural aspects of the decade, from music and fashion to comics and video games. Focusing on superficial and inoffensive elements of the past, nostalgia often builds upon and perpetuates idealized versions of the past. While shows like *Stranger Things* and *GLOW* have depicted '80s society and culture in ways that reinforce the conventional stereotype of the 1980s as a time of pop-cultural frivolity, other texts and authors have moved in a different direction, choosing to represent the less well-known but still important activist soul of the decade, focusing on subcultures and marginal areas at the forefront of struggles for social justice.

One example of a text that examines the progressive undercurrents of the 1980s is the series *Pose* (2018–2021), created by Ryan Murphy, Brad Falchuk, and Steven Canals for the cable network FX. During its three seasons, *Pose* told the stories of the people involved in the ballroom scene in New York, mainly Black and Latinx queer persons. While depicting different cultural and political perspectives and conflicting subcultures, the show posited itself as a form of collective memory for the contemporary LGBTQ community. The relationship between history and fiction is indeed a crucial and complex one. When fiction becomes a site of representation and reinterpretation of the past, it is necessary to analyze the ways in which the narrativization of history occurs, especially when it involves memory and nostalgia. *Pose* offers a case study of representation of the past through the language of memory and activism.

Representing History, History as Representation, and the "Other '80s"

The relationship between history and narrative involves, on the one hand, the fictional representation of historical periods or events and, on the other hand, the active construction of historical memory. Jerome De-Groot has argued that "cultural representations of history are more significant in the formation of historical imagination than 'actual' history," and, with respect to the 1980s, this tendency has been realized on multiple levels (270). The representation of the '80 in public opinion as well as in popular culture and nostalgic revivals is often shaped around the recurring themes of political conservatism and economic neoliberalism, situated within an opulent social scene and a festive show business and fashion world. Academic and "official" histories of the decade have emphasized these aspects, depicting the '80s as an almost exclusively Reaganocentric era, a time characterized by the overturning of '60s and '70s ideals, when hippies became yuppies. Some recent trends in historical research, however, have focused on the ways that social movements rooted in the '60s continued to evolve throughout the 1980s, developing into new and different forms of activism.

The mainstream narrative about the '80s emphasizes a double movement in American society: the growing relevance of conservatism and a decreasing interest in any form of participation in public and civic life, both symptoms of a more general disengagement (Foley 4). In the last decade however, a handful of scholars have shifted their attention from the general level of national politics to the grassroots movements and local politics: it is at this level that the persistence not only of leftist and liberal politics but, more broadly, of various forms of engagement can be seen. If, as Bradford Martin has noticed, the success of the mainstream image of the '80s was due to the effective ability and cultural power of the right to affirm itself and impose its views to shape the popular narrative, relevant cultural counter-movements were nevertheless operating in the society, movements that took the form of both organized campaigns as well as more spontaneous socio-cultural trends. From nuclear freeze campaigns to anti–AIDS or feminist activism and post-punk culture, the reality of everyday '80s life was one in which "diversity, community, engagement and activism resulted in cultural or social shifts" that often anticipated later trends (Troy 565). The secret history of the '80s is a history of resistance, not only as a defensive, rear-guard action, but as a fight for the acknowledgment of new rights.

The ways in which the '80s have been narrated and represented in pop-culture are paradigmatic of the power dynamics related to the representation of the past, especially in the nostalgic register, which is the dominant mode in which mainstream media tends to depict the recent past. Media and memory studies scholars have emphasized the role of media and especially of television in shaping the cultural view of the past, to such an extent that Andrew Hoskins concluded that "History is stuck with television as the primary mediator of memory" (345). Television in fact plays the role of historical mediator on multiple levels: as primary witness and keeper of historical moments and events, but also as a site for reinterpretation and representation of the past in various forms and genres. In the process, the construction of collective cultural memory via media and television is always filtered through present concerns (Niemeyer). It is crucial therefore to consider the role that different uses of memory and nostalgia play in the dynamics of representations of the past, especially in fictional forms that already mediate between invented stories and "real" history.

Defining Memory and Nostalgia as Strategies to Address the Past

Memory and nostalgia represent two ways of relating to the past, negotiating the relationship with history through different strategies, feelings, and purposes. Historians like Le Goff and LaCapra have noticed that, while memory cannot be identified as history per se, it is nevertheless "essential for historical elaboration" (Le Goff 281). During the 1980s, a specific field of memory studies came to prominence rooted in the early studies of Halbwachs on what he called *mémoire collective*. Originally articulated in the context of the linguistic and narrative turn and, more broadly, that of postmodernism and poststructuralism, the concept of collective memory imposed itself as "the new critical conjunction of history and theory" (Klein 128).

The term nostalgia, on the other side, coming from the Greek *nostos* (returning home) and *algos* (pain), was first used in a medical context in late seventeenth century by a Swiss physician to indicate a condition, homesickness, common among mercenaries (Lowenthal 46). Nostalgia refers to an attachment to a time that is supposed to be happier, a time that has been and cannot be anymore. Nostalgia is thus related to a concern with progress and modernity: "a bittersweet side-effect of modernity and a potential cause of a deadening hostility to the changes" (Atia and Davies 181). If memory studies flourished within the context of a postmodernist environment, the relation between postmodernism and nostalgia is more ambiguous and controversial. Linda Hutcheon has stressed the relationship between nostalgia, postmodernism, and irony, distinguishing a form of nostalgia that "does not simply repeat or duplicate memory" but is a real "social disease." In historiography, nostalgia, "denying or at least degrading the present," makes the idealized past the site of authenticity and, in doing so, it may realize a "betrayal of history" and of memory itself (Hutcheon 21). Politically, nostalgia has often been used by conservative parties: "Nostalgia operates as the search for a continuity of specific values and meanings from the past" (Pierson 141).

Media in general, especially television and, more recently, internet and social media, have generated what has been perceived as a dramatic acceleration of history, a flattening of events, and a general crisis of historical representation. Through these processes, media have often been seen as disruptive to the relation between history and memory, and as responsible for social-historical amnesia (Le Goff; Jameson). At the same time, memory studies have highlighted the relevance of media and narratives in the transmission of cultural and collective memory, especially intergenerationally: the production of cultural memory is a constructive process and an act of identity-formation, involving the active agency of individuals and publics (Erll; Rothberg; Plate and Smelik). Individuals, media, and society produce memory collectively in a way that is entangled with official history and shared in cultural products (Hagedoorn). When it comes specifically to the representation of the past in pop-culture, the register of nostalgia seems to be a preferred mode, and television has become a crucial actor in the production of nostalgia, both by producing nostalgic narratives and spreading them. The use of nostalgia in pop culture is not a novelty, but in the last decade, with the explosion of streaming services and the rise of prestige television, the nostalgic genre has become one of the main trends in the industry.

The '80s represents an interesting case for the analysis of this combination of memory and nostalgia as it occurs in the historical realm, in public opinion, and in pop culture, which seems to have "embraced the '80s, especially after 9/11" (Wetmore 2), leading to representations of the decade that often reproduce conservative attitude and ideals. The image of the '80s as a conservative era, however, emerged as a consequence of the cultural dominance of the conservative right, not as an exact historical portrait. As Foucault stated, "memory is a political force and a site of opposition," one in which different visions of the past may interact and negotiate their roles, making collective memory something "not stagnant but [something that] can be revised and contested" (Leavy). In this sense, some representations of the '80s have focused explicitly and with a specific purpose on alternative movements, staging a revised narrative of the decade while also acknowledging the pop-cultural allure of the '80s.

Pose *and the Representation of the Past*

Pose portrays a representation of 1980s that weaves together both a historical and nostalgic relationship with the past. In its central narrative, *Pose* follows a group of people active in the New York ballroom scene of late '80s. In the ballrooms, different teams (called houses), primarily of Black and Latinx queer performers, compete in drag costumes within various categories. *Pose*, however, manages to address this particular social and cultural milieu by following not only the ballroom scene itself, but also the personal struggles and everyday life of the characters, depicting at the same time two other interrelated subcultures: the downtown social and literary scene and the yuppies in the luxury Trump-era universe. Inspired by Jennie Livingston's 1990 documentary feature, *Paris Is Burning*, *Pose* broke records by assembling the largest cast of transgender actors in regular roles, as well as the largest recurring LGBTQ cast ever for a scripted series, and including numerous trans writers, directors, and consultants, in addition to members of the contemporary ball community. While the documentary, a "veritable treatise on gender performance"

Fig. 1. Indya Moore as "Angel" during a ballroom scene in the pilot of *Pose* (Color Force, 2018).

whose "influence on the modern culture of drag has been immeasurable," focused on the ball scene as "a self-contained underground" (Halter), *Pose*'s main interest, aside from the spectacular drag sequences, resides in the tensions between the characters' personal struggles and their problematic relationship with a hostile society. These struggles tend to arise from the characters' marginalization as trans women, queer persons, and cultural minorities rather than from issues related to their personal identity. Following two rival houses led by Abundance and Blanca, *Pose* offers a loving but disenchanted look at '80s society, one that manages to deconstruct idealized visions of the decade and to "highlight the problems that faced LGBTQ+ people, specifically those of colour" (Brown), while at the same time diving into '80s aesthetics and culture, emphasizing specific forms of civic resistance (fig. 1). *Pose* has been highly regarded by critics, hailed as a text of "utmost importance when it comes to learning how society worked in the '80s."

This focus on the past, with all its entanglements between fact and fiction, is one of the main aspects of Ryan Murphy's style. The balance between idealized (sometimes openly utopic) versions of the past and historical (even if dramatized) fidelity to the facts varies significantly from work to work in Murphy's oeuvre, elaborating in a very interesting way the complex relationship between memory, nostalgia, and pop-culture. Some of the most recent examples of Murphy's work, such as the miniseries *Hollywood* and the show *Ratched*, both aired on Netflix in 2020, tend strongly toward a uchronic rewriting of the actual past (or of some aspects of culture and society) in a way that manipulates the register of nostalgic narratives, pushing the boundaries between nostalgia and explicit utopia, while in other works, such as *Pose* or the anthology series *American Crime Story* (2016–present), the balance leans toward the metahistorical side. On yet another level, the anthology series *American Horror Story* articulates a balance between past, irony, and nostalgia that mixes the tropes of horror genres with a language that enacts a form of temporal drag, a performative appropriation of a given period "that rejects historical verisimilitude" (Geller and Banker 40) in favor of a sort of reflexive commentary. This is certainly the case of the ninth season of the show, *1984*. Set in the '80s and inspired by the slasher-era horror movies that take place in a summer camp setting, the season delivers a vision of the decade definitely more mainstream and pop than that articulated in *Pose*. At the same time, *1984* manages to exploit all the aesthetical and cultural nostalgic aspects of the decade, while maintaining the core elements of Murphy's style and agenda.

In the era of prestige television, spanning at least the decade of the 2010s, the role of the author has become one of the most important components in the production of a series, especially when embodied in the more encompassing figure of the showrunner: writer, producer, and often director. As Mittell noticed, the relevance of authorship is such that the audience frequently identifies a show not only through actors, but through authors. Authorship has become crucial "for understanding programming, delimiting potential appeals, tone, style, and genre [and] establishing an aesthetic framework" through which an audience may identify the political, ethical worldviews of certain series based on the previous work of their authors (105). Murphy's aesthetics and poetics are coherent and clear, with recurring themes that characterize almost all his works: a postmodernist language, a camp attitude, and a progressive agenda, all centered around a focus on and critique of American history and society. Murphy's stories are always extremely political and push a clear agenda based on the promotion of the visibility and rights of marginalized minorities.

"Camp" and "postmodern" are words that are frequently applied to the corpus of Murphy's shows and movies, even if he has sometimes referred to his style as "Baroque." Pastiche, appropriation through quotation, pop references or reusing, irony, intertextuality, parody, eclecticism: all the features of postmodernism are clearly recognizable in Murphy's works, starting with his first success, *Glee* (2009–2015), a high school musical-dramedy that Murphy envisioned explicitly as a "postmodern musical" (Roberts). As for camp, Susan Sontag formulated one of the first definitions, emphasizing the aesthetical aspects (outrageous, flamboyant, exaggerated, and ostentatious) as predominant;, however, the meanings of camp have shifted through time toward a clear political connotation, encompassing a strong form of activism: "a mode of artistic expression that promotes queer visibility and denotes its struggle for representation" (Clarke 62). The political import of Murphy's narratives channels these aesthetic and poetical features into a form of activism, not only through the stories that he tells, but also through casting politics and references selection. This critical and political attitude is tied to another characteristic feature of Murphy's artistry: a specific focus on American history, culture, and society realized as critique through satire and paradox.

Murphy's '80s: History, Fiction, and Activism

The image of the '80s that emerges from Murphy's work is the result of a balance, realized in different ways, between fidelity to the past (especially less well-known areas of the past), language and aesthetics that use nostalgic tropes, and the clear mission of promoting inclusive values. It is worth noting that the '80s are also the setting of the adaptation that Murphy directed in 2014 of the play *The Normal Heart*, in which the central theme is the spreading of HIV in the gay community. Murphy has been very open about the fact that his experience as a young gay man in the '80s plays a significant part in the formation not only of his character, but also of his poetics and style. Murphy has stated that *Pose* is "his most personal drama, [drawing] on details from his childhood, growing up gay in an Irish Catholic family in Indiana" (Brown). A show like *Pose* doesn't need to rely on the register of nostalgia, because its purpose is not to remember a happier past now gone, but to tell the story of suffering and struggles, and also of love and activism, that is intended to inspire new generations, promoting an awareness of this past and a collective memory of it.

Pose constructs an alternative to the conservative stereotype of the 1980s by organizing the narrative around the register of memory. Although standard-issue '80s themes and images, from the *Fame* (1980) soundtrack to *Wall Street* (1987) quotations, are integral parts of the storytelling, they operate to create the atmosphere, rather than functioning as nostalgic clichés. The core narrative consists of stories that are at the same time familiar and unusual—stories of love, chosen families, and bonding—but these stories take place against a historical background that emphasizes issues of class, gender, and sexuality.

Inclusion is thus the main purpose of the memory-driven and semi-nostalgic historical representation of *Pose*. *Pose* constructs a collective memory, especially for transgender people, and it has been identified as a site of what has been called trans-memory: "trans communities' reparative historical productions" (De Kosnik et al. 35). *Pose* is not only about ballrooms and drag; rather, it uses that famous and familiar setting for "centring trans people's experiences with poverty, violence, discrimination, and disease [...] experiences that most trans tipping-point media refrained from representing" (50). This mission is very clear not only to Murphy and the other writers, but also to members of the cast and crew, who, in many cases, have lived through that time and feel the responsibility for passing that memory to new generations (fig. 2). Both Dominique Jackson, who plays Elektra Abundance, and Mj Rodriguez, who plays Blanca, consider their work in *Pose* as a real game-changer for transgender lives and "like a form of activism," especially "at a time where the stakes are high" (Real). *Pose* was in production during the first year of Trump presidency, a time during which the president signed a ban on trans people serving in the U.S. military. Although one of the main characters in *Pose* works for the Trump Organization, Murphy chose to withdraw the Trump character after the 2016 election. Murphy and his cowriters clearly pay close attention to the ties between the representation of the past and action toward the present.

Another way in which *Pose* functions as a conduit for memory involves its engagement with the trauma of HIV. The '80s represents a form of collective trauma for the LGBTQ community, and Billy Porter, who plays the master of ceremonies of the balls in *Pose*, described the honor he felt in being part of *Pose* "as a survivor of that era" (Real). *Pose* explicitly addresses the theme of AIDS trauma, especially through the character of Blanca, who is diagnosed with HIV in the first episode of the series. In this sense, *Pose*, along with texts like *The Normal Heart*, participates in the construction of the traumatic heritage of the epidemic of HIV. *Pose* also dramatizes the sense in which the collective trauma of AIDS was characterized not only by the effects of the disease, but also by the stigmatization brought about by sectors of public opinion revolving around the religious right and the moral majority. At the same time, the AIDS crisis also triggered a growth of awareness and activism in the LGBTQ community (Halkitis; Hammack et al.).

A profile of Murphy published in December 2020 on the website of the Golden Globe Awards describes him as "The inclusive gatekeeper" and focuses on the author's activism in favor of minorities' inclusion in show business. Murphy has sponsored and supported The Half Initiative, which is dedicated to promoting the empowerment of women and minorities behind the camera. This form of activism is realized in Murphy's own productions through affirmative actions: since 2016, 63 percent

Fig. 2. Mj Rodriguez (Blanca) and Billy Porter (Pray Tell) in the series finale of *Pose* (Color Force, 2018).

of Murphy's company's productions have been directed by women, and Murphy has insisted on casting trans-women or queer people to play the parts of queer characters. Murphy sums up his approach: "Diversity and inclusion are [...] part of my business practice [...] it has helped change the system which is very different now than when I started. All of my work is about one thing: everybody should be who they want to be" (Gardiner).

In terms of storytelling, this approach is realized by Murphy's choice to tell narratives that might have a positive impact on the present in terms of representation and the promotion of other forms of activism. In this sense, Murphy's productions promote the message that looking at the past is instrumental to acting in the present and the future. Memory, especially in the arts, may have a performative nature: art can be "an act of active remembrance" that bridges the gap "between the lived past and the imagined future" (Plate and Smelik 3). This is exactly the axis around which Murphy's narratives revolve, and *Pose* exemplifies this commitment. Actors Laverne Cox and Jen Roberts both attributed to *Pose* a revolutionary role in the entertainment industry and in the wider society. In a *Variety* roundtable with transgender actors about discrimination in Hollywood, the two actors said that "*Pose* has changed the game" and that we live now in "a post-'Pose' world." They claim that the show has proved "that [trans people] can do the job, can lead shows, can write, can direct. We can tell our own stories, and it can be brilliant" (Setoodeh). Murphy said that the timing of *Pose* was "extremely significant given the swing in federal policy under the Trump administration" (Littleton): it is exactly this interaction between the representation of actual forms of activism in the past and the ongoing activism of the present that constitutes one of the series' most influential aspects. *Pose* "brings trans people into American cultural memory," not only through fictionalized personal histories and staged spectacles, but by "re-enacting how that scene impacted wider American culture" (De Kosnik et al. 50). It tells a story that must be remembered, not only for the sake of remembrance per se or for some form of nostalgic reverie, but as a call to action for the present day.

WORKS CITED

Atia, Nadia, and Jeremy Davies. "Nostalgia and the Shapes of History." *Memory Studies*, vol. 3, no. 3, 2010, pp. 181–86. doi:10.1177/1750698010364806.

Brown, Helen. "Transgender Pose Star Indya Moore: 'Religion Has Eliminated the Nuance in Humanity.'" *The Telegraph*, 18 Mar. 2019.

Clarke, Daniel. "My Freaks, My Monsters Queer Representation and The Camp in FX's American Horror Story (2011)." Gender, Sexuality, and Queerness in American Horror Story: Critical Essays, ed. by Harriet E.H. Earle. (2019): pp. 59–75.

De Groot, Jerome. "'Perpetually Dividing and Suturing the Past and Present': Mad Men and the Illusions of History." *Rethinking History*, vol. 15, no. 2, 2011, pp. 269–85.

De Kosnik, Abigail, et al. "Trans Memory as Transmedia Activism." Social Movements, Cultural Memory and Digital Media, eds. by Priska Daphi, Emily Keightley, Samuel Merrill. (2020): pp. 33–57.

Erll, Astrid. "Cultural Memory Studies: An Introduction." Cultural Memory Studies. An International and Interdisciplinary Handbook, eds. by Astrid Erll and Ansgar Nünning (2008): pp. 1–18.

Foley, Michael Stewart. *Front Porch Politics*. Hill & Wang, 2013.

Gardiner, Margaret. "Ryan Murphy: The Inclusive Gatekeeper." *Golden Globes*, 22 Dec. 2020.

Geller, Theresa L., and Anna Marie Banker. "'That Magic Box Lies': Queer Theory, Seriality, and American Horror Story." *The Velvet Light Trap*, vol. 79, 2017, pp. 36–49. doi:10.7560/vlt7904.

Hagedoorn, Berber. "Collective Cultural Memory as a TV Guide: 'Living' History and Nostalgia on the Digital Television Platform." *Acta Universitatis Sapientiae, Film and Media Studies*, vol. 14, no. 1, 2017, pp. 71–94. doi:10.1515/ausfm-2017-0004.

Halkitis, Perry. *The AIDS Generation: Stories of Survival and Resilience*. 1st ed., Oxford University Press, 2014.

Hammack, Phillip L., et al. "Gay Men's Health and Identity: Social Change and the Life Course." *Archives of Sexual Behavior*, vol. 47, no. 1, 2017, pp. 59–74. doi:10.1007/s10508-017-0990-9.

Hoskins, Andrew. "Memory Shocks." *Memory Studies*, vol. 8, no. 2, 2015, pp. 127–30.

Jameson, Fredric. *The Cultural Turn. Selected. Writings on the Postmodern 1983-1999*. Verso, 1998.

Klein, Kerwin Lee. "On the Emergence of Memory in Historical Discourse." *Representations*, vol. 69, 2000, pp. 127–50. doi:10.2307/2902903.

Leavy, Patricia. "The Memory-History-Popular Culture Nexus: Pearl Harbor as a Case Study in Consumer-Driven Collective Memory." *Sociological Research Online*, vol. 10, no. 1, 2005, pp. 1–16. doi:10.5153/sro.1021.

Le Goff, Jacques. *Histoire Et Mémoire*. Gallimard, 1988.

Littleton, Cynthia. "'Pose' Cast, Producers Talk Emotional, Empowering Journey to Make TV History." *Variety*, 5 Jan. 2018.

Lowenthal, David. *The Past Is a Foreign Country—Revisited*. 2nd ed., Cambridge University Press, 2015.

Mittell, Jason. *Complex TV: The Poetics of Contemporary Television Storytelling*. NYU Press, 2015.

Mulkerin, Tim. "Ryan Murphy's 'Pose' Is the History Lesson This Generation of Queer People Desperately Needs." *Mic*, 2 June 2018.

Niemeyer. *Media and Nostalgia: Yearning for the Past, Present and Future*. Palgrave Macmillan, 2014.

Plate, Liedeke, and Anneke Smelik. "Performing Memory in Art and Popular Culture: An Introduction." Performing Memory in Art and Popular Culture. eds. by Liedeke Plate and Anneke Smelik. (2015): pp. 1–22.

Real, Evan. "'Pose' Stars on Why the FX Show 'Feels Like a Form of Activism.'" *The Hollywood Reporter*, 3 Jan. 2019.

Roberts, Julia. "Ryan Murphy." *Interview Magazine*, 31 Jan. 2012.

Rothberg, Michael. "Introduction: Between Memory and Memory: From Lieux De Mémoire to Noeuds De Mémoire." *Yale French Studies*, no. 118/119, 2010, pp. 3–12. JSTOR, www.jstor.org/stable/41337077.

Setoodeh, Ramin. "Transgender Actors Roundtable: Laverne Cox, Chaz Bono and More on Hollywood Discrimination." *Variety*, 7 Aug. 2018.

Sontag, Susan, "Notes on Camp." Against Interpretation and Other Essays. Penguin (1966): pp. 275–292.

Troy, Gil. "Bradford Martin. The Other Eighties: A Secret History of America in the Age of Reagan." New York: Hill and Wang. 2011. Pp. xix, 242. $26.00." *The American Historical Review*, vol. 117, no. 2, 2012, pp. 564–65. doi:10.1086/ahr.117.2.564.

Wetmore, Kevin. *Uncovering Stranger Things: Essays on Eighties Nostalgia, Cynicism and Innocence in the Series*. McFarland, 2019.

Cinematically Satirizing AIDS Realities of the Reagan Decade in *Chocolate Babies*

KYLO-PATRICK R. HART

Five individuals stand together on a New York City street, all staring forward. Seconds later, they disperse in different directions. Two walk together to accost a local politician, Councilman Melvin Freeman (Bryan Webster), as he exits his Greenwich Village home; the others begin to surround them. Speaking first is Larva (Dudley Findlay, Jr.), a rotund, flamboyant, cross-dressing, HIV-positive Black man, who refers to the politician as a "pig dog ass" to get his attention because calling him "cunt bitch whore takes too long." This brief exchange efficiently sets the tone for the group interaction that follows. Immediately thereafter, Lady Marmalade (Michael Lynch), an aging, drug-injecting, HIV-positive Black transsexual, states, "Let the record show that 91% of AIDS babies are Black or Latino. You block their healthcare measures—what's up with that?" Larva, who regularly refers to himself as Larvetta Larvon Lavicomtess Delarva, follows quickly with, "Let the record show people of color die faster and in disproportionate numbers. You block treatment to the people." Next, Max Mo-Freak (Claude E. Sloan, Jr.), an HIV-positive Black diva who adorns his bald head with colorful gemstones and serves as the leader of this small group of activists, adds, "There's death in the street and blood on your hands. We want an AIDS hospice and health to this district now. We're dying and you do nothing" (fig. 1).

As the conflict continues to escalate, these three individuals begin to shout at the councilman about the local community's need for needle-exchange programs for drug addicts, and their perception that he is even deadlier than the virus itself. In his attempt to immediately exit this unpleasant situation, Freeman repeatedly states that they should call his office to express their concerns. When Larva becomes frustrated that the man is not taking them very seriously, he physically pushes Freeman and informs him, "We are Black faggots with a political agenda. We [are] your worst nightmare." Offended, the politician asks who Larva thinks he is talking to. "A murderer!" Max exclaims. Then, in an entirely unexpected development, Max, Larva, and Lady Marmalade produce knives and proceed to slash their own skin, gather some of their infected blood on their hands, and smear that blood on Freeman's face before he succeeds in running away. The two additional activists of the bunch—Jamela (Suzanne Gregg Ferguson), an HIV-positive, Black single mother and Max's heterosexual sister, and Sam (Jon Lee), Max's younger, HIV-negative, Asian American lover—look on as these various actions are unfolding, smiling and squealing with delight as they conclude.

Thus begins *Chocolate Babies*, independent director Stephen Winter's 1996 film about the ongoing attempts of this small group of radical AIDS activists to call attention and motivate improvements to the negative conditions being experienced by themselves and so many of the other residents of their New York City community as a result of the AIDS crisis. A reason this work is particularly noteworthy is that it is one of the only films about HIV/AIDS made and released in the United States during the pandemic's first two decades that features African American central characters with HIV/AIDS (Hart 63). Another reason is that, from start to finish, it intelligently highlights and satirizes common AIDS realities of the Reagan decade that were largely ignored by the president and so many other politicians of that era. During that decade, for example, AIDS activists regularly noted the government's apathy toward the AIDS crisis by stating, "We die. They do nothing" (Crimp and Rolston 82). This same message is communicated loudly and clearly in the opening moments of *Chocolate Babies*, with the aim of acknowledging that U.S. society would never begin to seriously address AIDS until the public at large truly comprehended its widespread, deleterious effects on a range of individuals (Sobnosky and Hauser 28). The primary goal of such activist rhetoric, as expressed by the film's central characters, is to place HIV/AIDS prominently on the public agenda once and for all (Sobnosky and Hauser 28).

Ronald Reagan was inaugurated as the 40th U.S. president in January 1981. Six months later, the Centers for Disease Control (CDC) began to discover what would later become identified as the country's first cases of acquired immune deficiency syndrome (AIDS) (Nelson 53). By April 1984, the CDC had received reports of more than 4,000 cases of AIDS, and nearly half of those infected individuals had died; by 1986, those numbers had grown to 17,000 and 8,000, respectively (Nelson 53). The syndrome, which was initially referred to by medical professionals as GRID

Fig. 1. "There's death in the street and blood on your hands," Max Mo-Freak (Claude E. Sloan, left) declares while confronting Councilman Melvin Freeman, as Lady Marmalade (Michael Lynch) looks on, during the opening minutes of *Chocolate Babies* (Open Cities Films, 1996).

(which stood for "gay-related immune deficiency") and socially constructed as a "gay plague," became concerning to greater numbers of Americans as it began to regularly affect members of other populations—including blood-transfusion recipients, children, drug addicts, hemophiliacs, minorities, and women, among others—and as its primary means of transmission became more widely known (Nelson 53–54). As a result, as Victoria Nelson has noted,

> The fear that immoral, irresponsible, if not socially deviant, individuals could spread the virus into broad segments of the population prompted calls for the testing and identification of the infected. In his 1987 address to the American Foundation for AIDS Research (AMFAR), President Reagan expressed concern that "innocent people" were being exposed to the virus…. This statement left the unfortunate impression that those who had died heretofore were not innocent or, at least, were responsible for their illness [Nelson 57].

Over the course of the Reagan decade and beyond, therefore, both AIDS and HIV, the virus that can lead to AIDS, were regarded as sensitive political issues as a result of their continuous association with stigmatized individuals (German and Courtright 67), and the pervasive social construction of an AIDS patient came to be someone who is "black, drug-using, homosexual, and urban—a geography of difference which is now part of the American iconography of the AIDS patient" (Gilman 266). It was not until near the end of the Reagan decade that increasing attention to heterosexual transmission of HIV/AIDS materialized in U.S. society (Gilman 269).

With its unexpected emergence and unpredictable course, the AIDS pandemic forced its way into the "anxious imagination of the American public" (Clark 9) over the course of the Reagan decade, and the greatest health crisis of the conservative Reagan era was undoubtedly the emergence and rapid spread of HIV/AIDS. Nevertheless, during the first several years of the pandemic, Ronald Reagan never once mentioned HIV or AIDS in political discourse (Slagle 93). In fact, "President Reagan did not give a talk about AIDS until May 1987, 72 months into the epidemic, a point at which 35,121 individuals had AIDS" (Rogers and Shefner-Rogers 408). According to political experts, Reagan regarded AIDS as a substantial budgetary threat and therefore simply opted to ignore it for as long as he could (Rogers and Shefner-Rogers 408). Thereafter, he and others frequently used conservative rhetoric to perpetuate perceptions of HIV/AIDS as deserved punishment for deviant and/or immoral behaviors (Slagle 94–95). It is perhaps entirely unsurprising, therefore, that groups of HIV/AIDS activists found it necessary to call attention to Reagan's indifference toward addressing the ongoing crisis as the decade of the 1980s progressed, as reflected in ACT UP's utilization of the slogan "SILENCE = DEATH" and that same organization's AIDSgate posters, featuring Reagan's face with evil red eyes and an urgent call for the continuing "political scandal" to be investigated (Griffin 36, 44).

During its opening moments, *Chocolate Babies* taps into several aspects of this disconcerting state of affairs, including the disproportionate impact of HIV/AIDS on urban communities of color and how politicians at various levels simply preferred to turn a blind eye to the AIDS realities present in their own communities, rather than working to achieve meaningful change, during the first decade of the AIDS crisis. As Lady Marmalade explains early on, "I got AIDS, dammit, and I got it by sucking dick, getting fucked, and sticking needles in my arm, and the government doesn't give a shit." Councilman Freeman's lack of action and concern in the film are shown to be even more egregious when it is revealed, through his burgeoning romantic entanglement with Sam, that he is a closeted gay man himself.

As Robert Mills points out, *Chocolate Babies* was made and released at a historical moment "when reflection on the failures and negligence of established activist practice was possible" (par. 3) and therefore is able to provide a "consciously satirical narrative that sees a group of drag queens and other social outcasts plot to overthrow their conservative, homophobic, and racially insensitive politicians" (par. 3). In this latter regard, Winter's satirical filmmaking approach in *Chocolate Babies* is what enables the film to deliver a powerful political message in the form of a gut punch. Mainstream movies about HIV/AIDS that were made and released during the first two decades of the AIDS crisis were typically created "from the outside," whether that be from a "normal-family perspective or through heterosexual vision" (MacKinnon 171–172). In contrast, Winter's film is created "from the inside" of the communities of color it chooses to represent, and the fact that its activist actions are being carried out by "a band of unlikely warriors" (Faires par. 1) serves to foreground various sorts of so-called "outcasts" and "deviants" that Reagan and so many others intentionally chose to ignore as they continued to die from AIDS with increasing frequency.

Of even greater import in this regard is the terminology used by the city's media professionals throughout the film to refer to this unique group of AIDS activists as they carry out frequent attacks on additional politicians. Their statements include "this gang of self-proclaimed raging, atheist, meat-eating, HIV-positive colored terrorists"; "the bizarre gay terrorists who are ultimately described by their victims as ugly Black women, overdressed homos, or freaks"; "the notorious drag-queen gang that has been rampaging the city and still remains at large"; and "this bunch of colored fags." Incorporation of such extreme, offensive, and discriminatory language to characterize these activists—which would never actually have been uttered on-air by media professionals during the period of the AIDS crisis in the United States—serves to give voice to the prejudice that continuously lurked just beneath the surface of acceptable discourse in relation to individuals most directly affected by HIV/AIDS and corresponding efforts to perpetuate systemic racial and sexual invisibilization (Mills par. 4). It further serves to challenge the widely held, inaccurate notion that individuals associated with AIDS during the pandemic's early years composed a sort of "uniform collective" (Mills par. 6).

The extreme actions presented as *Chocolate Babies* unfolds provide an intentionally uncomfortable viewing experience. Such discomfort begins in the opening scene (as previously discussed)—with its unique form of violent activism that "involves the blood of the infected taking the place of the critic's ink and the knife-wielder becoming the author of change" (Mills par. 3)—and reaches its apex during a later scene when Max, Larva, and Sam are serving brunch to the blindfolded Councilman Freeman after they have kidnapped him. During this latter encounter, Sam attempts to convince Max and Larva that Freeman is a better person than they initially believed him to be. When the topic of the desired AIDS hospice comes up, Freeman expresses the fear that its existence would further solidify their community's status as an AIDS ghetto, and that it would also divert funding from other needs such as daycare and housing for senior citizens. As

Fig. 2. Sam (Jon Kit Lee, left) attempts to comfort Melvin Freeman (Bryan Webster) after Max intentionally inserts his infected blood directly into the politician's mouth in *Chocolate Babies* (Open Cities Films, 1996).

he listens, however, Max is not persuaded by what he finds to be empty words, or by Sam's claim that Freeman can be trusted and wants to help them. As a result, he walks over and squats down beside Sam, revealing a blood-covered knife that was clean just moments before. Holding up his blood-filled palm, Max then proceeds to insert his infected blood directly into the councilman's mouth (fig. 2).

Because of their subject matter, it has been common for movies about HIV/AIDS, from their inception, to foreground imagery pertaining to destruction of the human body, and frequently in relation to themes of violence and/or mutilation (MacKinnon 172). Other common representational strategies have been to position AIDS bodies as an ever-lurking source of potential pollution (Gilman 256) and to portray "the individual living with AIDS as isolated, his very position echoing the classical iconographic position of melancholia" (Gilman 259), both of which apply quite well to the character Max. Given the satirical nature of its contents, these recurring representations are taken to their logical extremes in *Chocolate Babies* in the scene just described, as Max intentionally seeks to utilize violence and mutilation of his own body to reduce his melancholic feelings by infecting Freeman with his personal "pollution."

With regard to HIV/AIDS, the "archetype of blood plays into the imagination of the American people by crossing the preformed, anxiety-free boundaries of stigmatized others and by creating new and less easily assuaged fears of contagion," at least in part because potentially tainted blood is "disembodied and nonsexual," and its "degree of contamination [is] uncertain" (Clark 21). Over the course of the 1980s, numerous urban legends circulated throughout U.S. society about vengeful, AIDS-infected individuals who sought intentionally to spread HIV/AIDS to unsuspecting others via their own blood, whether through acts of unprotected sex or even leaving infected needles in padded seats for others to sit on, which made for fascinating yet quite frightening storytelling, as little evidence ever existed to support such claims (Clark 16). In the film, Max serves as a living, breathing embodiment of such urban myths. The blood-based behaviors of Max and his co-conspirators in *Chocolate Babies* shine light on the existence of such extreme claims from the Reagan decade, with Max's escalation of violence from smearing HIV-infected blood on human flesh to inserting it directly into another person's mouth in order to expedite intentional transmission signifying his ever-growing sense of desperation about the deleterious conditions he and others like him continue to experience as his health condition deteriorates. In this regard, it is noteworthy that Freeman refers to their community as an "AIDS ghetto," a term used to characterize a distinct type of misery- and despair-filled urban environment from which most inhabitants believe there is no means of escaping, which helps to explain the depth of Max's desperation (Haile et al. 436). Within such an environment, as Sander Gilman emphasizes, "The image of the body becomes the message. The AIDS patient remains the suffering, hopeless male, both the victim and the source of his own pollution" (262).

"Discourse about AIDS intersects with numerous other discourses, including those about reform of our medical system, civil rights protections for lesbians and gays, and the [efforts] of the government to regulate private behavior in the public interest" (Sobnosky and Hauser 27). All of these noteworthy topics are incorporated within the narrative of *Chocolate Babies*, with the final one emerging in relation to the so-called "AIDS acquisition files" that local politicians are rumored to be assembling. Max and his friends become concerned when they hear that government officials in the New York tri-state area have been compiling comprehensive lists of all individuals with HIV/AIDS, as it remains unclear what they plan to do with that information. This development continues to fuel their activist fires and causes Max to caution a small audience, "You want the government knowing who you are, and where you are, and who you['re] fucking, when you['re] fucking, and what your HIV status is even before you do? Hell no!" As the film progresses and their attacks on a growing number of politicians become more and more violent, Max and his fellow activists get so caught up with their goal of effecting desired change through radical means—even as it becomes increasingly evident they can no longer agree upon what forms such change should take—that they end up losing touch with their individual identities as well as with one another. (Such change is motivated by additional contributing factors, such as Max's emergent alcoholism and Lady Marmalade's ever-increasing drug use.) For these five individuals, HIV/AIDS is no longer simply a medical condition but rather an all-encompassing identity that has come to substantially define their everyday actions and interactions (Mills par. 5). But after Max gets shot when their kidnapping plan goes awry, the group spends increasing amounts of time apart from one another, and Sam chooses to get away by traveling the world. He returns to New York City a year later to find that their AIDS ghetto has since claimed the lives of both Jamela and Lady Marmalade and to reunite with Max—who has been experiencing night sweats, suffering from pneumonia and shingles, and coughing up blood—briefly before his former lover finally succumbs to AIDS. With these plot developments, another reality that the contents of *Chocolate Babies* communicates is that the activist ranks during the Reagan era were "continually thinned by the death of people with AIDS, which saps morale" (Sobnosky and Hauser 37).

In addition to its effective use of satire, another way that *Chocolate Babies* differs significantly from most other media offerings representing HIV/AIDS during the first two decades of the pandemic is that it intentionally endeavors to spread the word that all members of U.S. society—homosexual and heterosexual alike—are at risk of contracting AIDS (Gilman 269). This is accomplished through the inclusion of Jamela as one of the film's central characters and AIDS activists, and it is important because numerous studies have shown that heterosexuals do not typically adopt safer sexual practices unless they personally perceive themselves to be at risk for transmission (Clark 14). As such, the inclusion of an HIV-infected, heterosexual female character in the film provides viewers with more accurate social information about the true realities of the AIDS pandemic, and the range of individuals who needed to proactively protect themselves from its spread, than was typically made available to viewers of AIDS-themed media offerings during the Reagan decade itself.

When all is said and done, the use of satire throughout *Chocolate Babies* functions to provide a sort of revisionist history of the AIDS pandemic during the Reagan era, highlighting and commenting upon a range of topics that remained largely concealed from, or at least unspoken about by, the majority of individuals at that time. As critic Emanuel Levy emphasizes,

> As most AIDS stories have been serious dramas by and about white gay males, it's refreshing to see a political satire that not only revolves around men of color, but also refuses to label them as victims. Indeed, in its good moments, *Chocolate Babies* displays a zesty, often exuberant style that suits the chaotic story and its flashy drag queens [par. 4].

Critic Owen Levy further notes that Winter's "shrill, wacky take on a rather serious matter may just be the fresh dose of medicine the subject needs" (par. 3).

The effective use of satire enables *Chocolate Babies* to "defamiliarize" character types, images, and themes found in both U.S. society and AIDS movies of the Reagan decade by placing them in a unique context, with an atypical approach, in which they must necessarily be viewed "differently" and as "different," which then forces the film's audience members to devote significant intellectual energy to making sense of the intriguing on-screen developments as they unfold. As a result, active viewers of the film's contents emerge from the viewing experience with a range of information about the realities of the AIDS crisis in the United States during that era that was either overlooked or intentionally concealed from most of the individuals who lived through those years as they initially unfolded.

Works Cited

Clark, Kevin A. "Pink Water: The Archetype of Blood and the Pool of Infinite Contagion." *Power in the Blood: A Handbook on AIDS, Politics, and Communication*, edited by William N. Elwood, Lawrence Erlbaum Associates, 1999, pp. 9–24.

Crimp, Douglas, and Adam Rolston. *AIDS Demo Graphics*. Bay Press, 1990.

Faires, Robert. "Chocolate Babies." *Austin Chronicle*, 15 May 1998.

German, Kathleen M., and Jeffrey L. Courtright. "Politically Privileged Voices: Glaser and Fisher Address the 1992 Presidential Nominating Conventions." *Power in the Blood: A Handbook on AIDS, Politics, and Communication*, edited by William N. Elwood, Lawrence Erlbaum Associates, 1999, pp. 67–76.

Gilman, Sander L. *Disease and Representation: Images of Illness from Madness to AIDS*. Cornell University Press, 1988.

Griffin, Gabriele. *Representations of HIV and AIDS: Visibililty Blue/s*. Manchester University Press, 2000.

Haile, Rahwa, et al. "'Stuck in the Quagmire of an HIV Ghetto': The Meaning of Stigma in the Lives of Older Black Gay and Bisexual Men Living with HIV in New York City." *Culture, Health & Sexuality*, vol. 13, no. 4, 2011, pp. 429–442.

Hart, Kylo-Patrick R. *The AIDS Movie: Representing a Pandemic in Film and Television*. Routledge, 2000.

Levy, Emanuel. "Chocolate Babies." *Variety*, 29 July 1996.

Levy, Owen. "Festival Films." *Berlin Film Festival*, 1997.

MacKinnon, Kenneth. *The Politics of Popular Representation: Reagan, Thatcher, AIDS, and the Movies*. Fairleigh Dickinson University Press, 1992.

Mills, Robert. "On Queer Terrorism or: Corruptive Tactics in *Chocolate Babies*." *Peephole Journal*. n.d.

Nelson, Victoria S. "The Reagan Administration's Response to AIDS: Conservative Argument and Conflict." *Power in the Blood: A Handbook on AIDS, Politics, and Communication*, edited by William N. Elwood, Lawrence Erlbaum Associates, 1999, pp. 53–66.

Rogers, Everett M., and Corinne L. Shefner-Rogers. "Diffusion of Innovations and HIV/AIDS Prevention Research." *Power in the Blood: A Handbook on AIDS, Politics, and Communication*, edited by William N. Elwood, Lawrence Erlbaum Associates, 1999, pp. 405–414.

Slagle, R. Anthony. "Scapegoating and Political Discourse: Representative Robert Dornan's

Legislation of Morality through HIV/AIDS." *Power in the Blood: A Handbook on AIDS, Politics, and Communication*, edited by William N. Elwood, Lawrence Erlbaum Associates, 1999, pp. 93–104.

Sobnosky, Matthew J., and Eric Hauser. "Initiating or Avoiding Activism: Red Ribbons, Pink Triangles, and Public Argument about AIDS." *Power in the Blood: A Handbook on AIDS, Politics, and Communication*, edited by William N. Elwood, Lawrence Erlbaum Associates, 1999, pp. 25–38.

Film and Television Works Cited

The A-Team. Created by Frank Lupo and Stephen J. Cannell, Stephen J. Cannell Productions, MCA TV/NBCUniversal Television Distribution, 1983–1987.
Adventureland. Dir. Greg Mottola, Walt Disney Studios Motion Pictures, 2009.
Adventures in Babysitting. Dir. Chris Columbus, Buena Vista Pictures Distribution, 1987.
Against All Odds. Dir. Taylor Hackford, Columbia Pictures, 1984.
American Crime Story. Created by Scott Alexander, Larry Karaszewski, and Tom Rob Smith, 20th Television, 2016–present.
American Horror Story. Created by Ryan Murphy and Brad Falchuk, 20th Television, 2011–present.
American Psycho. Dir. Mary Harron, Columbia Pictures, 2000.
The Americans. Created by Joe Weisberg, 20th Television, 2013–2018.
Ant-Man. Dir. Peyton Reed, Walt Disney Studios Motion Pictures, 2015.
Ant-Man and the Wasp. Dir. Peyton Reed, Walt Disney Studios Motion Pictures, 2018.
Avengers: Endgame. Dir. Anthony Russo and Joe Russo, Walt Disney Studios Motion Pictures, 2019.
Baby Boom. Dir. Charles Shyer, United Artists, 1987.
The Baby-Sitters Club. Created by Jeanne Betancourt, Ann M. Martin, and Mary Plechette Willis, HBO, 1990.
The Baby-Sitters Club. Created by Rachel Shukert, Netflix, 2020–present.
The Baby-Sitters Club. Dir. Melanie Mayron, Columbia Pictures, 1995.
Back to School. Dir. Alan Metter, Orion Pictures, 1986.
Back to the Future. Dir. Robert Zemeckis, Universal Pictures, 1985.
Back to the Future 2. Dir. Robert Zemeckis, Universal Pictures, 1989.
Batwoman. Developed by Caroline Dries, Warner Bros. Television, 2019–present.
Beauty and the Beast. Directed by Bill Condon, Walt Disney Pictures and Mandeville Films, 2017.
Beauty and the Beast. 1991. Directed by Gary Trousdale and Kirk Wise, Walt Disney Pictures, Silver Screen Partners IV, and Walt Disney Feature Animation, 2002.
Better Off Dead. Directed by Savage Steve Holland, Warner Brothers, 1985.
Beverly Hills, 90210. Created by Darren Star, Fox Broadcasting Company, 1990–2000.
The Big Bang Theory. Created by Chuck Lorre and Bill Prady. Chuck Lorre Productions, Warner Bros. Television Distribution, 2007–2019.
Bill & Ted Face the Music. Dir. Dean Parasot, Oropin Pictures, 2020.
Black Lightning. Developed by Salim Akil, Warner Bros. Television, 2018–present.
Black Mirror: Bandersnatch. Dir. David Slade, Netflix, 2018.
Black Panther. Dir. Ryan Coogler, Walt Disney Studios Motion Pictures, 2018.
The Breakfast Club. Dir. John Hughes, Universal Pictures, 1985.
Call Me by Your Name. Dir. Luca Guadagnino, Sony Pictures Classics, 2017.
Can't Stop the Music. Dir. Nancy Walker, EMI Films, 1980.
Captain Marvel 2. Dir. Nia DaCosta, Walt Disney Studios Motion Pictures, 2022.
Carrie. Dir, Brian De Palma, United Artists, 1976.

Chernobyl. Created by Craig Mazin, HBO, 2019.
Chocolate Babies. Dir. Stephen Winter. Open City Films, 1996.
Cinderella. Dir. Clyde Geronimi, Hamilton Luske, and Wilfred Jackson, Walt Disney Productions, 1950.
Cinderella. Dir. Kenneth Branagh, Walt Disney Pictures, 2015.
Clueless. Dir. Amy Heckerling, Paramount Pictures, 1995.
Cobra Kai. Created by Josh Heald, Jon Hurwitz, and Hayden Schlossberg, Sony Pictures, 2018–2021.
Coming 2 America. Dir. Craig Brewer, Amazon Studios, 2021.
Conan the Barbarian. Dir. John Milius, Universal Pictures, 1982.
Conan the Destroyer. Dir. Richard Fleischer, Universal Pictures, 1984.
Creed. Dir. Ryan Coogler, Warner Bros. Pictures, 2015.
Creed II. Dir. Steven Caple, Jr., Metro-Goldwyn-Mayer, 2018.
The Dallas Buyers Club. Dir. Jean-Marc Vallée, Focus Features, 2013.
The Day After. Dir. Nicholas Meyer, ABC Circle Films, 1983.
Desperately Seeking Susan. Dir. Susan Seidelman, Orion Pictures, 1986.
The Dirt. Dir. Jeff Tremaine, Netflix, 2019.
Doctor Strange and the Multiverse of Madness. Dir. Sam Raimi, Walt Disney Studios Motion Pictures, 2022.
Donnie Darko. Dir. Richard Kelly, Pandora Cinema, 2001.
Dumbo. Dir. Ben Sharpsteen, Walt Disney Productions, 1941.
E.T.: The Extra-Terrestrial. Dir. Steven Spielberg, Universal Pictures, 1982.
The Facts of Life. Created by Dick Clair and Jenna McMahon, NBC, 1979–1988.
Falcon and the Winter Soldier. Created by Malcolm Spellman, Marvel Studios, 2021.
Fame. Dir. Alan Parker, Metro-Goldwyn-Mayer, 1980.
Family Ties. Created by Gary David Goldberg, NBC, 1982–1989.
Fatal Attraction. 1987. Dir. Adrian Lyne, Jaffe-Lansing Productions, 2002.
Ferris Bueller's Day Off. Dir. John Hughes, Paramount Pictures, 1986.
Firestarter. Dir. Mark L. Lester, Universal Pictures, 1984.
First Blood. Dir. Ted Kotcheff, Orion Pictures, 1982.
Footloose. Dir. Herbery Ross, Paramount Pictures, 1984.
Freaks and Geeks. Created by Paul Feig, NBC, 1999–2000.
Freddy vs. Jason. Dir. Ronny Yu, New Line Cinema, 2003.
Freddy's Dead: The Final Nightmare. Dir. Rachel Talalay, New Line Cinema, 1991.
Fuller House. Created by Jeff Franklin, Netflix, 2016–2020.
Game of Thrones. Created by David Benioff and D.B. Weiss, HBO, 2011–2019.
Ghostbusters. Dir. Ivan Reitman, Columbia Pictures, 1984.
Ghostbusters. Dir. Paul Feig, Columbia Pictures, 2016.
Glee. Created by Ryan Murphy, Brad Falchuk, and Ian Brennan, 20th Century Fox Television, 2009–2015.
GLOW. Created by Liz Flahive and Carly Mensch, Netflix, 2017–2019.
The Goldbergs. Created by Adam F. Goldberg, Sony Pictures Television, 2013-present.
The Goonies. Dir. Richard Donner, Warner Brothers, 1985.
Grease. Dir. Robert Kleiser, Paramount Pictures, 1978.
Gremlins. Dir. Joe Dante, Warner Bros., 1984.
Guardians of the Galaxy Vol. 2. Dir. James Gunn, Walt Disney Studios Motion Pictures, 2017.
Happy Days. Created by Garry Marshall, ABC, 1974–1984.
A Hard Day's Night. Dir. Richard Lester, United Artists, 1964.
Harold and Kumar Escape from Guantanamo Bay. Dir. Jon Hurwitz and Hayden Sclossberg, Warner Bros. Pictures, 2008.
Harold and Kumar Go to White Castle. Dir. Danny Leiner, New Line Cinema, 2004.
He-Man and the Masters of the Universe. Created by Lou Scheimer, Filmation, 1983–1985.
Hollywood. Created by Ryan Murphy and Ian Brennan, Netflix, 2020.
Home Alone 2: Lost in New York. Dir. Chris Columbus, Twentieth Century Fox, 1992.
Hot Tub Time Machine. Dir. Steve Pink, New Crime Productions, 2010.

Indiana Jones and the Temple of Doom. Dir. Steven Spielberg, Paramount Pictures, 1984.
Iron Eagle. Dir. Sidney J. Furie, TriStar Pictures, 1986.
Iron Man Dir. John Favreau, Paramount Pictures, 2008.
Iron Man 3. Dir. Shane Black, Walt Disney Studios Motion Pictures, 2013.
It: Chapter One. Dir. Andy Muschietti, Warner Bros. Pictures, 2017.
Jailhouse Rock. Dir. Richard Thorpe, Metro-Golden-Mayer, 1957.
Jem and the Holograms. Created by Christy Marx, Sunbow Productions and Marvel Pro-
    ductions, 1988.
The Jungle Book. Dir. Wolfgang Reitherman, Walt Disney Productions, 1967.
Just One of the Guys. Dir. Lisa Gottlieb, Columbia Pictures, 1985.
Justice League. Dir. Zack Snyder, Warner Bros. Pictures, 2017.
The Karate Kid. Dir. John G. Avildsen, Columbia Pictures, 1984.
The Karate Kid Part II. Dir. John G. Avildsen, Columbia Pictures, 1986.
The Karate Kid Part III. Dir. John G. Avildsen, Columbia Pictures (1989).
Knight Rider. Created by Glen A. Larson, Universal Television, 1982–1986.
MacGyver. Created by Lee David Zlotoff, CBS Television Distribution, 1985–1992.
Mad Men. Created by Matthew Weiner, AMC, 2007–2015.
Magnum, P.I. Created by Donald P. Bellisario and Glen A. Larson, CBS, 1980–1988.
Man of Steel. Dir. Zack Snyder, Warner Bros. Pictures, 2013.
The Mandalorian. Created by John Favreau, Lucasfilm, 2019-present.
Married...With Children. Created by Michael G. Moye and Ron Leavitt, Colubia Pictures
    Television, 1987–1997.
The Mary Tyler Moore Show. Created by James L. Brooks and Allan Burns, 20th Television,
    1970–1977.
Miami Vice. Created by Anthony Yerkovich, NBCUniversal Television Distribution,
    1984–1990.
Monster Squad. Developed by Stanley Ross Ralph, NBC, 1987.
Ms. Marvel. Created by Bisha K. Ali, Marvel Studios, 2021-present.
Murphy Brown. Created by Diane English, Warner Bros. Television, 1988–1998.
My Little Pony. Creative Director, Jay Bascal, Hasbro and Sunbow Productions, 1986–1987.
My Little Pony: Friendship is Magic. Created by Lauren Faust, Allspark (Hasbro),
    2010–2019.
My Little Pony 'n' Friends. Created by Bonnie Zacherle and Hasbro, Sunbow Productions
    and Marvel Productions, 1987.
My Little Pony: Rescue at Midnight Castle. Dir. John Gibbs, Sunbow Productions and Mar-
    vel Productions, 1984.
My Little Pony: The Movie. Dir. Michael Joens, Marvel Productions, 1986.
The New Mutants. Dir. Josh Boone, 20th Century Studios, 2020.
A Nightmare on Elm Street. Dir. Wes Craven, New Line Cinema, 1984.
A Nightmare on Elm Street 2: Freddy's Revenge. Dir. Jack Sholder, New Line Cinema, 1985.
A Nightmare on Elm Street 3: Dream Warriors. Dir. Chuck Russell, New Line Cinema, 1987.
A Nightmare on Elm Street 4: The Dream Master. Dir. Renny Harlin, New Line Cinema,
    1988.
9 to 5. Dir. Colin Higgins, 20th Century Fox, 1980.
The Normal Heart. Dir. Ryan Murphy, HBO, 2014.
The Office. Created by Ricky Gervais and Stephen Merchant, BBC Worldwide, 2001–2003.
The 100. Created by Jason Rothenberg, Alloy Entertainment, 2014–2020.
Orange is the New Black. Created by Jenji Kohan, Lionsgate Television, 2013–2019.
Ordinary People. Dir. Robert Redford, Paramount Pictures, 1980.
Paris Is Burning. Dir. Jennie Livingston, Off-White Productions, 1990.
Poltergeist. Dir. Tobe Hooper, Metro-Goldwyn-Mayer, 1982.
Pose. Created by Ryan Murphy, Brad Falchuk, and Steve Canals, 20th Television, 2018–2021.
Pretty in Pink. Dir. Howard Deutch, Paramount Pictures, 1986.
Pulp Fiction. Dir. Quentin Tarantino, Miramax Films, 1994.
Punky Brewster. Created by David W. Duclon, 2021-present.
Purple Rain. Dir. Albert Magnoli, Warner Brothers, 1984.

Queer Eye. Created by David Collins and Michael Williams, Bravo, 2003–2007.

Rambo: First Blood Part II. Dir. George P. Cosmatos, TriStar Pictures, 1985.

Rambo III. Dir. Peter MacDonald, TriStar Pictures, 1988.

Ratched. Created by Evan Romansky, Touchstone Television.20th Television, 2020-present.

Real Genius. Dir. Martha Coolidge, Tri-Star Pictures, 1985.

Revenge of the Nerds. Dir. Jeff Kanew, 20th Century Fox, 1984.

Risky Business. Dir. Paul Brickman, Warner Bros., 1983.

Riverdale. Developed by Roberto Aguirre-Sacasa, Warner Bros. Television, 2017-present.

RoboCop. Dir. Paul Verhoeven, Orion Pictures, 1987.

Rock of Ages. Dir. Adam Shankman, New Line Cinema, 2012.

Rock Star. Dir. Stephen Herek, Warner Bros. Pictures, 2001.

Rocky. Dir. John G. Avildsen, United Artists, 1976.

Saved by the Bell. Created by Sam Bobrick, NBC Universal Television Distribution, 2020-present.

Shang-Chi and the Legend of the Ten Rings. Dir. Destin Daniel Cretton, Marvel Studios, 2021.

She-Ra and the Princesses of Power. Created by Noelle Stevenson, DreamWorks Animation Television and Mattel Creations, 2018–2020.

She-Ra: Princess of Power. Created by Larry DiTillio and J. Michale Straczynski, Filmation, 1985–1987.

The Simpsons. Created by Matt Groening, 20th Television, 1989-present.

Sixteen Candles. Dir. John Hughes, Universal Pictures, 1984.

Sleeping Beauty. Dir. Clyde Geronimi, Walt Disney Productions, 1959.

Small Time. Dir. Shane Meadows, British Film Institute, 1996.

Snow White and the Seven Dwarfs. Dir. David Hand, Walt Disney Productions, 1937.

Some Kind of Wonderful. Dir. Howard Deutch, Paramount Pictures, 1987.

The Souvenir. Dir. Joanna Hogg, BBC Films, 2019.

Stand by Me. Dir. Rob Reiner, Columbia Pictures, 1986.

Star Wars: The Force Awakens. Dir. J.J. Abrams, Walt Disney Studios Motion Pictures, 2015.

Star Wars: The Last Jedi. Dir. Rian Johnson, Walt Disney Studios Motion Pictures, 2017.

Star Wars: The Rise of Skywalker. Dir. J.J. Abrams, Walt Disney Studios Motion Pictures, 2019,

Stranger Things. Created by the Duffer Brothers, Netflix Streaming Services. 2016-present.

Suicide Squad. Dir. David Ayer, Warner Bros. Pictures, 2016.

Summer of '84. Dir. François Simard, Anouk Whissell, and Yoann-Karl Whissell, Brightlight Pictures, 2018.

Super 8. Dir. J.J. Abrams, Paramount Pictures, 2011.

Super Friends. Created by E. Nelson Birdwell, Carmine Infantino, and Julius Schwartz, Hanna-Barbera Productions, 1973, 1980–1982.

Super Friends: The Legendary Super Powers Show. Created by E. Nelson Birdwell, Carmine Infantino, and Julius Schwartz, Hanna-Barbera Productions 1984–1985.

The Terminator. Dir. James Cameron, Orion Pictures, 1984.

This Is England. Dir. Shane Meadows, Warp Films, 2006.

This Is England '86. Created by Shane Meadows, Warp Films, 2010.

This Is England '88. Created by Shane Meadows, Warp Films, 2011.

This Is England '90. Created by Shane Meadows, Warp Films, 2015.

Thor. Dir. Kenneth Branagh, Marvel Studios, 2011.

Thor: Ragnarok. Dir. Taika Waititi, Marvel Studios, 2017.

Valley Girl. Dir. Martha Coolidge, Atlantic Releasing, 1983.

A Very Harold and Kumar 3D Christmas. Dir. Todd Strauss-Schulson, New Line Cinema, 2011.

Walker. Created by Anna Fricke, Stick to Your Guns Productions, 2021.

Walker, Texas Ranger. Created by Albert S. Ruddy, The Ruddy-Greif Company, 2001.

The Walking Dead. Developed by Frank Darabont, AMC Studios, 2010-present.

Wall Street. Dir. Oliver Stone, 20th Century Fox, 1987.

WandaVision. Created by Jac Schaeffer, Marvel Studios, 2021.

Watchmen. Dir. Zack Snyder, Warner Bros. Pictures, 2009.

The Wedding Singer. Dir. Frank Coraci, New Line Cinema, 1998.

Weird Science. Dir. John Hughes, Universal Pictures, 1985.

Welcome to the Dollhouse. Dir. Todd Solondz, Suburban Pictures, 1995.

Wes Craven's New Nightmare. Dir. Wes Craven, New Line Cinema, 1994.

The Wizard of Oz. Dir. Richard Fleming and King Vidor, Metro-Goldwyn-Mayer, 1939.

Wonder Woman. Dir. Patty Jenkins, Warner Bros. Pictures, 2017.

Wonder Woman 1984. Dir. Patty Jenkins, Warner Bros. Pictures, 2020.

Working Girl. Dir. Mike Nichols, 20th Century Fox, 1988.

Xanadu. Dir. Robert Greenwald, Universal Pictures, 1980.

Young Sheldon. Created by Chuck Lorre and Steven Molaro, Warner Bros. Television Distribution, 2017–present.

About the Contributors

Jack **Anderson** completed a master of research thesis titled *The Spatial Cosmology of the Stalin Cult: Ritual, Myth and Metanarrative* at the University of Glasgow in 2017. He is the author of "Return, Remembrance and Redemption," which featured in the *Journal of British Cinema and Television* and two book chapters in C. Martin and D. Olsen (eds), *The Undead Child: Representations of Childhoods Past, Present, and Preserved.*

Allan W. **Austin** is a professor of history at Misericordia University. His and Patrick L. Hamilton's *All New, All Different* won the Popular Culture Association's John G. Cawelti Award and the Midwest Popular Culture/American Culture Association's Best Book for Use in the Classroom. He has written and edited books on Japanese American, Asian American, Quaker, and popular culture history.

Ilaria **Biano** is an independent postdoctoral researcher in cultural and intellectual history, with an interest in the intersections between history, religion, and popular culture. She holds a Ph.D. in political studies, history and theory from the University of Turin, and she was a fellow of the Italian Institute for Historical Studies. She has published on identity, trauma, memory, and nostalgita on television in several journals and books.

Ann M. **Ciasullo** is a professor of English and women's and gender studies at Gonzaga University. She has published on a wide range of topics, including women-in-prison narratives, bromance films, gender and humor in *Mad Magazine*, and gender and nostalgia in the television series *Mad Men*. She is working on a book on Francis Ford Coppola's 1983 teen film *The Outsiders*.

Carrie **Clanton** is a Melbourne, Australia–based academic specializing in anthropology and media. She holds a Ph.D. in cultural studies from Goldsmiths College, University of London. She is particularly interested in pop culture nostalgia as a potential form of political critique, and she has written on topics ranging from surrealism to hauntology, to the Southern U.S. She is working on a project about soundtracks and everyday life.

Craig **Clark** is a Ph.D. candidate at Northumbria University. His thesis is an intertextual analysis of film and television characters' use of LSD and the representation of its effects on their perceptual experience. He presented two papers at conferences in 2021 on the American Dream: "Interpreting the American Dream as a Nostalgic Genre" and "Satirising the American Dream."

Morgan E. **Foster** earned her Ph.D. at the University of Wisconsin–Milwaukee, where she worked as a research and teaching assistant. Her research interests include girlhood studies, young adult literature, and popular culture. In her own tween years, she could be found babysitting or reading *The Baby-Sitters Club* for ideas.

Kristen **Galvin** is an assistant professor and director of art history in the Department of Visual and Performing Arts at the University of Colorado, Colorado Springs. Her research and teaching explore intersections across contemporary art, film and media, performance, gender and sexuality, memory, popular music, and subcultural studies. She is working on a book on hypernostalgia, old and new media cultures, and Americanness.

Lilly J. **Goren** is a professor of political science and global studies at Carroll University. Her published books include Mad Men *and Politics* (2015, co-edited with Linda Beail); *Women and the White House* (2012, co-edited with Justin Vaughn), as well as articles in *Politic & Gender, Society, Political Research Quarterly, White House Studies*, and *The Forum: A Journal of Applied Research in Contemporary Politics*.

Helena I. **Gurfinkel** is a professor of English at Southern Illinois University Edwardsville. She is the editor of *PLL: Papers on Language and Literature* and author of *Outlaw Fathers in Victorian and Modern British Literature: Queering Patriarchy*. She is currently at work on a monograph on the Soviet-era film and TV adaptations of Oscar Wilde's works.

Patrick L. **Hamilton** is a professor of English at Misericordia University. His and Allan W. Austin's *All New, All Different* won the 2019 John G. Cawelti Award from the Popular Culture Association and the Midwest Popular Culture/American Culture Award for Best Book for Use in the Classroom. He has also published works on race and gender in superhero comics and popular culture, as well as contemporary Chicano/a fiction.

Kylo-Patrick R. **Hart** is the chair of the Department of Film, Television and Digital Media at Texas Christian University, where he teaches courses in film and television history and queer media studies. He is the author of *The AIDS Movie* and *Queer Males in Contemporary Cinema*, founding coeditor of the academic journal *Queer Studies in Media & Popular Culture*, and a recipient of the Leroy F. Aarons Award for Lifetime Contributions to LGBTQ Education and Research.

Stephen **Hock** is an associate professor of English at Virginia Wesleyan University. He is the editor of *Trump Fiction: Essays on Donald Trump in Literature, Film, and Television* (2020) and the coeditor (with Jeremy Braddock) of *Directed by Allen Smithee* (2001). His work has appeared in a number of journals and edited collections.

Melanie **Hurley** is a Ph.D. candidate in the Department of English at Memorial University of Newfoundland. Her dissertation uses iconology, feminist theory, and film theory to determine how Disney's Cinderella signifies in popular culture and scholarly literature in relation to discourses about girlhood and womanhood. She has research interests in fairy tales, picture books, and girl-centered animation.

Randy **Laist** is a professor of English at Goodwin University and the University of Bridgeport. He is the author of several books, including *Cinema of Simulation: Hyperreal Hollywood in the Long 1990s* and *The Twin Towers in Film: A Cinematic History of the World Trade Center*. He has edited previous collections of essays in the fields of popular culture, literary criticism, and pedagogy.

John **Misak** is an assistant professor of humanities and the director of technical communication at the New York Institute of Technology. His research seeks to create a connection between students' lived narrative experiences with games and media and traditional literature. He also explores the effectiveness of incorporating STEM principles in humanities classes in order to enable transfer of learning between disciplines.

Myrna **Moretti** is a Ph.D. candidate in the Screen Cultures program at Northwestern University. Her research focuses on new media, affect, discourse analysis, and everyday life during the 1980s and early 1990s. She is also a filmmaker with a focus on documentary and experimental video.

John **Quinn** holds a Ph.D. in narratology and lectures on screen and performance at the University of the West of Scotland. His publications have discussed the representation of masculinity in popular film and television, with a particular focus on nostalgia and the aesthetics of populist politics. His research includes eighties action cinema and demagoguery, celebrity in professional wrestling, and the construction and dissemination of contemporary legend in Netflix docuseries.

Valerie **Surrett** is an assistant professor of English at the University of North Georgia, Gainesville, where she teaches and writes about cyborg life in popular culture as well as representations of prison in American fiction and film. Her earlier work can be found in *The Journal of Contemporary Thought* as well as the edited collection, *Artificial Humans in Children's Literature*.

Erika **Tiburcio Moreno** is an assistant professor of late modern history at Carlos III University and of history education at the Complutense University. Her research interests include intersectionality and horror studies and violence in media. She has published articles and reviews in *The Historical Journal of Film, Radio and Television*, and *Fotocinema. Revista Científica de Cine y Fotografía*, among others. She is the author of *Y nació el asesino en serie* (2019).

Index